Design BB2947

Empty-Nester
HOMES

206 *Exciting Plans for Empty Nesters, Retirees and Couples Without Children*

HOME PLANNERS, INC.
TUCSON, ARIZONA

TABLE OF CONTENTS

Published by Home Planners, Inc.
Editorial and Corporate Offices:
3275 West Ina Road, Suite 110
Tucson, Arizona 85741

Distribution Center:
29333 Lorie Lane
Wixom, Michigan 48393

Rickard D. Bailey, *President and Publisher*
Cindy J. Coatsworth, *Publications Manager*
Paulette Mulvin, *Editor*
Paul D. Fitzgerald, *Book Designer*

Photo Credits
Front and Back Covers: ©1993 Andrew D. Lautman

First Printing, January 1994

10   9   8   7   6   5   4   3   2

ISBN softcover: 1-881955-13-3
ISBN hardback: 1-881955-12-5

On the front and back covers: This comfortable ranch design (BB2947)—shown
in reverse on the front cover—is the choice of Diane and Julius Perillo of
Frankfort, New York. Its small square footage and convenient one-level plan
work well for their lifestyle. For additional information about this design, see
page 52.

1½-STORY HOMES

Perhaps more than any other type, 1½-story homes lend themselves well to the empty-nester lifestyle. Because they usually contain a master bedroom on the first floor and secondary bedrooms on the second floor, they create convenience for the empty-nester homeowner and provide privacy when family members or guests are visiting. The designs profiled in this section bring a new sense of style to this classic configuration. The homes are long on open floor planning—an important enhancement in a medium-sized home—and contain all the features you may have discovered you now require in a home. Look for amenity-filled gathering areas, studios, well-appointed master suites, thoughtful outdoor living areas, and even space for a home office. Both two- and three-bedroom versions in contemporary and traditional styles can be found. Note the special livability on the second floors of some plans. Designs BB3438 and BB3315 are especially good examples.

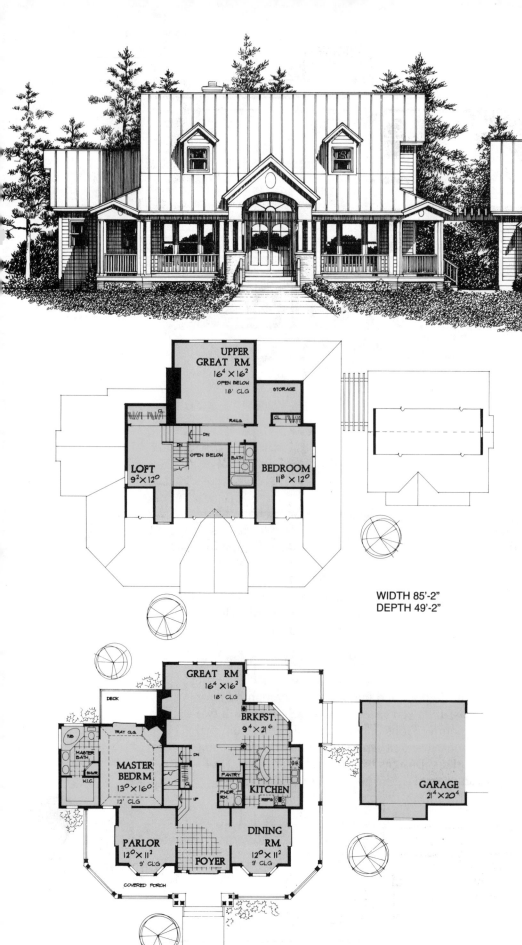

UPPER GREAT RM.
16⁴ × 16²
OPEN BELOW
18' CLG

STORAGE

CL.

RAIL.

DN

UP

OPEN BELOW

BATH

LOFT
9² × 12⁰

BEDROOM
11⁸ × 12⁰

WIDTH 85'-2"
DEPTH 49'-2"

GREAT RM
16⁴ × 16²
18' CLG

BRKFST.
9⁴ × 21⁶

DECK

TRAY CLG.

TUB

MASTER BATH

SHWR.

W.I.C.

MASTER BEDRM
13⁰ × 16⁰
12' CLG

DN

PANTRY

PDR. RM.

KITCHEN

REF'G.

UP

GARAGE
21⁴ × 20⁴

PARLOR
12⁰ × 11²
9' CLG

FOYER

DINING RM.
12⁰ × 11²
9' CLG

COVERED PORCH

Design BB3468

First Floor: 1,618 square feet
Second Floor: 510 square feet
Total: 2,128 square feet

L

● There's nothing lacking in this contemporary farmhouse. A wraparound porch ensures a favorite spot for enjoying good weather. A large great room sports a fireplace and lots of natural light. Grab a snack at the kitchen island/snack bar or in the bright breakfast room. The vaulted foyer grandly introduces the dining room and parlor—the master bedroom is just off this room. Inside it: tray ceiling, fireplace, luxury bath and walk-in closet. Stairs lead up to a quaint loft/bedroom—perfect for study or snoozing—a full bath and an additional bedroom. Designated storage space also makes this one a winner.

QUOTE ONE™

Cost to build? See page 214 to order complete cost estimate to build this house in your area!

Design BB3438

First Floor: 1,489 square feet
Second Floor: 741 square feet
Total: 2,230 square feet

A unique farmhouse plan which provides a grand floor plan, this home is comfortable in country or suburban settings. Formal entertaining areas share first-floor space with family gathering rooms and work and service areas. The master suite is also on this floor for convenience and privacy. Upstairs is a guest bedroom, private bath and loft area that makes a perfect studio. Special features make this a great place to come home to.

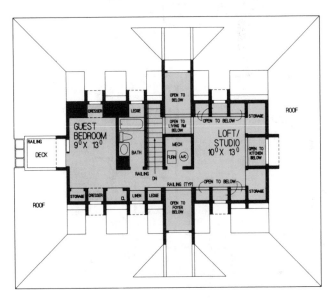

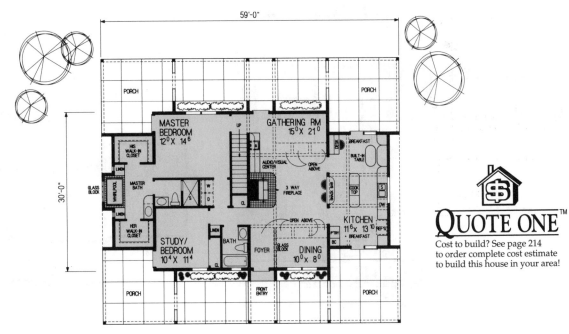

Quote One™

Cost to build? See page 214 to order complete cost estimate to build this house in your area!

Design BB3462

First Floor: 1,395 square feet
Second Floor: 813 square feet
Total: 2,208 square feet

L

● Get off to a great start with this handsome family farmhouse. Covered porches front and rear assure comfortable outdoor living while varied roof planes add visual interest. Inside, distinct formal and informal living zones provide the best accommodations for any occasion. The columned foyer opens to both the dining and living rooms. The central kitchen services the large family room with an island work counter and snack bar. For everyday chores, a laundry room is conveniently located and also provides access to the garage. On the first floor you'll find the master bedroom suite. It enjoys complete privacy and luxury with its double closets and master bath with double-bowl vanity, whirlpool tub and separate shower. Upstairs, three family bedrooms extend fabulous livability.

RAILING

VERANDA

MASTER BEDROOM
11⁰ X 15⁰

WHIRLPOOL

GREAT RM
13⁶ X 15⁴

KITCHEN
9¹⁰ X 11⁸

BATH

SNACK BAR
D.W. SINK

REFR.

DN

UP

PANTRY

PDR.

LAUNDRY
W. D.

DINING ROOM
11⁰ X 11⁰

CL.

FOYER

LIVING ROOM
12⁰ X 13⁴

GARAGE
23⁰ X 24⁸

VERANDA

RAILING

Width 53'-8"
Depth 57'

BEDROOM
11⁰ X 13⁰

OPEN BELOW

STORAGE

BATH

DN

LINEN

BEDROOM
12⁸ X 12⁰

DESK

BEDROOM
12⁰ X 14⁴

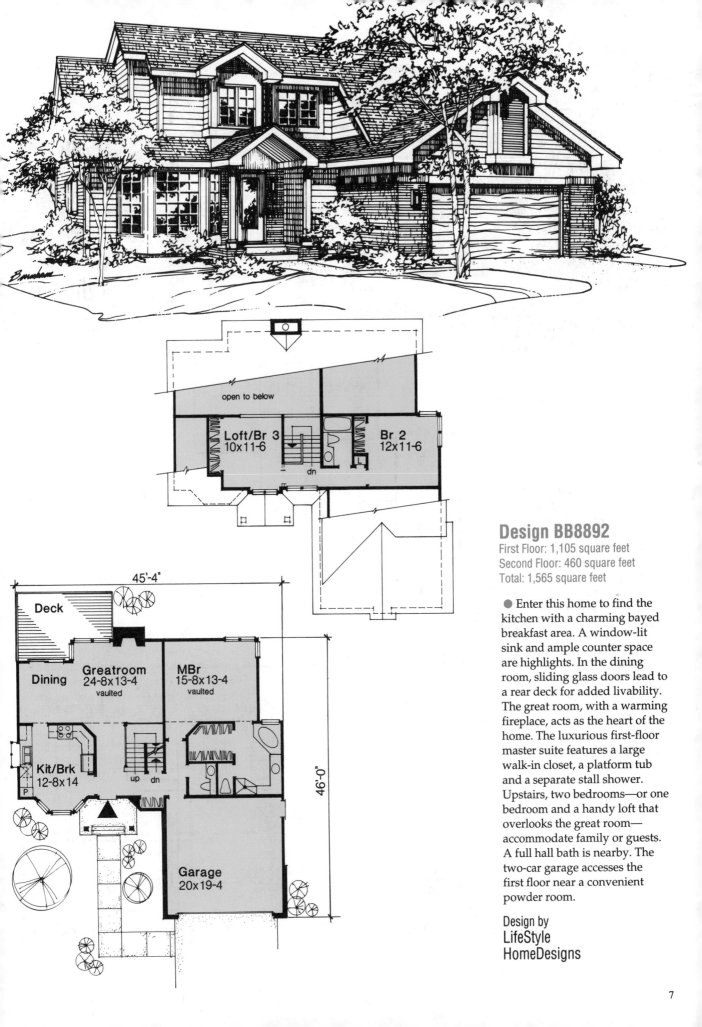

Loft/Br 3
10x11-6

Br 2
12x11-6

open to below

dn

Design BB8892

First Floor: 1,105 square feet
Second Floor: 460 square feet
Total: 1,565 square feet

● Enter this home to find the kitchen with a charming bayed breakfast area. A window-lit sink and ample counter space are highlights. In the dining room, sliding glass doors lead to a rear deck for added livability. The great room, with a warming fireplace, acts as the heart of the home. The luxurious first-floor master suite features a large walk-in closet, a platform tub and a separate stall shower. Upstairs, two bedrooms—or one bedroom and a handy loft that overlooks the great room— accommodate family or guests. A full hall bath is nearby. The two-car garage accesses the first floor near a convenient powder room.

Design by
LifeStyle
HomeDesigns

45'-4"

Deck

Dining

Greatroom
24-8x13-4
vaulted

MBr
15-8x13-4
vaulted

Kit/Brk
12-8x14

up   dn

46'-0"

Garage
20x19-4

Design BB3461

First Floor: 1,391 square feet
Second Floor: 611 square feet
Total: 2,002 square feet

L

● A Palladian window set in
a dormer provides a nice introduction to this 1½-story country
home. The two-story foyer
draws on natural light and a
pair of columns to set a comfortable, yet elegant mood. The living room, to the left, presents a
grand space for entertaining.
From full-course dinners to family suppers, the dining room will
serve its purpose well. The
kitchen delights with an island
work station and openness to
the keeping room. Here, a
raised-hearth fireplace provides
added comfort. Sleeping accommodations are comprised of
four bedrooms, one a first-floor
master suite. With a luxurious
private bath, including dual
lavatories, this room will surely
be a favorite retreat. Upstairs,
three secondary bedrooms meet
the needs of the growing family.

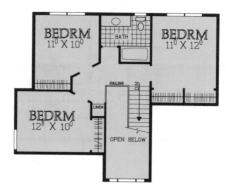

QUOTE ONE™

Cost to build? See page 214
to order complete cost estimate
to build this house in your area!

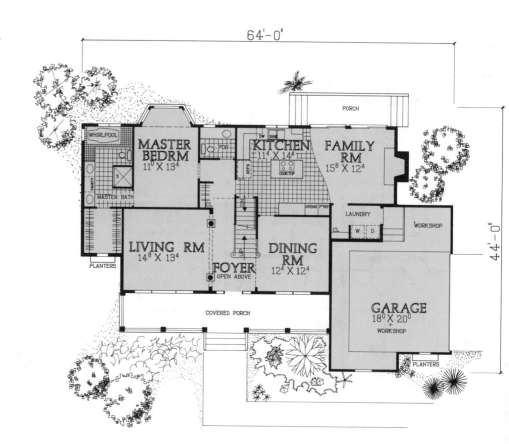

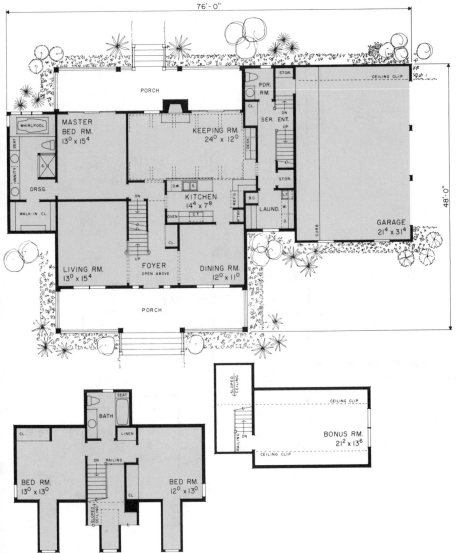

76'-0"

PORCH

MASTER BED RM.
13⁰ x 15⁴

WHIRLPOOL

SEAT

VANITY

DRSG.

S.

WALK-IN CL.

LIVING RM.
13⁰ x 15⁴

FOYER
OPEN ABOVE

UP

DINING RM.
12⁰ x 11⁰

KEEPING RM.
24⁰ x 12⁰

DESK

KITCHEN
14⁴ x 7⁸

DW

OVEN

CL

REF'G

STOR.

PDR. RM.

CL

SER. ENT.

DN

UP

STOR.

B.C.

LAUND.

W.

D.

CURB

GARAGE
21⁴ x 31⁴

CEILING CLIP

PORCH

48'-0"

BATH

SEAT

LINEN

CL

CL

BED RM.
13⁰ x 13⁰

DN RAILING

CL

SLOPED CEILING

BED RM.
12⁰ x 13⁰

SLOPED CEILING

RAILING

DN

BONUS RM.
21² x 13⁶

CEILING CLIP

CEILING CLIP

Design BB3566

First Floor: 1,635 square feet
Second Floor: 586 square feet
Total: 2,221 square feet
Bonus Room: 321 square feet

L **D**

● Don't be fooled by the humble appearance of this farmhouse. All the amenities abound. Covered porches are located to both the front and rear of the home. A grand front entrance opens into living and dining rooms. The family will surely enjoy the ambience of the keeping room with its fireplace and beamed ceiling. A service entry, with laundry nearby, separates the garage from the main house. An over-the-garage bonus room allows for room to grow or a nice study. Two quaint bedrooms and full bath make up the second floor. Each bedroom features a lovely dormer window.

QUOTE ONE™

Cost to build? See page 214 to order complete cost estimate to build this house in your area!

Design BB2510

First Floor: 1,191 square feet
Second Floor: 533 square feet
Total: 1,724 square feet

L **D**

● Hometown comfort abounds in this darling
1½-story home. Vertical siding and stone lend
interest to the facade. Inside, a family room with a
bay window interacts easily with the in-line
kitchen. Notice the large, walk-in pantry nearby.
The rear dining area opens to the living room—a
fireplace here will keep all warm and snug. The
master bedroom is situated on the first floor and
enjoys direct access to a private rear terrace. A full
bath and washer/dryer space complete the
amenities on this floor. Upstairs, two secondary
bedrooms provide accommodations for the small
family or guests. One of the bedrooms enjoys a
walk-in closet.

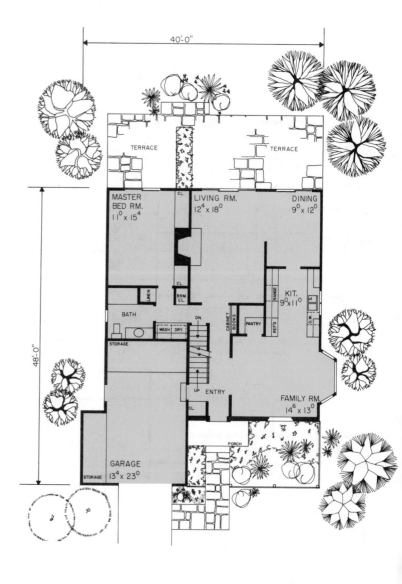

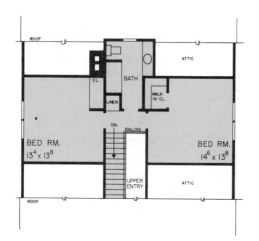

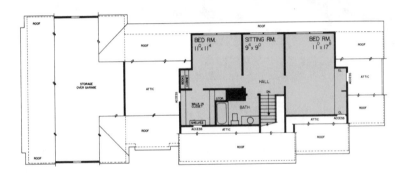

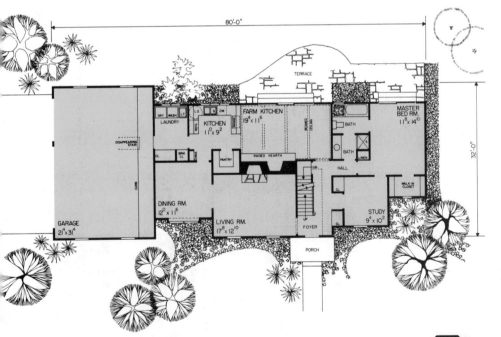

Design BB2563

First Floor: 1,500 square feet
Second Floor: 690 square feet
Total: 2,190 square feet

L **D**

● This charming Cape Cod definitely will capture your heart with its warm appeal. This home offers you and your family a lot of livability. Upon entering this home, to your left, is a nice-sized living room with fireplace. Adjacent is a dining room. An efficient kitchen and a large, farm kitchen eating area with fireplace will be enjoyed by all. A unique feature on this floor is the master bedroom with a full bath and walk-in closet. Also take notice of the first-floor laundry, the pantry and a study for all of your favorite books. Note the sliding glass doors in the farm kitchen and master bedroom. Upstairs you'll find two bedrooms, one with a walk-in closet. Also here, a sitting room and a full bath are available. Lastly, this design accommodates a three-car garage.

QUOTE ONE™

Cost to build? See page 214
to order complete cost estimate
to build this house in your area!

CUSTOMIZABLE

Custom Alterations? See page 221
for customizing this plan to your
specifications.

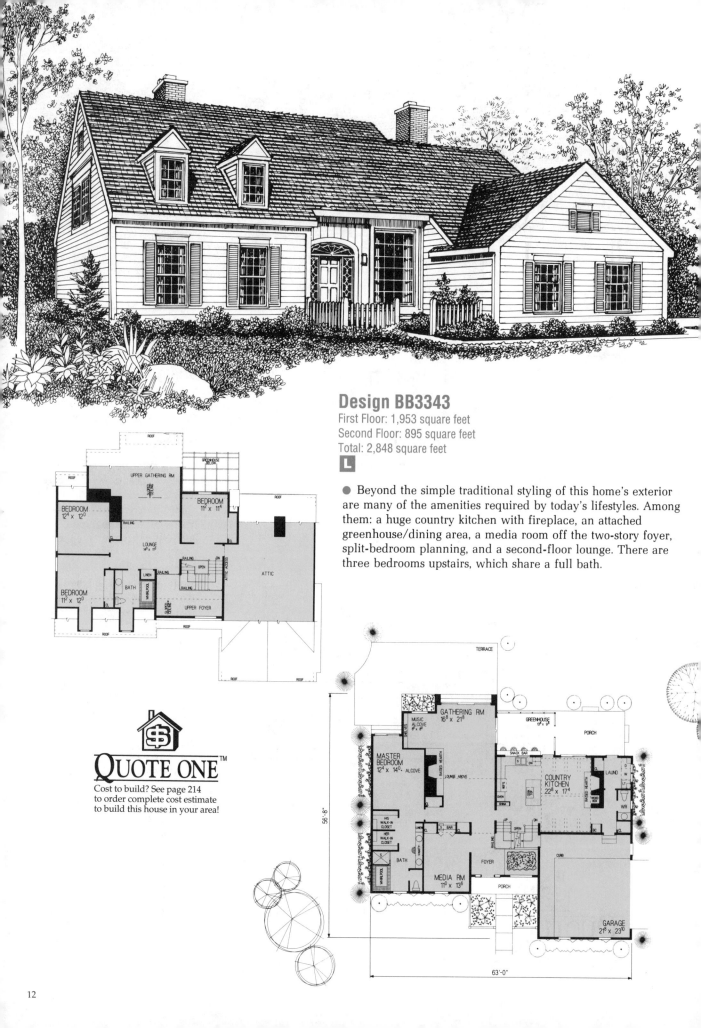

Design BB3343

First Floor: 1,953 square feet
Second Floor: 895 square feet
Total: 2,848 square feet

L

● Beyond the simple traditional styling of this home's exterior are many of the amenities required by today's lifestyles. Among them: a huge country kitchen with fireplace, an attached greenhouse/dining area, a media room off the two-story foyer, split-bedroom planning, and a second-floor lounge. There are three bedrooms upstairs, which share a full bath.

QUOTE ONE™

Cost to build? See page 214 to order complete cost estimate to build this house in your area!

Design BB8891

First Floor: 1,689 square feet
Second Floor: 534 square feet
Total: 2,223 square feet

Design by
LifeStyle
HomeDesigns

● Interesting lattice detail, a combination of brick and shingle siding and rounded accent walls make this home unique in appearance. Inside, smaller front living and dining rooms are augmented by larger rear-oriented family and breakfast areas. A courtyard circled off the family room focuses the start of yard development and highlights the forms of the house. The luxurious and stylish master bedroom suite has a very special bath with a platform tub divided from the glass-walled shower. Upstairs, two bedrooms and a loft share ample proportions and a hall bath. The two-car garage connects to the laundry/mudroom.

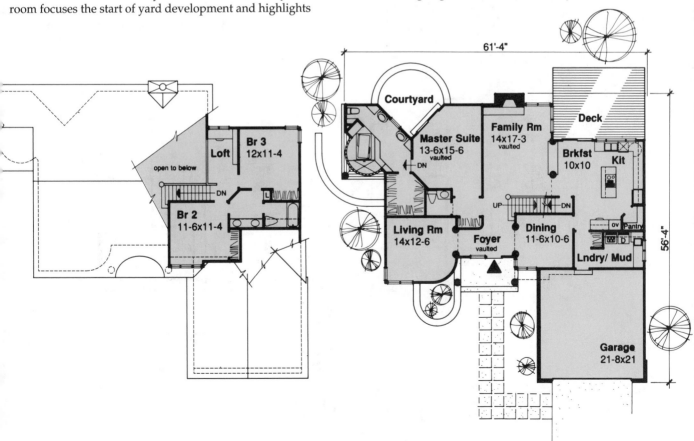

13

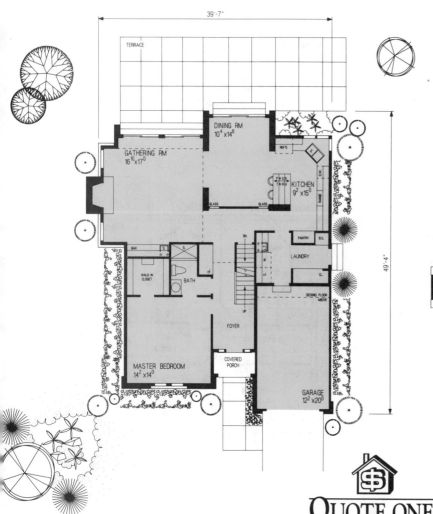

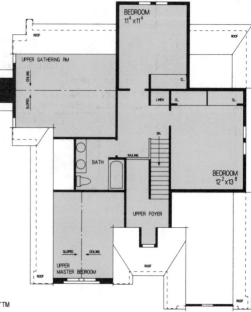

Design BB3302

First Floor: 1,326 square feet
Second Floor: 542 square feet
Total: 1,868 square feet

L

● A cottage fit for a king! Appreciate
the highlights: a two-story foyer, a rear
living zone (gathering room, terrace, and
dining room), pass-through snack bar in
kitchen, a two-story master bedroom.
Two upstairs bedrooms share a full bath.

Design BB3331

First Floor: 1,115 square feet
Second Floor: 690 square feet
Total: 1,805 square feet

L

● Who could guess that this compact design contains three bedrooms and two full baths? The kitchen has indoor eating space in the dining room and outdoor eating space on an attached deck. A fireplace in the two-story gathering room welcomes company.

California Engineered Plans and California Stock Plans are available for this home. Call 1-800-521-6797 for more information.

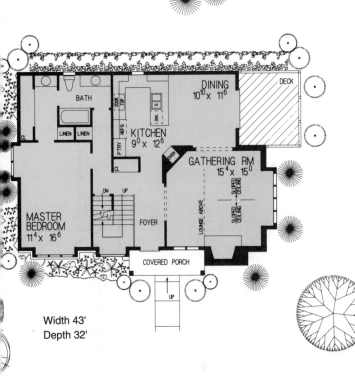

Width 43'
Depth 32'

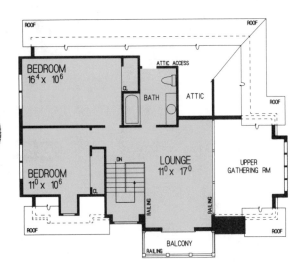

QUOTE ONE™

Cost to build? See page 214 to order complete cost estimate to build this house in your area!

Design BB2967

First Floor: 1,877 square feet
Second Floor: 467 square feet
Total: 2,344 square feet

L

● Special interior amenities
abound in this unique
1½-story Tudor. Living
areas include an open
gathering room/dining room
area with fireplace and
pass-through to the breakfast room. Quiet time can be
spent in a sloped-ceiling
study. Look for plenty of
workspace in the island
kitchen and workshop/
storage area. Sleeping areas
are separated for utmost
privacy: an elegant master
suite on the first floor, two
bedrooms and a full bath on
the second. Note the un-
usual curved balcony seat
in the stairwell and the
second floor ledge—a per-
fect spot for displaying
plants or collectibles.

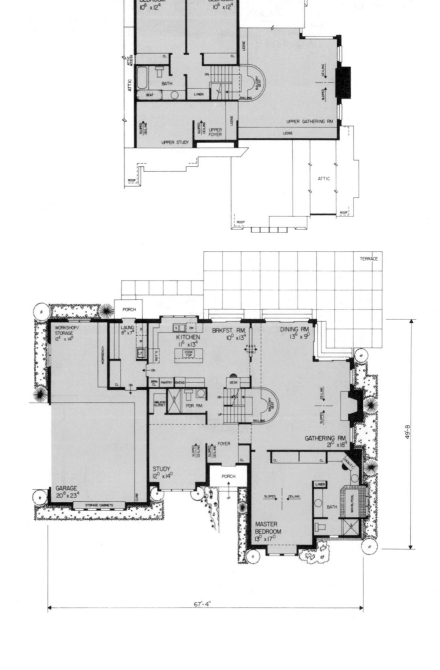

Design BB2964

First Floor: 1,441 square feet
Second Floor: 621 square feet
Total: 2,062 square feet

● Tudor houses have their own unique exterior design features. They include: gable roofs, simulated beam work, stucco and brick surfaces, diamond-lite windows, muntins, panelled doors, varying roof planes and hefty cornices. This outstanding two-story features a first-floor master bedroom, plus two more with lounge upstairs. The living room is dramatically spacious. It has a two-story sloping ceiling which permits it to look upward to the lounge. Large glass areas across the rear further enhance the bright, cheerful atmosphere of this area as well as the bedroom, dining and breakfast rooms. The open staircase to the upstairs has plenty of natural light as does the stairway to the basement recreation area.

Design BB8897

First Floor: 834 square feet
Second Floor: 722 square feet
Total: 1,556 square feet

● In this contemporary interpretation of the traditional cottage, wood and stone accents create a homey feel. The foyer leads to a vaulted living room with a three-sided fireplace, which can be viewed from the dining room. The country kitchen across the rear gives a great family focus on outdoor living with a nearby deck. The kitchen utilizes an efficient layout to maximize counter and cupboard space. On the second floor, three bedrooms comfortably accommodate the family. The master bedroom enjoys a private bath with two lavatories. A walk-in closet will also gain appreciation.

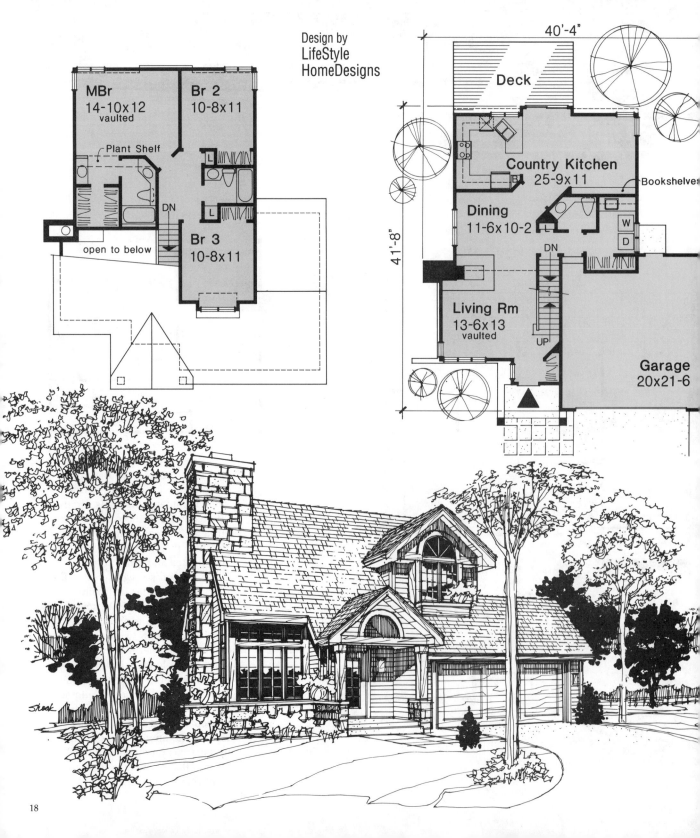

Design by
LifeStyle
HomeDesigns

MBr
14-10x12
vaulted

Plant Shelf

Br 2
10-8x11

DN

open to below

Br 3
10-8x11

40'-4"

Deck

Country Kitchen
25-9x11

Bookshelves

Dining
11-6x10-2

41'-8"

W
D

Living Rm
13-6x13
vaulted

DN

UP

Garage
20x21-6

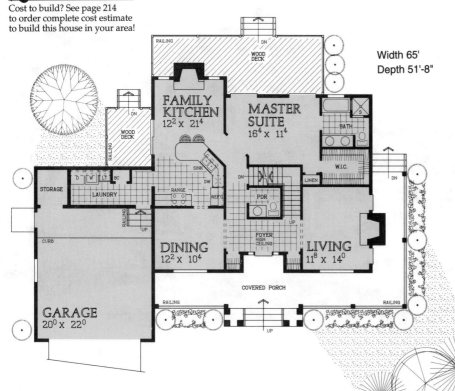

BEDROOM
10⁴ x 14⁰
+ DORMER

DESK   BOOKS   DESK
HALL

BEDROOM
11⁸ x 14⁰
+ DORMER

RAILING

LINEN

DN

BATH

OPEN TO
FOYER BELOW

LEDGE   LEDGE

QUOTE ONE™
Cost to build? See page 214
to order complete cost estimate
to build this house in your area!

RAILING   DN

WOOD
DECK

Width 65'
Depth 51'-8"

DN

WOOD
DECK

RAILING

FAMILY
KITCHEN
12² x 21⁴

MASTER
SUITE
16⁴ x 11⁴

BATH

SINK

DW

RANGE

DN

REFG

W.I.C.

LINEN

DN

STORAGE

D   W   LT   BC

LAUNDRY

RAILING

UP

PDR

FOYER
HIGH
CEILING

UP

DINING
12² x 10⁴

LIVING
11⁸ x 14⁰

CURB

GARAGE
20⁰ x 22⁰

COVERED PORCH

RAILING   RAILING

UP

Design BB3467

First Floor: 1,276 square feet
Second Floor: 658 square feet
Total: 1,934 square feet

L

● Bold and beautiful, this
Neo-classic farmhouse will
delight family and friends alike.
Lap wood siding combined with
a standing seam metal roof provides a wealth of visual appeal.
Inside, living takes off with a
great kitchen and family room
combination. Or take in brunch
on the wood deck located just
off this area. For more formal
occasions, a split dining room
and living room—with a fireplace—will serve well. A
covered wraparound porch is
accessible from both rooms and
makes outdoor living a pleasure. Located at the rear of the
first floor, the master bedroom
extends the finest accommodations including a private bath
and a walk-in closet. Upstairs,
two bedrooms with dormers
will comfortably lodge family
and guests.

CUSTOMIZABLE

Custom Alterations? See page 221
for customizing this plan to your
specifications.

19

Design BB2500

First Floor: 1,851 square feet
Second Floor: 762 square feet
Total: 2,613 square feet

L **D**

● The large family will enjoy
the wonderful living patterns of
this charming home. Don't miss
the covered rear porch and the
many features of the family
room. The master suite, conveniently separated from the family
bedrooms on the second floor,
has its own bath and a huge
walk-in closet. Two more giant-
sized storage areas—one a linen
closet—are found upstairs.

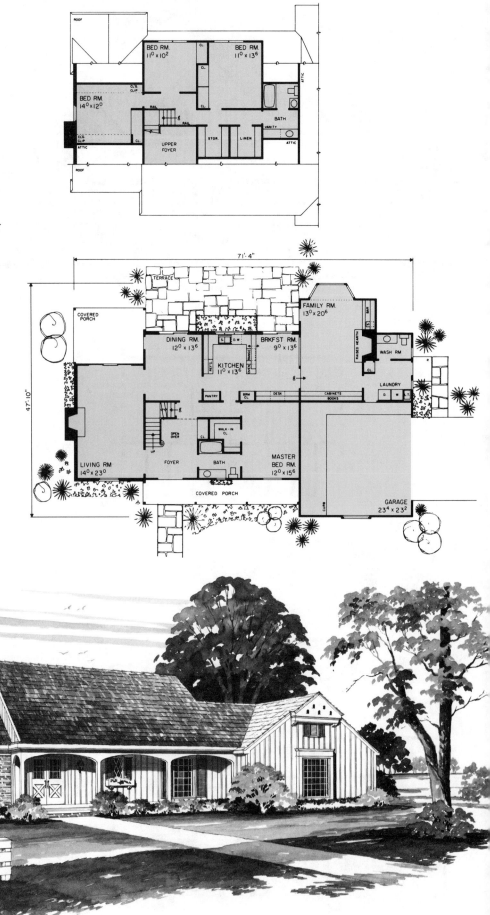

Design BB3351

First Floor: 1,794 square feet

Second Floor: 887 square feet

Total: 2,681 square feet

L **D**

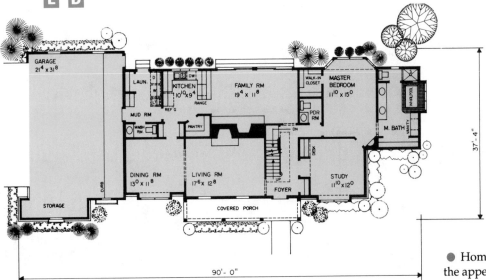

Quote One™

Cost to build? See page 214
to order complete cost estimate
to build this house in your area!

● Home-grown comfort is the key to
the appeal of this traditionally styled
home. From the kitchen with attached
family room to the living room with
fireplace and attached formal dining
room, this plan has it all. Notice the
first-floor master bedroom with
whirlpool tub and adjacent study. A
nearby powder room turns the study
into a convenient guest room. On the
second floor are three more bedrooms
with ample closet space and a full
bath. The two-car garage has a large
storage area.

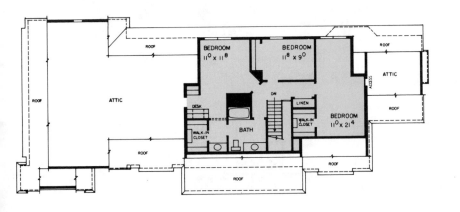

Design BB3315

First Floor: 2,918 square feet
Second Floor: 330 square feet
Total: 3,248 square feet

L

● Besides the covered front veranda, look for another full-width veranda to the rear of this charming home. The master bedroom, breakfast room, and gathering room all have French doors to this outdoor space. A handy wet bar/tavern enhances entertainment options. The upper lounge could be a welcome haven.

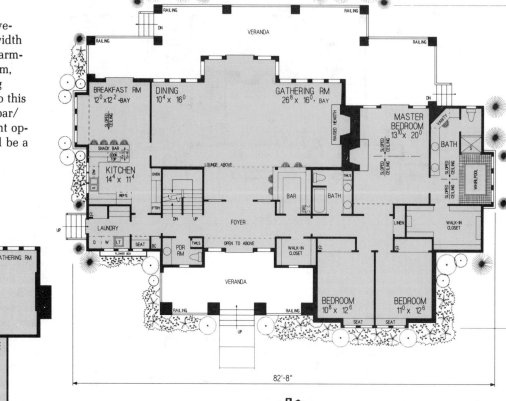

Quote One™

Cost to build? See page 214
to order complete cost estimate
to build this house in your area!

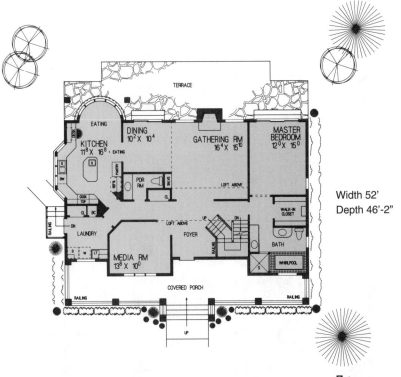

TERRACE

EATING

KITCHEN
11⁸ X 16⁸ · EATING

DINING
10² X 10⁴

GATHERING RM
16⁴ X 15¹⁰

MASTER
BEDROOM
12⁰ X 15⁰

PANTRY

PDR
RM

LOFT ABOVE

COOK
TOP

WALK-IN
CLOSET

CL

LAUNDRY

LOFT ABOVE

UP   DN

FOYER

RAILING

BATH

WHIRLPOOL

MEDIA RM
13⁸ X 10⁰

COVERED PORCH

RAILING

RAILING

UP

Width 52'
Depth 46'-2"

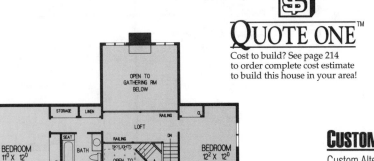

OPEN TO
GATHERING RM
BELOW

STORAGE   LINEN

RAILING   CL

LOFT

SEAT

BATH

RAILING

DN

BEDROOM
11⁰ X 12⁰

CL

SKYLIGHTS

OPEN TO
FOYER
BELOW

BEDROOM
12² X 12⁰

PLANT LEDGE

Design BB3321

First Floor: 1,636 square feet
Second Floor: 572 square feet
Total: 2,208 square feet

L **D**

● Cozy and completely functional, this 1½-story bungalow has many amenities not often found in homes its size. The covered porch at the front opens at the entry to a foyer with angled staircase. To the left is a media room, to the rear the gathering room with fireplace. Attached to the gathering room is a formal dining room with rear terrace access. The kitchen features a curved casual eating area and island work station. The right side of the first floor is dominated by the master suite. It has access to the rear terrace and a luxurious bath. Upstairs are two family bedrooms connected by a loft area overlooking the gathering room and foyer.

QUOTE ONE™

Cost to build? See page 214
to order complete cost estimate
to build this house in your area!

CUSTOMIZABLE

Custom Alterations? See page 221
for customizing this plan to your
specifications.

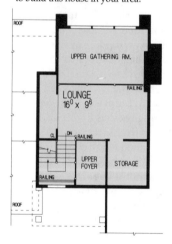

Quote One™

Cost to build? See page 214 to order complete cost estimate to build this house in your area!

Design BB3330
First Floor: 1,394 square feet
Second Floor: 320 square feet
Total: 1,714 square feet

● Outdoor living and open floor planning are highlights of this moderately sized plan. Amenities include a private hot tub on a wooden deck that is accessible via sliding glass doors in both bedrooms, and a two-story gathering room. An optional second-floor plan allows for a full 503 square feet of space with a balcony.

Design BB8894

First Floor: 846 square feet
Second Floor: 400 square feet
Total: 1,246 square feet

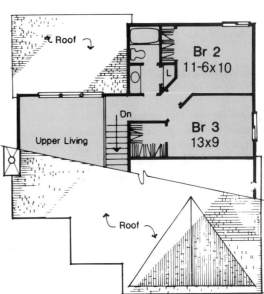

Roof

Br 2
11-6x10

Upper Living

Dn

Br 3
13x9

Roof

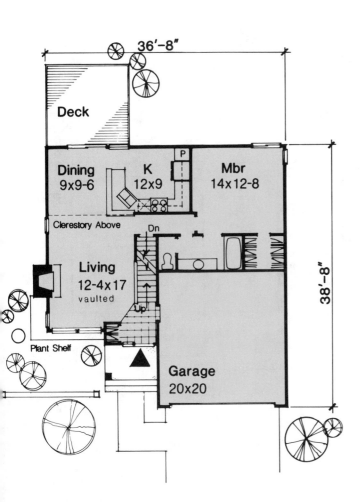

36'-8"

Deck

Dining
9x9-6

K
12x9

P

Mbr
14x12-8

Clerestory Above

Dn

Living
12-4x17
vaulted

Up

38'-8"

Plant Shelf

Garage
20x20

● A sloping roofline and wood siding lend a fresh look to this stunning starter home. Inside options include a second floor that can be built unfinished and completed as budgets allow. On the first floor, a tiled entryway reveals a vaulted living room with a fireplace. A rear kitchen serves a dining room that accesses a rear deck for outside enjoyments. Master-suite enhancements include corner windows, a walk-in closet and private passage to a full bath. Two bedrooms on the second floor include one with a walk-in closet and share a full hall bath.

Design by
LifeStyle
HomeDesigns

Design BB2892

First Floor: 1,623 square feet
Second Floor: 160 square feet
Total: 1,783 square feet

● What a striking contemporary! It houses an efficient floor plan with many outstanding features. The foyer has a sloped ceiling and an open staircase to the basement. To the right of the foyer is the work center. Note the snack bar, laundry and covered dining porch, along with the step-saving kitchen. Both the gathering and dining rooms overlook the backyard. Each of three bedrooms has access to an outdoor area. The second-floor loft could be used as a sewing room, den or lounge.

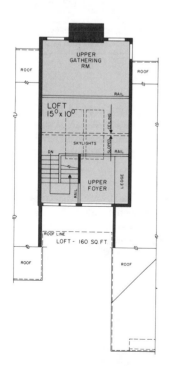

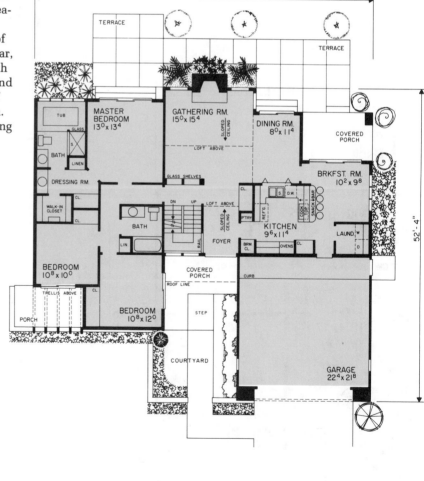

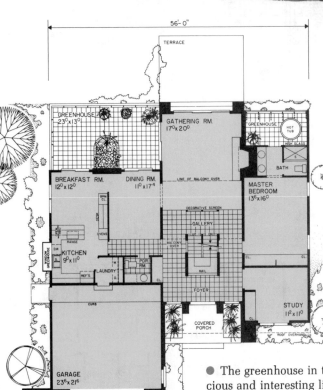

56'-0"

TERRACE

GREENHOUSE
23⁰x13⁰

GATHERING RM.
17⁰x20⁰

GREENHOUSE

HOT
TUB

HIGH GLASS

BATH

BREAKFAST RM.
12⁰x12⁰

DINING RM.
11⁰x17⁴

LINE OF BALCONY OVER

MASTER
BEDROOM
13⁶x16⁰

OVENS

RANGE

DECORATIVE SCREEN

KITCHEN
9⁴x11⁰

GALLERY

LAUNDRY

PDR.
RM.

BALCONY
OVER

RAIL

CL.

CL.

FOYER

STUDY
11²x11⁰

GARAGE
23⁶x21⁶

COVERED
PORCH

CURB

ROOF OVERHANG

ROOF OVERHANG

Design BB2884 First Floor: 1,855 square feet
Second Floor: 837 square feet; Total: 2,692 square feet

L

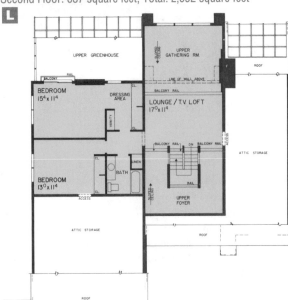

UPPER GREENHOUSE

UPPER
GATHERING RM.

ROOF

BALCONY

RAIL

LINE OF WALL ABOVE

BEDROOM
15⁴x11⁴

DRESSING
AREA

BALCONY RAIL

LOUNGE / T.V. LOFT
17⁰x11⁴

VANITY

CL.

BALCONY RAIL

DN BALCONY RAIL

ATTIC STORAGE

LINEN

CL.

BATH

RAIL

BEDROOM
13⁰x11⁴

ACCESS

UPPER
FOYER

ATTIC STORAGE

ROOF

ROOF

● The greenhouse in this design enhances its energy-efficiency and allows for spacious and interesting living patterns. Being a one-and-a-half story design, the second floor could be developed at a later date when the space is needed. The greenhouses add an additional 418 sq. ft. to the above quoted figures.

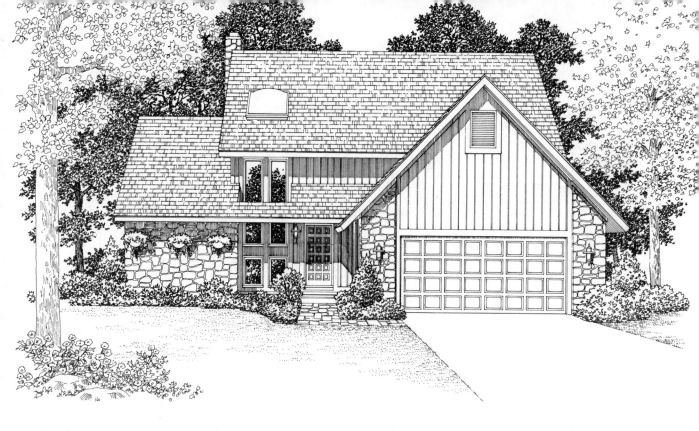

Design BB2905

First Floor: 1,342 square feet
Second Floor: 619 square feet
Total: 1,961 square feet

L D

● All of the livability in this plan is in the back! Each first floor room, except the kitchen, has access to the rear terrace via sliding glass doors. A great way to capture an excellent view. This plan is also ideal for a narrow lot seeing that its width is less than 50 feet. Two bedrooms and a lounge, overlooking the gathering room, are on the second floor.

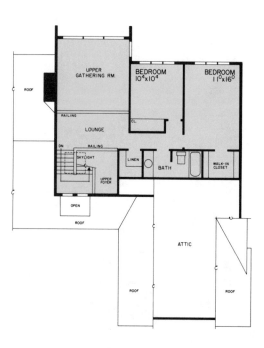

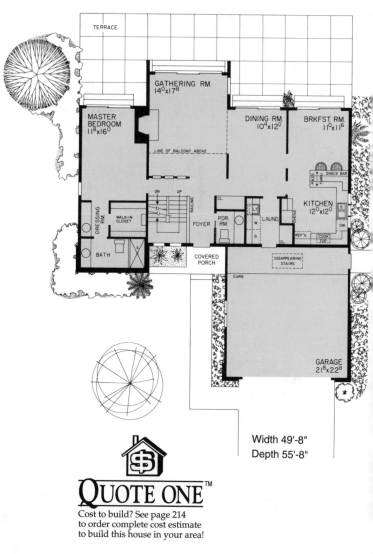

Width 49'-8"
Depth 55'-8"

QUOTE ONE™
Cost to build? See page 214
to order complete cost estimate
to build this house in your area!

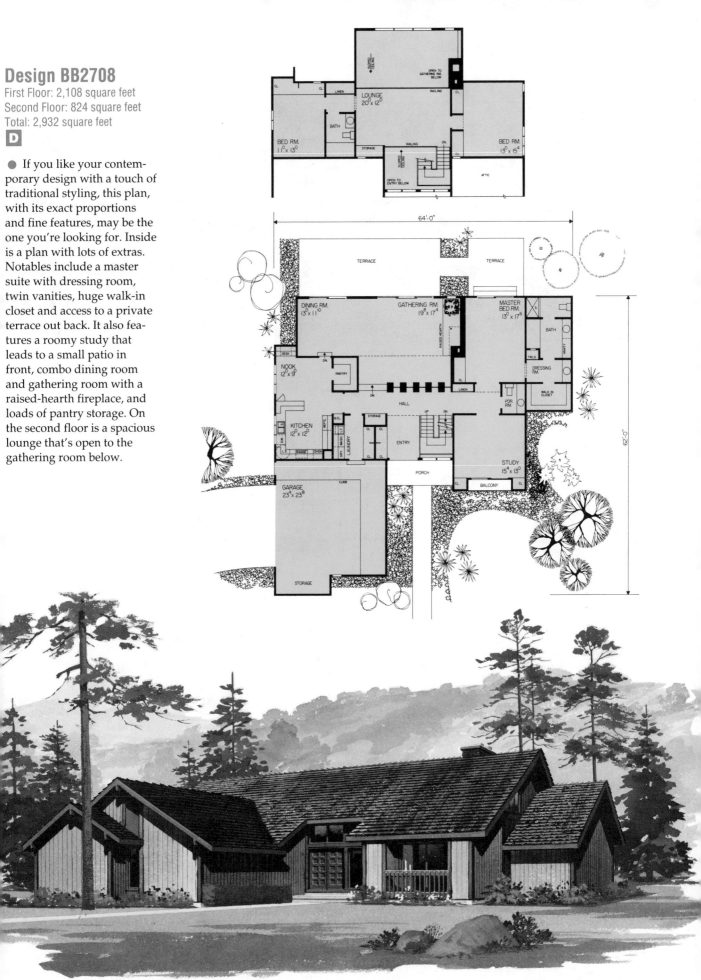

Design BB2708

First Floor: 2,108 square feet
Second Floor: 824 square feet
Total: 2,932 square feet

D

● If you like your contemporary design with a touch of traditional styling, this plan, with its exact proportions and fine features, may be the one you're looking for. Inside is a plan with lots of extras. Notables include a master suite with dressing room, twin vanities, huge walk-in closet and access to a private terrace out back. It also features a roomy study that leads to a small patio in front, combo dining room and gathering room with a raised-hearth fireplace, and loads of pantry storage. On the second floor is a spacious lounge that's open to the gathering room below.

Width 66'-8"
Depth 62'-4"

Design BB2729

First Floor: 1,590 square feet
Second Floor: 756 square feet
Total: 2,346 square feet

L

● A sheltered walkway and double front doors make a welcome entrance to this remarkable contemporary home. The two-story entry and sunken gathering room (with a raised-hearth fireplace) add dimension. Indoor/outdoor living relationships are incorporated into the design; each of the first-floor living areas opens to a terrace. The first-floor master suite, which includes a large walk-in closet, dressing room, and separate shower and tub, offers much privacy. Two additional second-floor bedrooms feature private baths and dressing rooms.

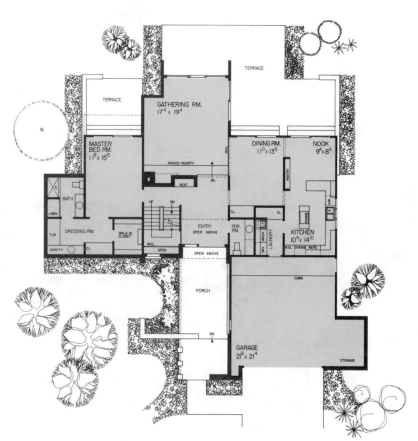

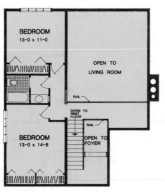

BEDROOM
13-0 x 11-0

OPEN TO
LIVING ROOM

RAIL

DOWN TO
FIRST
FLOOR

BEDROOM
13-0 x 14-8

RAIL

OPEN TO
FOYER

58'- 0"

RAIL

DECK

GREENHOUSE
WINDOW

DINING
13-0 x 11-8

SLIDING GL. DOOR

SLIDING GL. DOOR

SUN SPACE

LIVING ROOM
17-6 x 23-0

SLIDING GL. DOOR

RAIL

BREAKFAST
DECK

KITCHEN
13-0 x 12-0

MASTER BEDROOM
15-8 x 15-2

SLOPED CEILING

CEILING

BALCONY ABOVE

SOLAR
GREENHOUSE

BREAKFAST
11-4 x 9-8

DOWN TO
BASEMENT

PANTRY

SLOPED CEILING

DRESSING

WALK - IN
CLOSET

64'- 8"

STORAGE

LAUNDRY

D W

UP TO
SECOND
FLOOR

DOWN

FOYER

AIR LOCK
ENTRY

DOWN

GARAGE
21-4 x 21-8

Design BB4334

First Floor: 1,838 square feet
Second Floor: 640 square feet
Total: 2,478 square feet

● Grand sloping rooflines and a design created for southern orientation are the unique features of this contemporary home. Outdoor living is enhanced by a solar greenhouse off the breakfast room, a sun space off the master bedroom, a greenhouse window in the dining room, a casual breakfast deck, and full-width deck to the rear. The split-bedroom plan allows for the master suite (with fireplace, and huge walk-in closet) to be situated on the first floor and two family bedrooms and a full bath to find space on the second floor. Be sure to notice the balcony overlook to the sloped-ceiling living room below.

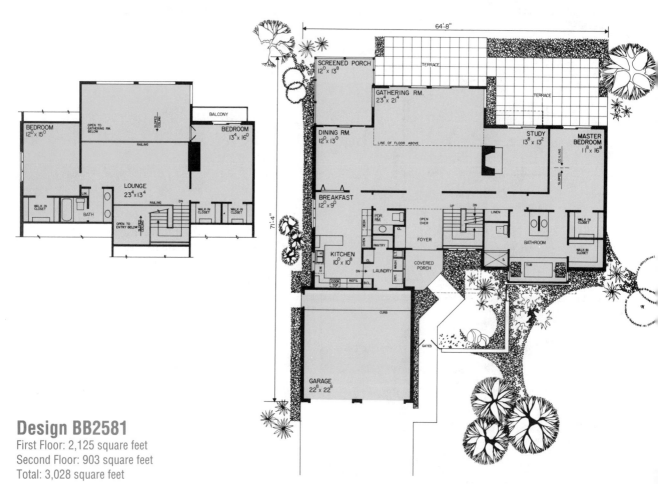

Design BB2581

First Floor: 2,125 square feet
Second Floor: 903 square feet
Total: 3,028 square feet

● A study with a fireplace! What a fine attraction to find in this lovely three-bedroom home. And the fine features certainly do not stop there. The gathering room has a sloped ceiling and two sliding glass doors to the rear terrace. The study and master bedroom (which has first floor privacy and convenience) also have glass doors to the wrap-around terrace. Adjacent to the gathering room is a formal dining room and screened-in porch. The efficient kitchen with its many built-ins has easy access to the first floor laundry. The separate breakfast nook has a built-in desk. The second floor has two bedrooms each having at least one walk-in closet. Also, a lounge overlooking the gathering room below and a balcony. Note the oversized two-car garage for storing bikes and lawn mowers. The front courtyard adds a measure of privacy to the covered porch entrance.

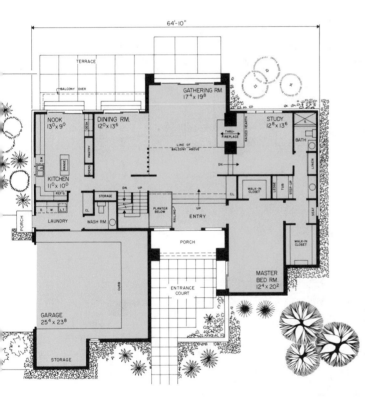

Design BB2771

First Floor: 2,087 square feet
Second Floor: 816 square feet
Total: 2,903 square feet

● This design will provide an abundance of livability for your family. The second floor is highlighted by an open lounge which overlooks both the entry and the gathering room below.

Quote One™

Cost to build? See page 214
to order complete cost estimate
to build this house in your area!

Design BB3347

First Floor: 1,915 square feet
Second Floor: 759 square feet
Total: 2,674 square feet

L

● Open living is the key to
the abundant livability of this
design. The gigantic gathering room/dining room area
shares a through-fireplace
with a unique sunken con-
versation area. An L-shaped
kitchen has a pass-through
snack bar to the breakfast
room. On the second floor,
two bedrooms are separated
by a lounge with a balcony
overlook.

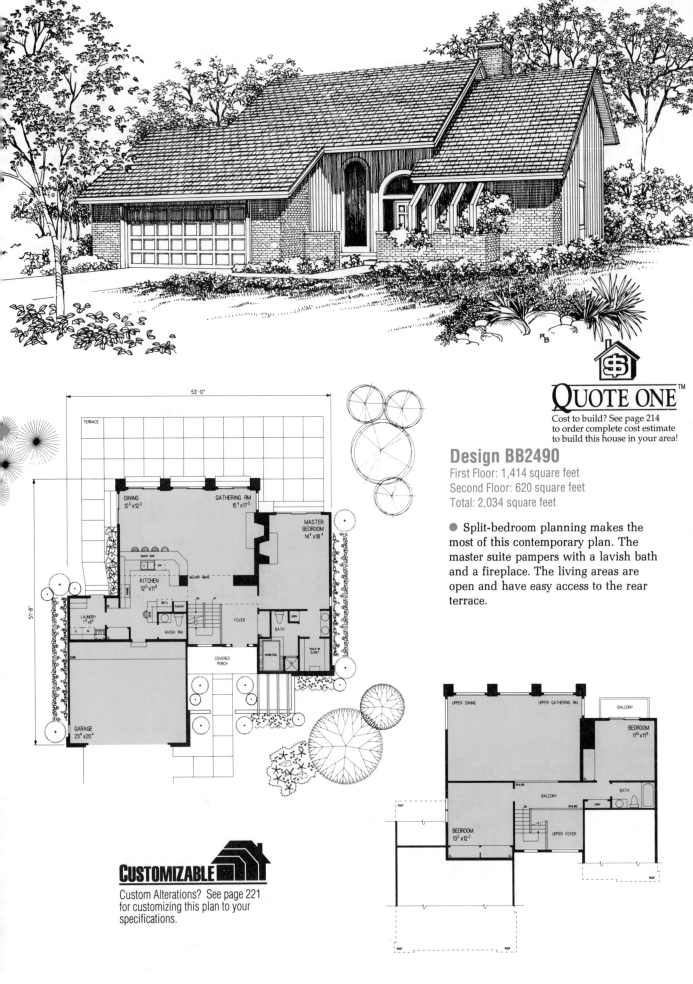

QUOTE ONE™

Cost to build? See page 214
to order complete cost estimate
to build this house in your area!

Design BB2490

First Floor: 1,414 square feet
Second Floor: 620 square feet
Total: 2,034 square feet

● Split-bedroom planning makes the
most of this contemporary plan. The
master suite pampers with a lavish bath
and a fireplace. The living areas are
open and have easy access to the rear
terrace.

CUSTOMIZABLE

Custom Alterations? See page 221
for customizing this plan to your
specifications.

Design BB3455

First Floor: 1,408 square feet
Second Floor: 667 square feet
Total: 2,075 square feet

L D

● Whether you're just starting out or looking to retire, this 1½-story, sun-country design will make an excellent home. The focal point of the first floor, the two-story living room utilizes a central fireplace and columns for comfort and elegance. Open to the living room, the dining room complements this space with its influx of natural light. The kitchen services this room easily and also enjoys a cozy breakfast nook. An island work counter in the kitchen guarantees ease in food preparation. Note the service entry to the garage; a full washer/dryer set-up adds convenience to laundry chores. On the second floor you'll find a skylit balcony—a dramatic yet purposeful design feature—leading to two bedrooms.

QUOTE ONE™

Cost to build? See page 214 to order complete cost estimate to build this house in your area!

Design BB8896

First Floor: 668 square feet
Second Floor: 691 square feet
Total: 1,359 square feet

● A raised foyer gives the inside of this home added dimension. A bright, vaulted living room includes a fireplace and easy access to the rear dining room—perfect for entertaining. The kitchen and breakfast room offer efficiency in meal preparation and serving. A coat closet and a powder room are situated near the two-car garage. The master bedroom suite is removed from two bedrooms—or one bedroom and a loft.

Design by
LifeStyle
HomeDesigns

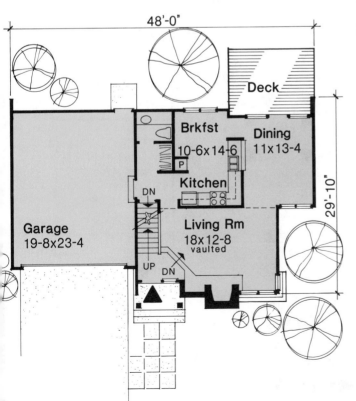

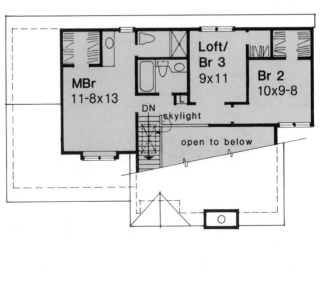

Design BB3558

First Floor: 2,328 square feet
Second Floor: 603 square feet
Total: 2,931 square feet

 L **D**

● This home will keep even the most active family from feeling cramped. A broad foyer opens to a living room that measures 24 feet across and features sliding glass doors to a rear terrace and a covered porch. Adjacent to the kitchen is a conversation area with additional access to the covered porch, a snack bar, fireplace and a window bay. A butler's pantry leads to the formal dining room. Placed conveniently on the first floor, the master suite features a roomy bath with a huge walk-in closet and dual vanities. Two large bedrooms are found on the second floor.

Width 69'-4"
Depth 66'

BEDRM
11⁰ X 11⁴

BEDRM
11⁰ X 15⁰

OPEN BELOW
RAILING

LINEN

DN
RAILING

BEDRM
11² X 13⁴

BATH

Design BB3458

First Floor: 1,617 square feet
Second Floor: 725 square feet
Total: 2,342 square feet

L D

● Palladian windows adorn the facade
of this excellent, fully functional plan.
The foyer introduces the formal zones of
the house with a volume living room to
the left and a dining room to the right.
The kitchen easily services this area and
also enjoys a large breakfast room on the
other side. A step away, the service entry
presents a washer and dryer as well as
passage to the two-car, side-load garage.
A curb in the garage expands to storage
space or becomes a perfect spot for a
workbench. For sleeping, four bedrooms
each exhibit uniqueness. The master
suite—on the ground level—has terrace
access, a generous, private bath and a
walk-in closet. Upstairs, a balcony overlooking the two-story family room leads
to the secondary bedrooms. A compartmented bath with dual lavs adds to convenience.

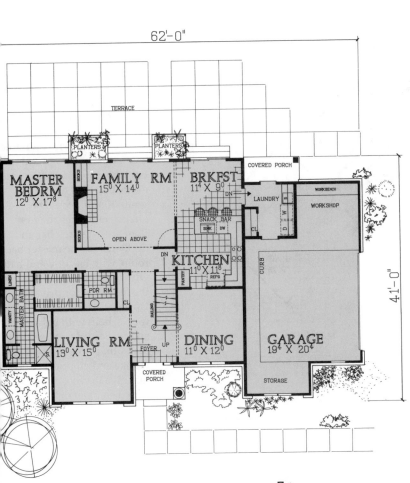

62'-0"

41'-0"

TERRACE

PLANTERS

PLANTERS

COVERED PORCH

MASTER
BEDRM
12⁰ X 17⁸

FAMILY RM
15⁰ X 14⁰

BRKFST
11⁴ X 9⁰

LAUNDRY

WORKBENCH

WORKSHOP

BOOKS

SNACK BAR

SINK DW

DN

OPEN ABOVE

KITCHEN
11⁰ X 11⁸

PANTRY

REF'S

CL

CURB

MASTER BATH

VANITY

LINEN

PDR RM

CL

RAILING

DN

LIVING RM
13⁰ X 15⁰

DINING
11⁰ X 12⁰

GARAGE
19⁴ X 20⁴

FOYER UP

COVERED PORCH

STORAGE

QUOTE ONE™

$

Cost to build? See page 214
to order complete cost estimate
to build this house in your area!

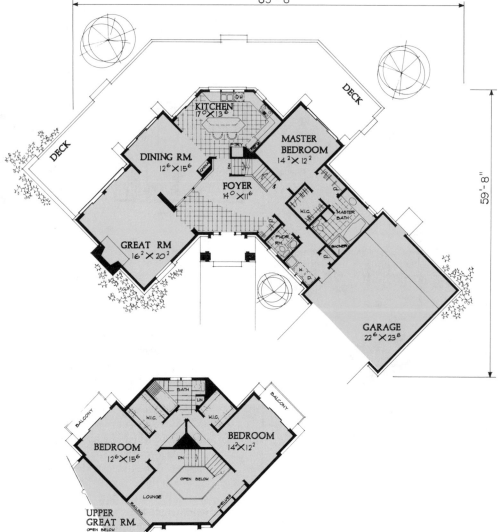

Design BB3310

First Floor: 1,668 square feet
Second Floor: 905 square feet
Total: 2,573 square feet

● If you're looking for a different angle on a new home, try this enchanting transitional house. The open foyer creates a rich atmosphere. To the left you'll find a great room with raised-brick hearth and sliding glass doors that lead out onto a wraparound deck. The kitchen enhances the first floor with a snack bar and deck access. The master bedroom, with balcony and bath with whirlpool, is located on the first floor for privacy. Upstairs, two family bedrooms, both with balconies and walk-in closets, share a full bath. Don't overlook the lounge and elliptical window that give the second floor added charisma.

Cost to build? See page 214 to order complete cost estimate to build this house in your area!

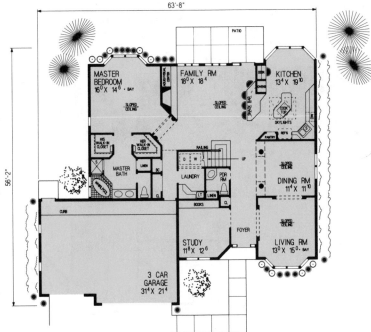

Design BB3441

First Floor: 2,022 square feet
Second Floor: 845 square feet
Total: 2,867 square feet

L

● Special details make the difference
between a house and a home. A snack
bar, audio/visual center and a fireplace make the family room livable.
A desk, island cooktop, bay and skylights enhance the kitchen area. The
dining room features two columns
and a plant ledge. The first-floor master suite includes His and Hers walk-
in closets, a spacious bath and a bay
window. On the second floor, one
bedroom features a walk-in closet and
private bath, while two additional
bedrooms share a full bath.

**California Engineered Plans and
California Stock Plans are available
for this home. Call 1-800-521-6797 for
more information.**

Custom Alterations? See page 221
for customizing this plan to your
specifications.

Cost to build? See page 214
to order complete cost estimate
to build this house in your area!

Design BB3403

First Floor: 2,240 square feet
Second Floor: 660 square feet
Total: 2,900 square feet

 L

QUOTE ONE™

Cost to build? See page 214
to order complete cost estimate
to build this house in your area!

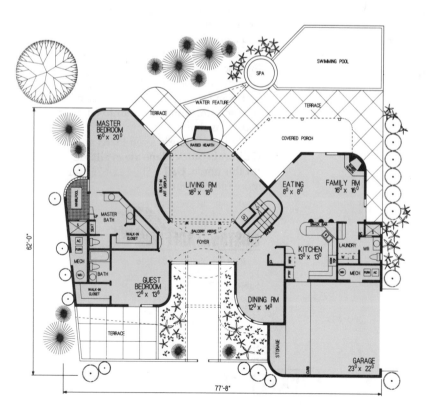

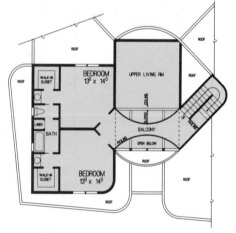

● There is no end to the distinctive features in this Southwestern contemporary. Formal living areas are concentrated in the center of the plan, perfect for entertaining. To the right of the plan, the kitchen and family room function well together as a working and living area. Also note the separate laundry room. The optional guest bedroom or den and the master bedroom are located to the left of the plan. Upstairs, the remaining two bedrooms are reached by a balcony.

California Engineered Plans and California Stock Plans are available for this home. Call 1-800-521-6797 for more information.

ONE-STORY HOMES
Under 2,000 Square Feet

A natural for empty-nesters, the smaller one-story home may be the first consideration for many. However, those looking to down-size in terms of space and number of rooms do not necessarily want to lose anything in the way of features. The homes in this section will not disappoint! They range in size from just over 1,200 square feet to just under 2,000 square feet and offer all the livability of homes that are much larger. Some contain formal living and dining spaces for elegant entertaining. Others have open, casual gathering areas for more relaxed living. A few even offer both formal and informal living areas to suit both needs. All feature convenient floor plans with extra-special master suites and integrated outdoor livability. These will be especially good choices for empty-nesters who are looking for a plan that can be converted to universal design in the future, should physical limitations become a consideration. Of special interest are the one-story Tudors (see pages 60-65) and the volume-look traditionals (see pages 90-92).

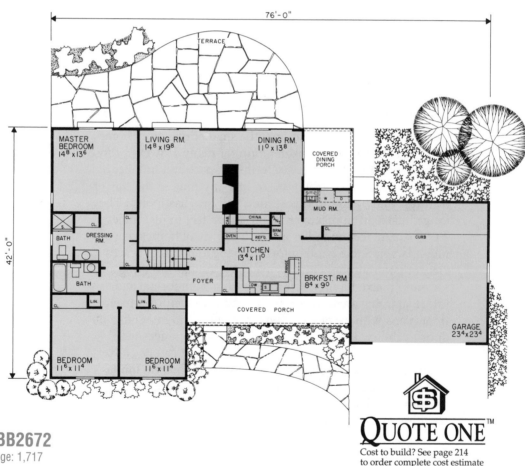

TERRACE

MASTER
BEDROOM
14^8 x 13^6

LIVING RM.
14^8 x 19^8

DINING RM.
11^0 x 13^8

COVERED
DINING
PORCH

CL

BATH

DRESSING
RM.

CL

CL

MUD RM.

W   D

BATH

CAB

CHINA

PANT

BRM

CL

OVEN

REFG

BRM
CL

CURB

KITCHEN
13^4 x 11^0

FOYER

DN

DW   S

RANGE

BRKFST. RM.
8^4 x 9^0

LIN

LIN

CL

CL

COVERED PORCH

BEDROOM
11^6 x 11^4

BEDROOM
11^6 x 11^4

GARAGE
23^4 x 23^4

76'-0"

42'-0"

$$S$$
Quote One™
Cost to build? See page 214
to order complete cost estimate
to build this house in your area!

Design BB2672
Square Footage: 1,717

L D

● The traditional appearance of this one-story is emphasized by its covered porch, multi-paned windows, narrow clapboard and vertical wood siding. Not only is the exterior eye-appealing but the interior has an efficient plan and is very livable. The front U-shaped kitchen will work with the breakfast room and mud room, which houses the laundry facilities. An access to the garage is here. Outdoor dining can be enjoyed on the covered porch adjacent to the dining room. Both of these areas, the porch and dining room, are convenient to the kitchen. Sleeping facilities consist of three bedrooms and two full baths. Note the three sets of sliding glass doors leading to the terrace.

Design BB3466

Square Footage: 1,800

L **D**

● Small but inviting, this one-story ranch-style farmhouse is the perfect choice for a small family or empty-nesters. It's loaded with amenities even the most particular homeowner can appreciate. For example, the living room and dining room each have plant shelves, sloped ceilings and built-ins to enhance livability. The living room also sports a warming hearth. The master bedroom contains a well-appointed bath with dual vanity and walk-in closet. The additional bedroom has its own bath with linen storage. The kitchen is separated from the breakfast nook by a clever bar area. Access to the two-car garage is through a laundry area with washer/dryer hookup space.

CUSTOMIZABLE

Custom Alterations? See page 221 for customizing this plan to your specifications.

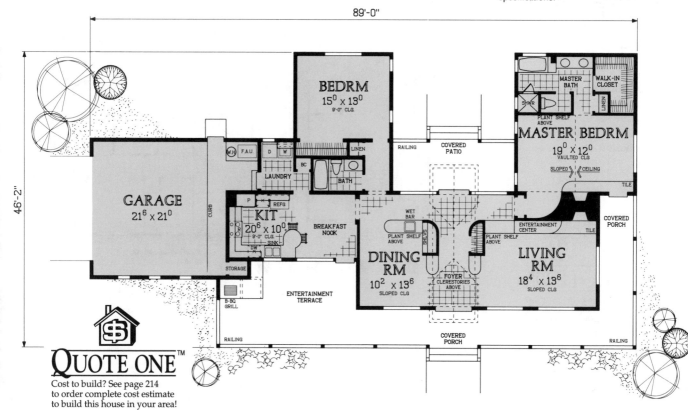

QUOTE ONE™

Cost to build? See page 214 to order complete cost estimate to build this house in your area!

45

Design BB3314

Square Footage: 1,951

● Formal living areas in this plan are joined by a sleeping wing that holds three bedrooms. Two verandas and a screened porch enlarge the plan and enhance indoor/outdoor livability. Notice the abundance of storage space.

California Engineered Plans and California Stock Plans are available for this home. Call 1-800-521-6797 for more information.

QUOTE ONE™

Cost to build? See page 214 to order complete cost estimate to build this house in your area!

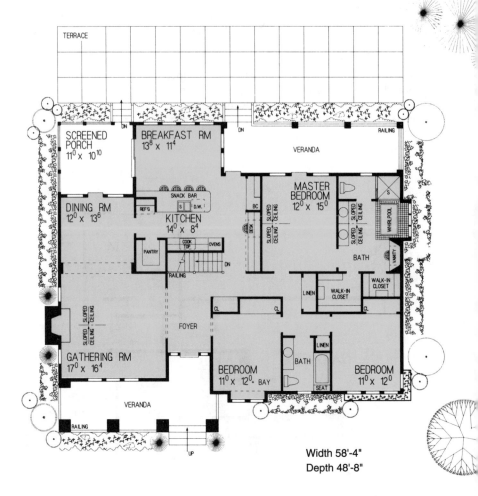

Width 58'-4"
Depth 48'-8"

Design BB3465

Square Footage: 1,410

● An L-shaped veranda employs tapered columns to support a standing-seam metal roof. Horizontal siding with brick accents and multi-pane windows enhance the exterior of this home. Most notable, however, is the metal roof with its various planes. Complementing this is a massive stucco chimney that captures the ambi-ence of the West. A hardworking interior will delight those building within a modest budget. A 36' front room provides plenty of space for both living and family dining activities. A fireplace makes a delightful focal point. The kitchen, set aside, will be free of annoying cross-room traffic. Adjacent to the kitchen is the passage-way to the garage. To one side is the laundry area, to the other, the stairs to the basement. The centrally located main bath has twin lavatories and a nearby linen closet. One of the two secondary bedrooms has direct access to the veranda. The master bedroom is flanked by the master bath and its own private covered porch.

Quote One™

Cost to build? See page 214 to order complete cost estimate to build this house in your area!

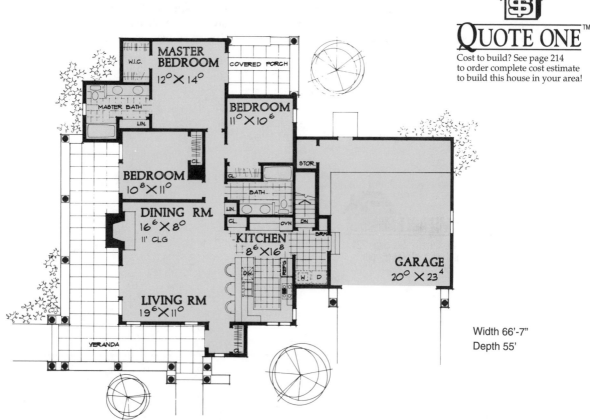

MASTER BEDROOM 12⁰ X 14⁰

W.I.C.

COVERED PORCH

MASTER BATH

LIN.

BEDROOM 11⁰ X 10⁶

BEDROOM 10⁸ X 11⁰

STOR.

BATH

DINING RM. 16⁶ X 8⁰
11' CLG

LIN.
CL.

OVN
DN

KITCHEN 8⁶ X 16⁸

DRM.

GARAGE 20⁰ X 23⁴

W   D

LIVING RM 19⁶ X 11⁰

VERANDA

Width 66'-7"
Depth 55'

47

Design BB3460
Square Footage: 1,389

● A double dose of charm, this special farmhouse plan offers two elevations in its blueprint package. With this one, a delightful wraparound porch provides excellent outdoor livability. Inside, a formal living/dining room combination has a warming fireplace and a cheery bay window. The kitchen separates this area from the more casual family room. In the kitchen, you'll find an efficient snack bar that services the family room, as well as a pantry for additional storage space. Three bedrooms include two family bedrooms served by a full bath, and a lovely master suite with its own private bath with separate lavatories. Notice the location of the washer and dryer—convenient to all of the bedrooms.

Custom Alterations? See page 221 for customizing this plan to your specifications.

44'-8"

FAMILY RM
VAULTED CLG
12⁴ x 12⁰

MASTER BEDRM
VAULTED CLG
13⁰ x 12⁰

MASTER BATH

BEDRM
VAULTED CLG
10⁰ x 10⁸

PLANT SHELF ABOVE

COVERED PORCH

SNACK BAR

PANTRY

KIT
12⁴ x 10⁰

DW

SINK

REFG

LAUNDRY

D   W

LINEN

BATH

BEDRM
VAULTED CLG
10⁰ x 10⁸

54'-6"

BAY WINDOW

DINING

LIVING RM
VAULTED CLG
13¹⁰ x 19⁰

PLANT SHELF ABOVE

F.U.   W.H

ENTRY

HALF WALL

CURB

COVERED PORCH

GARAGE
21⁴ x 23⁸

● A front porch, a decorative dormer and interesting roof planes set this elevation apart from its sister elevation on the previous page. The floor plan remains the same and very livable with bedrooms that include two family bedrooms served by a full bath and a lovely master suite with its own private bath with separate lavatories. Notice the location of the washer and dryer—convenient to all of the bedrooms.

California Engineered Plans and California Stock Plans are available for this home. Call 1-800-521-6797 for more information.

QUOTE ONE™

Cost to build? See page 214 to order complete cost estimate to build this house in your area!

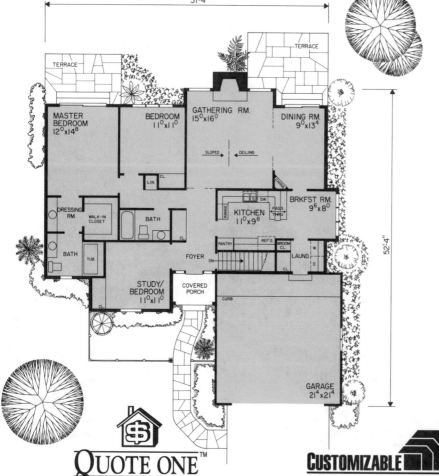

51'-4"

TERRACE

TERRACE

MASTER BEDROOM
12⁰x14⁸

BEDROOM
11⁰x11⁰

GATHERING RM.
15⁰x16⁰

DINING RM.
9⁰x13⁴

SLOPED ← CEILING

LIN CL.

DRESSING RM.

WALK-IN CLOSET

BATH

OTHER

BRKFST RM.
9⁶x8⁰

PASS THRU

RANGE

KITCHEN
11⁰x9⁸

BATH

TUB

PANTRY

REF G.

BROOM CL.

FOYER

DN

LAUND.

W

D

CL.

STUDY/ BEDROOM
11⁰x11⁰

COVERED PORCH

CURB

CL.

GARAGE
21⁴x21⁴

52'-4"

Design BB2878

Square Footage: 1,521

L   D

● This charming one-story traditional design offers plenty of livability in a compact size. Thoughtful zoning puts all bedroom sleeping areas to one side of the house apart from household activity in the living and service areas. The home includes a spacious gathering room with a sloped ceiling as well as a formal dining room and a separate breakfast room. There's also a handy pass-through between the breakfast room and an efficient, large kitchen. The laundry is strategically located adjacent to garage and breakfast/kitchen areas for handy access. A master bedroom enjoys its own suite with a private bath and a walk-in closet. A third bedroom can double as a sizable study just off the central foyer.

California Engineered Plans and California Stock Plans are available for this home. Call 1-800-521-6797 for more information.

QUOTE ONE™

Cost to build? See page 214 to order complete cost estimate to build this house in your area!

CUSTOMIZABLE

Custom Alterations? See page 221 for customizing this plan to your specifications.

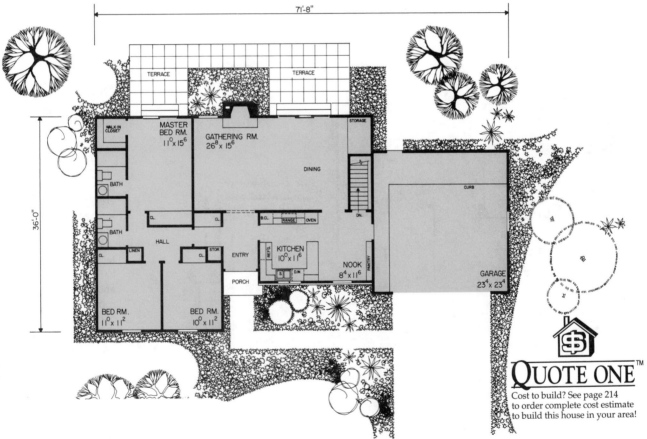

Quote One™
Cost to build? See page 214
to order complete cost estimate
to build this house in your area!

Design BB2597
Square Footage: 1,515

L **D**

● Whether it be a starter house you are after, or one in which to spend your retirement years, this pleasing frame home will provide a full measure of pride in ownership. The contrast of vertical and horizontal lines, the double front doors and the coach lamp post at the garage create an inviting exterior. Efficiently planned, the floor plan functions in an orderly manner. The 26-foot gathering room has a delightful view of the rear yard and will take care of those formal dining occasions. There are two full baths serving the three bedrooms. Additional features include: plenty of storage facilities, two sets of glass doors to the terraces, a fireplace in the gathering room, a basement and an attached two-car garage to act as a buffer against the wind.

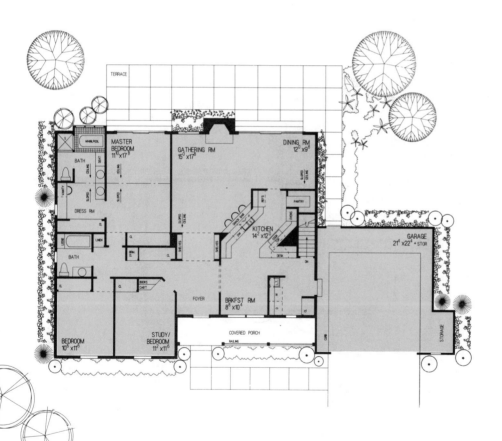

TERRACE

MASTER BEDROOM 11⁰ x17⁸

GATHERING RM 15⁰ x17⁸

DINING RM 12⁰ x9⁸

WHIRLPOOL

BATH

DRESS RM

BATH

LINEN

PANTRY

KITCHEN 14² x12¹

GARAGE 21⁰ x22⁴ + STOR

BEDROOM 10⁶ x11⁶

STUDY/ BEDROOM 11² x11⁰

BOOKS CABT

FOYER

BRKFST RM 8⁸ x10⁴

STORAGE

COVERED PORCH

RAILING

Width 75'
Depth 43'-5"

Design BB2947
Square Footage: 1,830

● This charming one-story traditional home greets visitors with a covered porch. A galley-style kitchen shares a snack bar with the spacious gathering room. An ample master suite includes a luxury bath with a whirlpool tub and a separate dressing room. Two additional bedrooms, one that could double as a study, are located at the front of the home.

California Engineered Plans and California Stock Plans are available for this home. Call 1-800-521-6797 for more information.

QUOTE ONE™

Cost to build? See page 214 to order complete cost estimate to build this house in your area!

CUSTOMIZABLE

Custom Alterations? See page 221 for customizing this plan to your specifications.

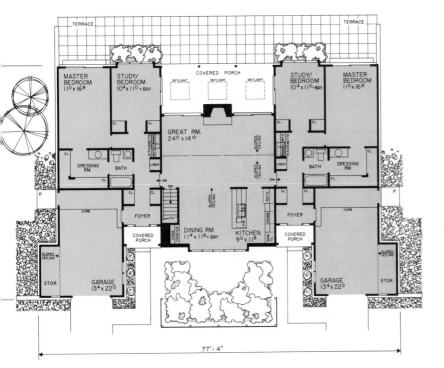

Floor plan labels:

TERRACE · TERRACE

COVERED PORCH

MASTER BEDROOM 11⁰ x 16⁸ · STUDY/BEDROOM 10⁴ x 11⁰ + BAY · SKYLIGHT · SKYLIGHT · SKYLIGHT · STUDY/BEDROOM 10⁴ x 11⁰ + BAY · MASTER BEDROOM 11⁰ x 16⁸

GREAT RM. 24⁰ x 14¹⁰

DRESSING RM. · BATH · LINEN · SLOPED CEILING · SLOPED CEILING · LINEN · BATH · DRESSING RM.

CL · CL · DN · DN · CL · CL

FOYER · SLOPED CEILING · FOYER

CURB · CURB

COVERED PORCH · DINING RM. 11⁴ x 11⁸ + BAY · KITCHEN 9⁰ x 11⁸ · COVERED PORCH

CHINA COUNTER · RANGE · REF'G.

SLOPED CEILING · STOR. · GARAGE 13⁴ x 22⁰ · GARAGE 13⁴ x 22⁰ · STOR. · SLOPED CEILING

77'-4"

Design BB2869

Square Footage: 1,986

● This traditional one-story design offers the economical benefits of shared living space without sacrificing privacy. The common area of this design is centrally located between the two private, sleeping wings. The common area, 680 square feet, is made up of the great room, dining room and kitchen. Sloping the ceiling in this area creates an open feeling as will the sliding glass doors on each side of the fireplace. These doors lead to a large covered porch with skylights above. Separate outdoor entrances lead to each of the sleeping wings. Two bedrooms, dressing area, full bath and space for an optional kitchenette occupy 653 square feet in each wing. Additional space will be found in the basement which is the full size of the common area. Don't miss the covered porch and garage with additional storage space.

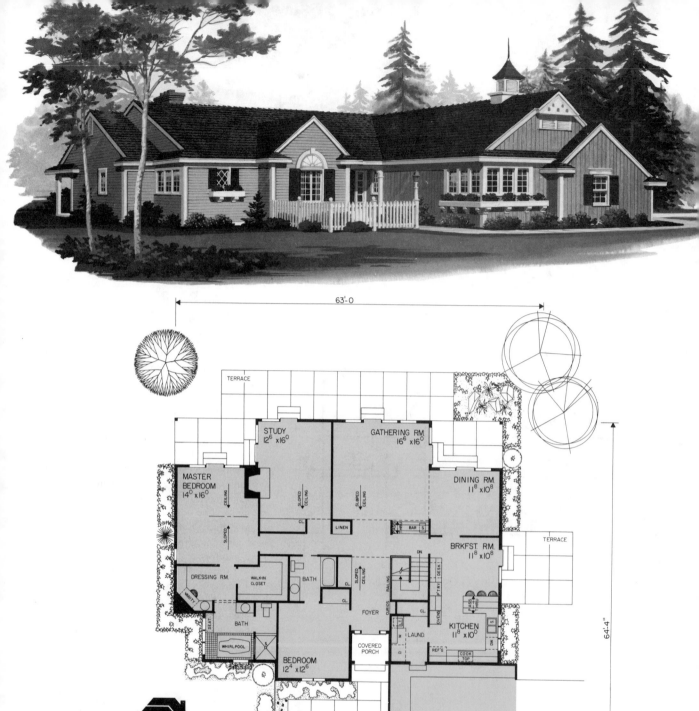

63'-0

TERRACE

STUDY
12⁶ x 16⁰

GATHERING RM.
16⁶ x 16⁰

MASTER
BEDROOM
14⁰ x 16⁰

SLOPED CEILING

SLOPED CEILING

CL

DINING RM.
11⁸ x 10⁸

TERRACE

SLOPED

LINEN

BAR S.

BRKFST. RM.
11⁸ x 10⁸

DRESSING RM.

WALK-IN CLOSET

BATH

CL

SLOPED CEILING

DN

PTRY. DESK

64'-4"

VANITY

SEAT

BATH

FOYER

CURIO/RAILING

CL

OVEN

CL

KITCHEN
11⁸ x 10⁰

WHIRLPOOL

BEDROOM
12⁴ x 12⁶

COVERED PORCH

LAUND.

REF'G.

COOK TOP

COURTYARD

GARAGE
21⁴ x 21⁴

STORAGE

CUSTOMIZABLE

Custom Alterations? See page 221
for customizing this plan to your
specifications.

Design BB2931
Square Footage: 2,032

● Little details make the difference.
Consider these that make this such a
charming showplace: Picket-fenced
courtyard, carriage lamp, window
boxes, shutters, muntined windows,
multi-gabled roof, cornice returns, vertical and horizontal siding with corner

boards, front door with glass side lites,
etc. Inside this appealing exterior there
is a truly outstanding floor plan for the
small family or empty-nesters. The
master bedroom suite is long on luxury, with a separate dressing room, private vanities, and whirlpool bath. An

adjacent study is just the right retreat.
There's room to move and — what a
warm touch! — it has its own fireplace.
Other attractions: roomy kitchen and
breakfast area, spacious gathering
room, rear and side terraces, and an
attached two-car garage with storage.

QUOTE ONE™

Cost to build? See page 214
to order complete cost estimate
to build this house in your area!

TERRACE

COVERED PORCH

SKYLIGHT   SKYLIGHT   SKYLIGHT

BRKFST RM
13² x 11⁸

LIVING RM
13⁰ x 17²

DINING
8⁸ x 9¹⁰

LAUNDRY
8⁴ x 7⁸

STORAGE
11⁰ x 8⁴

SLOPED CEILING   SLOPED CEILING

SNACK BAR

DW   S

KITCHEN
13² x 9⁶

COOK TOP

RAILING

P'TRY

CL

OVEN   REF'G

DN

BATH

FOYER

S

CL

BATH

WALK-IN
CLOSET

LINEN

STUDY/
BEDROOM
10⁰ x 10⁴

PORCH

GARAGE
19⁸ x 20⁴

CL   CL

SLOPED CEILING   SLOPED CEILING

MASTER
BEDROOM
13⁴ x 13⁰

BEDROOM
13⁴ x 10⁸

SEAT

52'-6"

58'-0"

Design BB3340
Square Footage: 1,611

L

● You may not decide to build this design simply because of its delightful covered porch. But it certainly will provide its share of enjoyment if this plan is your choice. Notice also how effectively the bedrooms are arranged out of the traffic flow of the house. One bedroom could double nicely as a TV room or study. The living room/dining area is highlighted by a fireplace, sliding glass doors to the porch, and an open staircase with built-in planter to the basement.

Design BB2565

Square Footage: 1,540

● This modest-sized floor plan has much to offer in the way of livability. With three elevations to choose from—Tudor, Colonial or contemporary—and a flexible floor plan, you're sure to find a pleasing combination. The expansive living room features a fine raised-hearth fireplace and a beamed ceiling. The kitchen will delight with its island range and adjacent breakfast nook. A laundry room and service entrance to the garage are a step away. The open stairwell to the basement is handy and leads to what may be developed into a recreation area. Three bedrooms—or have two and a study—include a private master bedroom with its own bath. For convenience in deciding what is right for you, all elevations are included in the blueprint package.

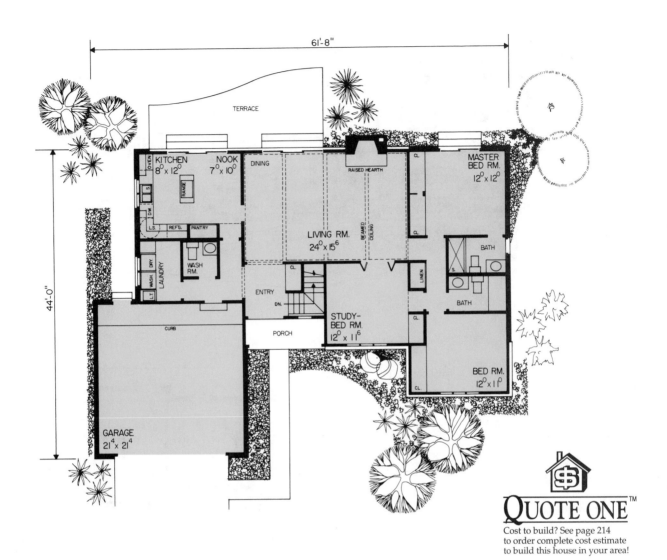

61'-8"

44'-0"

TERRACE

KITCHEN
8⁰ x 12⁰

OVEN

RANGE

NOOK
7⁰ x 10⁰

DINING

RAISED HEARTH

MASTER
BED RM.
12⁰ x 12⁰

CL.

CL.

LIVING RM.
24⁰ x 15⁶

BEAMED CEILING

BATH

S.

REF'G.

PANTRY

DW

L.S.

WASH RM.

LAUNDRY

WASH

DRY

LT.

CL.

ENTRY

DN.

LINEN

BATH

PORCH

STUDY-
BED RM.
12⁰ x 11⁶

CL.

CURB

GARAGE
21⁴ x 21⁴

CL.

BED RM.
12⁰ x 11⁰

QUOTE ONE™
Cost to build? See page 214
to order complete cost estimate
to build this house in your area!

57

Design BB8889
Square Footage: 1,283

● This fine ranch home offers
distinction with its Palladian
windows, shingle siding and
stone enhancements. The vaulted great room focuses on a fireplace. The dining room shares
views with this room. A pass-
through from the kitchen
assures ease in serving meals.
A vaulted breakfast room enjoys
access to a rear deck for added
enjoyment. Three bedrooms
include a master bedroom with
a private bath. As a starter home
or a retirement home, this
design has it all!

Design by
LifeStyle
HomeDesigns

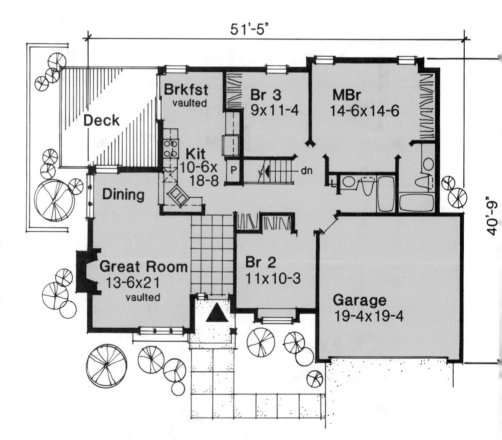

51'-5"

40'-9"

Deck

Brkfst
vaulted

Br 3
9x11-4

MBr
14-6x14-6

Kit
10-6x
18-8

P

dn

Dining

Great Room
13-6x21
vaulted

Br 2
11x10-3

Garage
19-4x19-4

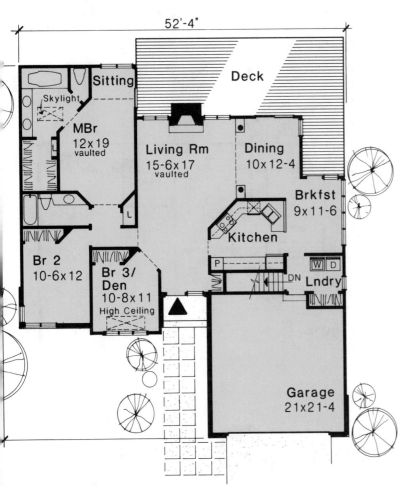

Design BB8890
Square Footage: 1,630

● This home design effectively separates living and sleeping zones for added comfort. A vaulted living room offers a fireplace flanked by bright windows. Columns define the dining room which accesses a rear wraparound deck. The well-designed kitchen easily serves the airy breakfast room. A nearby laundry room makes chores a breeze. In the sleeping wing, the master bedroom suite impresses with its vaulted ceiling, sitting room and skylit bathroom with dual vanities, compartmented toilet and walk-in closet. Bedroom 3 could also be a den, perfect for home computing.

Design by
LifeStyle
HomeDesigns

Design BB2802

Square Footage: 1,729

L **D**

● Here's yet another exterior
elevation choice for the plan
featured on the preceding two
pages. This elegant Tudor
shows off the same great livability. It does so through the effec-
tive use of half-timbered stucco
and brick as well as with an
authentic bay window in front.
The covered porch serves as a
fitting introduction to all the
inside amenities. The gathering
room gains a lot of the attention
with its rustic appeal and outside access. The house gourmet
can't miss with the full-sized
kitchen to work in. Also noteworthy is the expanse of storage
space present in the two-car
garage and the huge amount of
room available for a workbench.

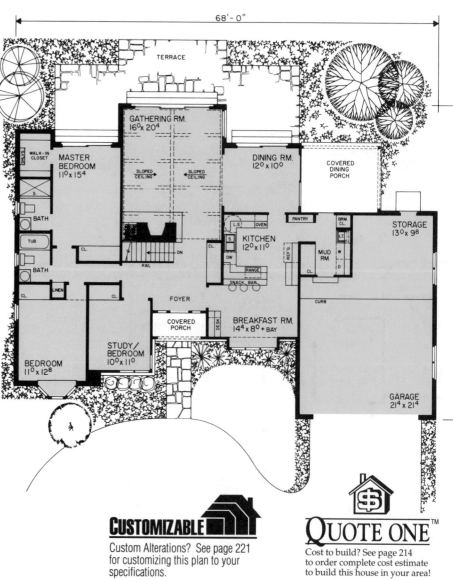

OPTIONAL NON-BASEMENT

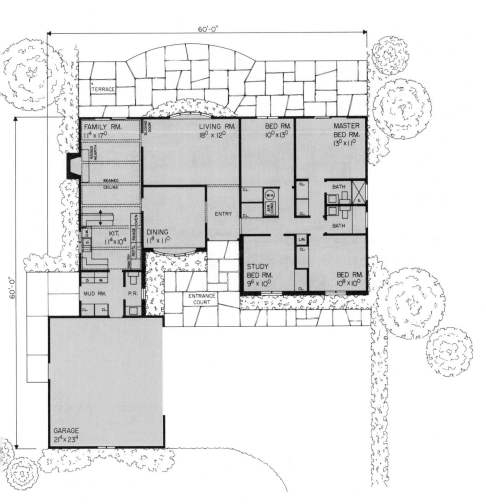

Design BB2170
Square Footage: 1,646

● An L-shaped home with an enchanting Olde English styling. The wavy-edged siding, the simulated beams, the diamond lite windows, the unusual brick pattern and the interesting roof lines all are elements which set the character of authenticity. The center entry routes traffic directly to the formal living and sleeping zones of the house. Between the kitchen-family room area and the attached two-car garage is the mud room. Here is the washer and dryer with the extra powder room nearby. The family room is highlighted by the beamed ceilings, the raised hearth fireplace and sliding glass doors to the rear terrace. The work center with its abundance of cupboard space will be fun in which to function. Four bedrooms, two full baths and good closet space are features of the sleeping area.

Design BB3373
Square Footage: 1,376

● This charmingly compact plan has three facades from which to choose: Greek Revival (BB3373), Tudor (BB3374) or Southwestern (BB3375). The interior plan contains a large living room/dining room combination, a media room, a U-shaped kitchen with a breakfast room and two bedrooms. If the extra space is needed, the media room could serve as a third bedroom. Note the terrace to the rear of the plan off the dining room and the sloped ceilings throughout.

California Engineered Plans and California Stock Plans are available for Design BB3373. Call 1-800-521-6797 for more information.

QUOTE ONE™

Cost to build? See page 214 to order complete cost estimate to build this house in your area!

Design BB3374
Square Footage: 1,375

Design BB3375

Square Footage: 1,378

L D

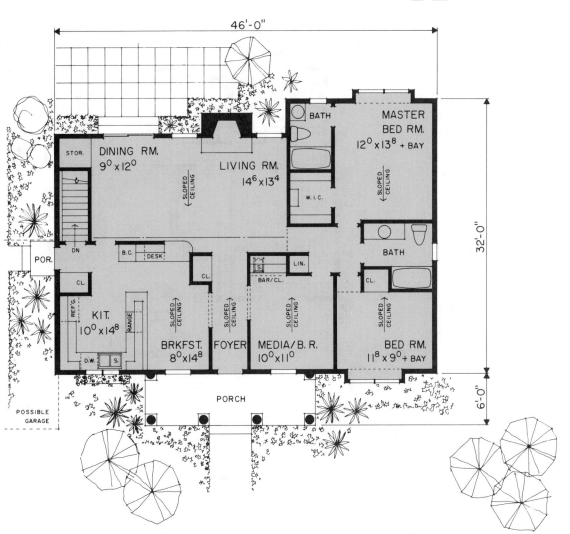

46'-0"

STOR.

DINING RM.
9⁰ x 12⁰

LIVING RM.
14⁶ x 13⁴

SLOPED CEILING

BATH

W.I.C.

MASTER BED RM.
12⁰ x 13⁸ + BAY

SLOPED CEILING

32'-0"

DN

POR.

CL.

B.C.   DESK

CL.

BAR/CL.

S   LIN.

BATH

CL.

REF'G.

KIT.
10⁰ x 14⁸

RANGE

SLOPED CEILING

SLOPED CEILING

SLOPED CEILING

SLOPED CEILING

D.W.   S.

BRKFST.
8⁰ x 14⁸

FOYER

MEDIA/B.R.
10⁰ x 11⁰

BED RM.
11⁸ x 9⁰ + BAY

PORCH

6'-0"

POSSIBLE GARAGE

Design BB2607
Square Footage: 1,208

 L

● This English Tudor cottage will delight young and old with its warm, open interior. The front porch gives way to the main living area of the house. With a fireplace and windows that overlook both front and rear yards, this space becomes a most pleasant one to inhabit. The dining room features a built-in china cabinet—built-in bookshelves are just around the corner. The U-shaped kitchen is wonderfully efficient with its double sink, dishwasher, pantry and adjacent eating bay. A laundry area and half bath also occupy this end of the house. At the other end, two bedrooms share a full bath.

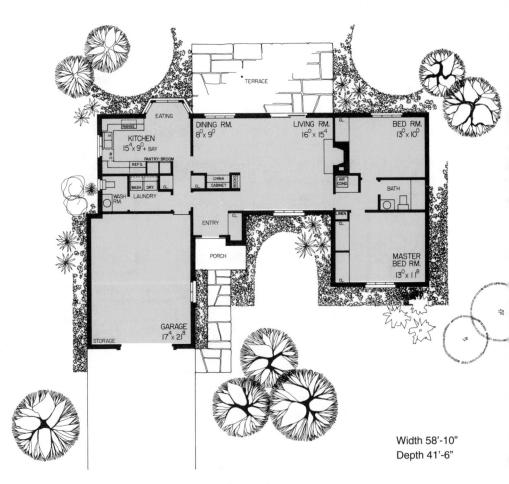

Width 58'-10"
Depth 41'-6"

OPTIONAL BASEMENT

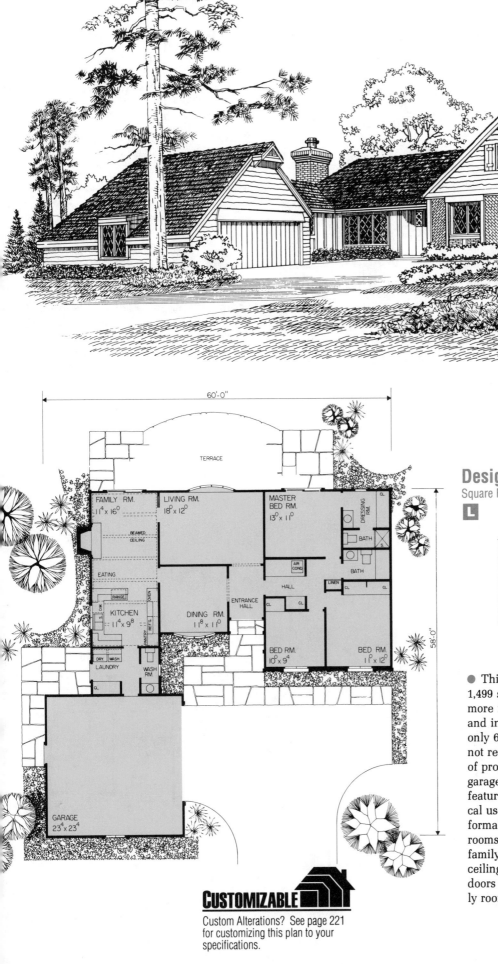

60'-0"

TERRACE

FAMILY RM.
11⁴ x 16⁰

LIVING RM.
18⁰ x 12⁰

MASTER
BED RM.
13⁰ x 11⁰

DRESSING
RM.

BEAMED
CEILING

BATH

EATING

BATH

AIR
COND.

RANGE
OVEN

HALL

LINEN
CL.
CL.

KITCHEN
11⁴ x 9⁸

DW.
S.
REF'G.
PANTRY

ENTRANCE
HALL

DINING RM.
11⁸ x 11⁰

CL.
CL.

DRY.
WASH.

LAUNDRY
CL.

WASH.
RM.

BED RM.
10⁰ x 9⁴

BED RM.
11⁰ x 12⁰

58'-0"

GARAGE
23⁴ x 23⁴

QUOTE ONE™

Cost to build? See page 214
to order complete cost estimate
to build this house in your area!

Design BB2606
Square Footage: 1,499

L

MASTER BED RM.

LINEN

BATH

ENT.
HALL

DN.

HALL

CL.

BED RM.
CL.

BED RM.

OPTIONAL BASEMENT

● This modest sized house with its
1,499 square feet could hardly offer
more in the way of exterior charm
and interior livability. Measuring
only 60 feet in width means it will
not require a huge, expensive piece
of property. The orientation of the
garage and the front drive court are
features which promote an economical use of property. In addition to the
formal, separate living and dining
rooms, there is the informal kitchen/
family room area. Note the beamed
ceiling, the fireplace, the sliding glass
doors and the eating area of the family room.

Design BB3355
Square Footage: 1,387

L D

● Though it's only just under 1,400 total
square feet, this plan offers three bedrooms (or
two with study) and a sizable gathering room
with fireplace and sloped ceiling. The galley
kitchen provides a pass-through snack bar and
has a planning desk and attached breakfast
room. Besides two smaller bedrooms with a
full bath, there's an extravagant master suite
with large dressing area, double vanity and
raised whirlpool tub. The full-length terrace to
the rear of the house extends the living potential to the outdoors.

CUSTOMIZABLE

Custom Alterations? See page 221
for customizing this plan to your
specifications.

Cost to build? See page 214
to order complete cost estimate
to build this house in your area!

QUOTE ONE™

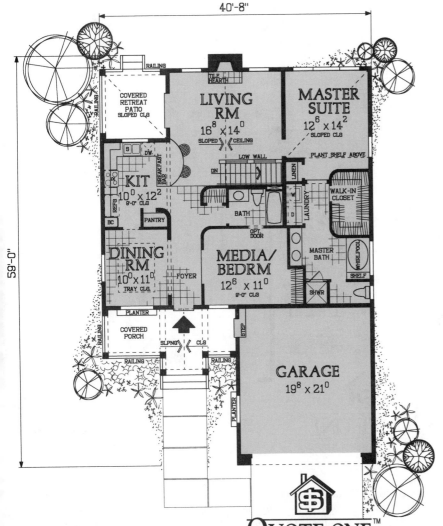

Design BB3442

Square Footage: 1,273

L **D**

● For those just starting out or the empty-nester, this unique one-story plan is sure to delight. A covered-porch introduces a dining room with a coffered ceiling and views out two sides of the house. The kitchen is just off this room and is most efficient with a double sink, dishwasher and pantry. The living room gains attention with a volume ceiling, fireplace and access to a covered patio. The master bedroom also features a volume ceiling while enjoying the luxury of a private bath. In it, a walk-in closet, washer/dryer, double-bowl vanity, garden tub, separate shower and compartmented toilet comprise the amenities. Not to be overlooked, a second bedroom may easily convert to a media room or study—the choice is yours.

CUSTOMIZABLE

Custom Alterations? See page 221 for customizing this plan to your specifications.

QUOTE ONE

Cost to build? See page 214 to order complete cost estimate to build this house in your area!

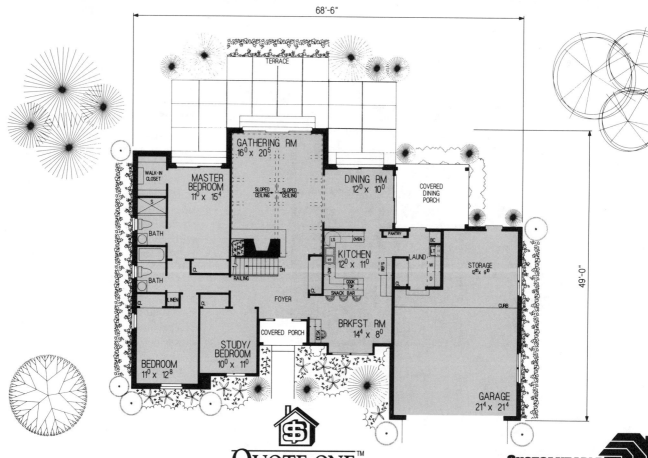

Design BB3345
Square Footage: 1,738

L

Quote One™

Cost to build? See page 214
to order complete cost estimate
to build this house in your area!

CUSTOMIZABLE

Custom Alterations? See page 221
for customizing this plan to your
specifications.

● This quaint shingled cottage offers an unexpected amount of living space in just over 1,700 square feet. The large gathering room with fireplace, dining room with covered porch, and kitchen with breakfast room handle formal parties as easily as they do the casual family get-together. Three bedrooms, one that could also serve as a study, are found in a separate wing of the house. Give special attention to the storage space in this home and the extra touches that set it apart from many homes of equal size.

esign BB3481A

quare Footage: 1,901

In just under 2,000 square feet, this pleasing one-
ory home bears all the livability of houses twice its
ze. A combined living and dining room offers ele-
nce for entertaining; with two elevations to choose
om, the living room can either support an octagonal
ay or a bumped-out nook. The U-shaped kitchen
nds easy access to the breakfast nook and rear fami-
room; sliding glass doors lead from the family
om to a back stoop. The master bedroom has a
uaint potshelf and a private bath with a spa tub, a
ouble-bowl vanity, a walk-in closet and a compart-
iented toilet. With two additional family bed-
ooms—one may serve as a den if desired—and a
all bath with dual lavatories, this plan offers the best
accommodations. Both elevations come with the
lueprint package.

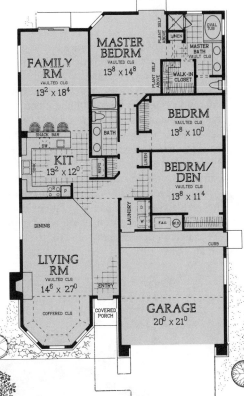

Design BB3481B

Square Footage: 1,908

L

Width 42'-4"
Depth 63'-10"

CUSTOMIZABLE

Custom Alterations? See page 221
for customizing this plan to your
specifications.

Design BB2505

Square Footage: 1,366

● This plan offers you a choice of three distinctively different exteriors—each is detailed in the set of blueprints you receive. One, with traditional flair, sets the pace with its use of vertical siding. The two remaining exteriors both exhibit contemporary styling—one makes use of raised and varying roof planes. Whichever you choose, the floor plan stays the same. In less than 1,400 square feet, the amenities abound. A large, central gathering room enjoys the warmth of a raised-hearth fireplace and the companionship of a formal dining room. The galley-style kitchen also services a bayed breakfast nook. Three bedrooms comprise the sleeping wing of the house. The master bedroom enjoys a walk-in closet and a private bath.

CUSTOMIZABLE

Custom Alterations? See page 221 for customizing this plan to your specifications.

QUOTE ONE™

Cost to build? See page 214 to order complete cost estimate to build this house in your area!

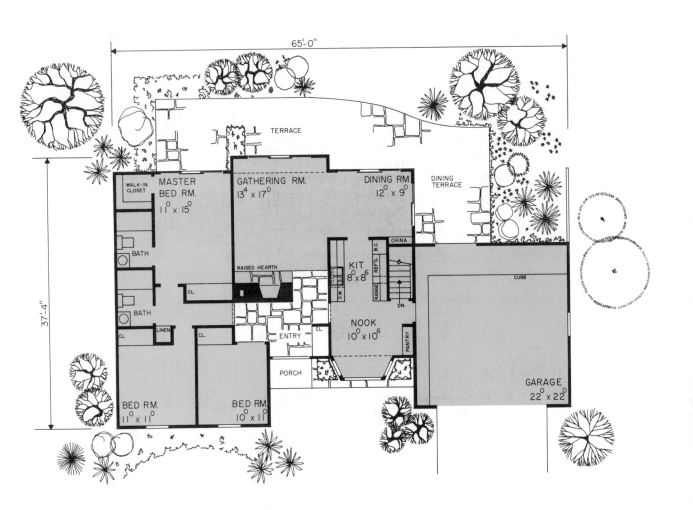

65'-0"

37'-4"

TERRACE

WALK-IN CLOSET

MASTER BED RM.
11⁰ x 15⁰

GATHERING RM.
13⁴ x 17⁰

DINING RM.
12⁰ x 9⁰

DINING TERRACE

BATH

CHINA

REFG. B.C.

KIT.
8⁰ x 8⁶

RAISED HEARTH

CL.

BATH

D.W. S

RANGE

DN.

CURB

CL.

LINEN

CL.

ENTRY

CL.

NOOK
10⁰ x 10⁶

PANTRY

PORCH

GARAGE
22⁰ x 22⁰

BED RM.
11⁰ x 11⁰

BED RM.
10⁰ x 11⁰

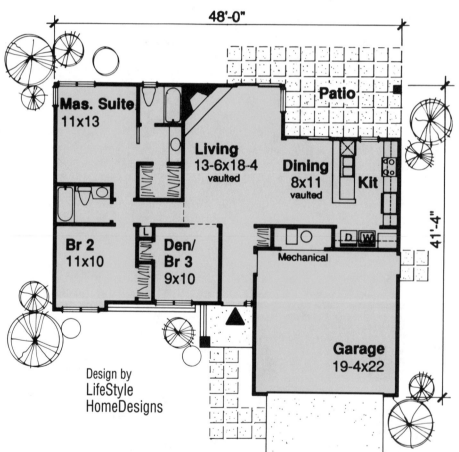

48'-0"

41'-4"

Mas. Suite
11x13

Living
13-6x18-4
vaulted

Patio

Dining
8x11
vaulted

Kit

Br 2
11x10

Den/
Br 3
9x10

Mechanical

Garage
19-4x22

Design by
LifeStyle
HomeDesigns

Design BB8895
Square Footage: 1,159

● Fine starter livability is present in this handsome ranch home. At the heart of the home is the vaulted living room with a corner fireplace and views of the rear patio. The dining room connects to this area and is easily serviced by the efficient kitchen. You'll find a washer and dryer tucked into a neat kitchen alcove. Three bedrooms include one that could double as a den. In the master suite, a walk-in closet and a compartmented bath gain attention. A basement stairway can be built in place of the laundry/mechanical space.

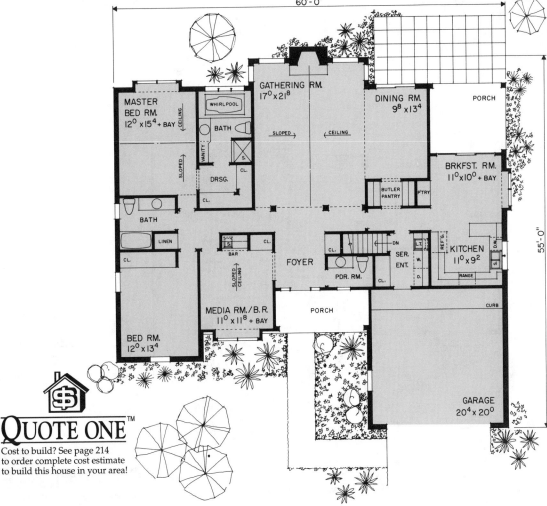

GATHERING RM.
17⁰ x 21⁸

DINING RM.
9⁸ x 13⁴

PORCH

MASTER
BED RM.
12⁰ x 15⁴ + BAY

WHIRLPOOL

BATH

SLOPED   CEILING

VANITY

DRSG.

CL.

BRKFST. RM.
11⁰ x 10⁰ + BAY

BATH

LINEN

CL.

BAR

SLOPED
CEILING

BUTLER
PANTRY

P'TRY

REF'G.

KITCHEN
11⁰ x 9²

DW.

FOYER

PDR. RM.

CL.

DN

SER.
ENT.

W.

D.

RANGE

MEDIA RM./B.R.
11⁰ x 11⁸ + BAY

PORCH

CURB

BED RM.
12⁰ x 13⁴

GARAGE
20⁴ x 20⁰

60'-0"

55'-0"

Quote One™

Cost to build? See page 214
to order complete cost estimate
to build this house in your area!

Design BB3376

Square Footage: 1,999

L   D

● Small families or empty nesters
will appreciate the layout of this traditional ranch. The foyer opens to the
gathering room with fireplace and
sloped ceiling. The dining room is
open to the gathering room for entertaining ease and contains sliding
doors to a rear terrace. The breakfast
room also provides access to a covered porch for dining outdoors. The
media room to the left of the home
offers a bay window and a wet bar, or
it can double as a third bedroom.

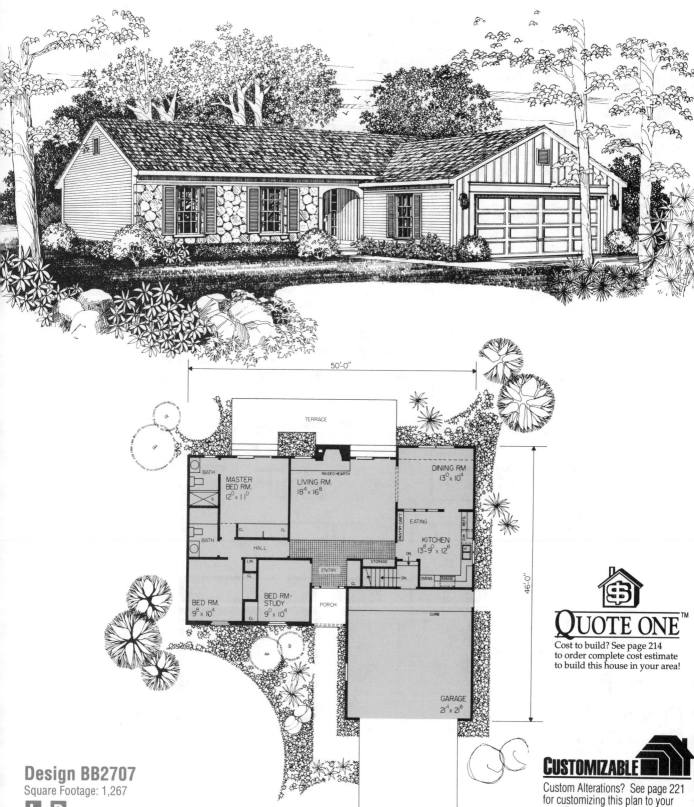

TERRACE

BATH

MASTER BED RM.
12⁰ x 11⁰

LIVING RM.
18⁴ x 16⁸

RAISED HEARTH

DINING RM
13⁰ x 10⁴

BATH

CL

CL

HALL

EATING

KITCHEN
13-9⁰ x 12⁸

PANTRY CAB'T

DW REF'S

LIN

CL

STORAGE

BED RM.
9⁸ x 10⁴

BED RM-STUDY
9⁰ x 10⁴

CL

ENTRY

CL

DN.

DN.

OVENS RANGE

PORCH

CURB

GARAGE
21⁴ x 21⁸

50'-0"

46'-0"

QUOTE ONE™

Cost to build? See page 214
to order complete cost estimate
to build this house in your area!

CUSTOMIZABLE

Custom Alterations? See page 221
for customizing this plan to your
specifications.

Design BB2707
Square Footage: 1,267

L D

● Here is a charming Early American adaptation that will serve as a picturesque and practical retirement home. Also, it will serve admirably those with a small family in search of an efficient, economically built home. The living area, highlighted by the raised hearth fireplace, is spacious. The kitchen features eating space and easy access to the garage and basement. The dining room is adjacent to the kitchen and views the rear yard. Then, there is the basement for recreation and hobby pursuits. The bedroom wing offers three bedrooms and two full baths. Don't miss the sliding doors to the terrace from the living room and the master bedroom. Storage units are plentiful including a pantry cabinet in the eating area of the kitchen. This plan will be efficient and livable.

esign BB2805

uare Footage: 1,547

Choices abound with the intro-
uction of three exteriors for one
bulous floor plan. On this page, a
dditional exterior delights with its
mployment of various exterior
uilding materials. The next two
ages display a Tudor exterior as
ell as a contemporary one. Inside
ch, you'll find yourself at home.
grand living room connects to a
ning room. A pair of sliding glass
oors offers passage to a covered
ar porch—skylights here offer an
dditional degree of livability. The
-shaped kitchen expands into a
pacious breakfast room—also
ith access to the rear porch. Three
edrooms—or two and a TV room
study—comprise the sleeping
uarters. Don't miss the large stor-
ge area in the garage—perfect for
l of your seasonal items. An
ptional non-basement plan adds
the flexibility of this design.

Width 60'-4"
Depth 51'-5"

OPTIONAL NON-BASEMENT

QUOTE ONE™
Cost to build? See page 214
to order complete cost estimate
to build this house in your area!

75

Design BB2806
Square Footage: 1,584

L D

● Like the home on the last page, this Tudor provides an excellent facade for this same floor plan. Shown with a side-entry garage, the authenticity in the facade is not lost. The breakfast room presents the perfect atmosphere for high tea or family dinners. Nearby, the combination living/dining room provides an elegant entertaining area. In the master bedroom, a walk-in closet and a private bath will delight.

Width 58'-10"
Depth 50'-10"

COVERED PORCH

SKYLIGHT | SKYLIGHT | SKYLIGHT

BRKFST. RM.
13⁴ x 11¹⁰

LIVING RM.
13⁴ x 17²

DINING RM.
8⁰ x 9¹⁰

MUD RM.

STORAGE

KITCHEN
13⁴ x 9⁶

SNACK BAR

DW S.

OVEN REF'G.

PANT.

RAILING

DN

FOYER

DESK

SLOPED CEILING

TV/STUDY
BEDROOM
10⁰ x 10⁴

BATH

BATH

WALK-IN CLOSET

LIN.

COVERED PORCH

CL.

CL.

GARAGE
19⁸ x 19⁰ + STOR.

CURB

MASTER BEDROOM
13⁶ x 12⁰

BEDROOM
13⁶ x 10⁸ + BAY

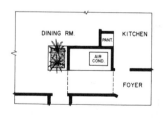

DINING RM.

KITCHEN

PANT.

AIR COND.

FOYER

OPTIONAL NON-BASEMENT

esign BB2807
uare Footage: 1,576

D

In this contemporary ren-
tion of the plan featured on
e preceding two pages, a
onderful exterior empha-
zes a most desirable floor
lan. Notice the slight redefi-
tion of the front bed-
ooms—to maintain the sleek
ylings of a contemporary,
e bumped-out wall and bay
indow are replaced with a
ush wall and vertical siding.

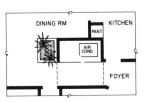

OPTIONAL NON-BASEMENT

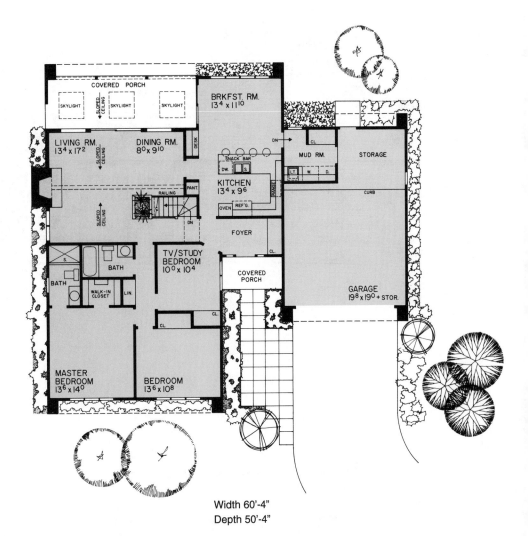

Width 60'-4"
Depth 50'-4"

77

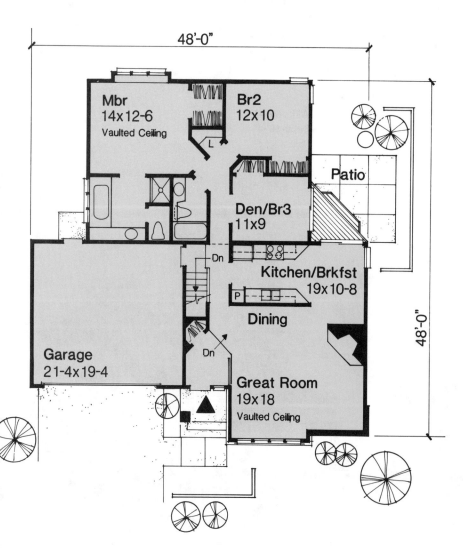

Mbr
14x12-6
Vaulted Ceiling

Br2
12x10

Patio

Den/Br3
11x9

Kitchen/Brkfst
19x10-8

Dn

Dining

Garage
21-4x19-4

Dn

Great Room
19x18
Vaulted Ceiling

48'-0"

48'-0"

Design BB8893
Square Footage: 1,368

● Modern flair in this one-story home offers great curb appeal. Inside, flexible living patterns accommodate the growing family. The raised foyer leads to the vaulted great room. A fireplace and dining space make this a cozy space. The galley-style kitchen opens to a breakfast nook. Sliding glass doors here lead to a private patio. The sleeping zone in this home includes two secondary bedrooms—one could easily serve as a den. The master bedroom features a vaulted ceiling, bumped-out windows, a walk-in closet and a spacious bath.

Design by
LifeStyle
HomeDesigns

Design BB8888
Square Footage: 1,850

● For all the room you need, this design takes precedence. A front den or office is highlighted by a massive brick fireplace and lots of bright windows. Use this space, too, to accommodate house guests. The living room also features a fireplace as well as a high ceiling. The gourmet kitchen enjoys an island and a sunny breakfast nook. The formal dining room opens to the rear deck and spa. Two bedrooms are situated on the left side of the plan. In the master bedroom suite, large proportions, deck access and a luxury bath are popular enhancements. A large walk-in closet and a linen closet assure you meet storage needs.

Design by
LifeStyle
HomeDesigns

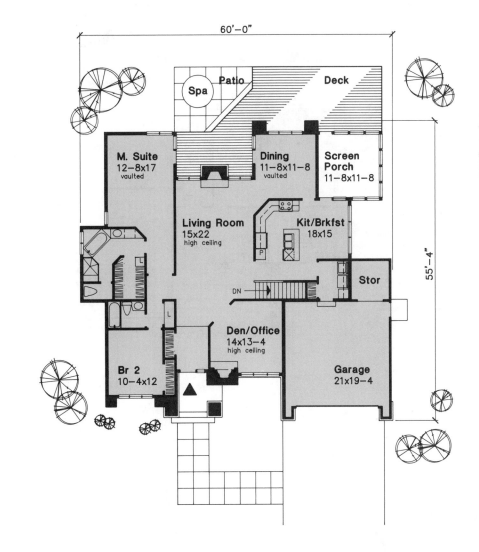

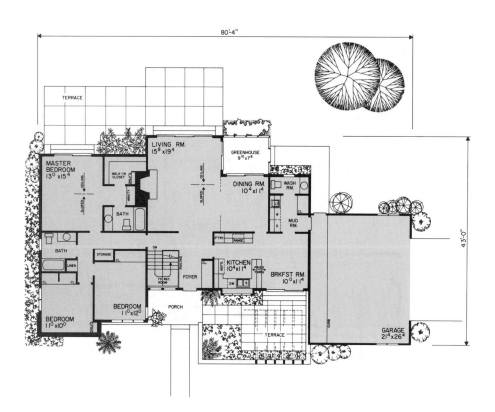

80'-4"

TERRACE

MASTER
BEDROOM
13⁰ x15⁴

WALK-IN
CLOSET

VANITY

BATH

LIVING RM.
15⁸ x19⁴

SLOPED CEILING

GREENHOUSE
9¹⁰ x7⁸

DINING RM.
10⁴ x11⁴

WASH
RM.

MUD
RM.

BATH

STORAGE

CL

LINEN

CL

DN

TO REC.
ROOM

FOYER

P'TRY

RANGE

REF'G

KITCHEN
10⁴ x11⁴

PASS
THRU

BRKFST RM.
10⁰ x11⁴

43'-0"

BEDROOM
11⁰ x10⁰

BEDROOM
11⁰ x12⁰

PORCH

TERRACE

GARAGE
21⁴ x26⁴

Design BB2871
Square Footage: 1,905

D

● A greenhouse area off the dining room and living room provides a cheerful focal point for
this comfortable three-bedroom
Trend home. The spacious living
room features a cozy fireplace and
sloped ceiling. In addition to the
dining room, there's a less formal
breakfast room just off the modern
kitchen. Both kitchen and breakfast areas look out into a front terrace. Stairs just off the foyer lead
down to a recreation room. Master
bedroom suite opens to a terrace.
A mud room and washroom off
the garage allow rear entry to the
house during inclement weather.

Design BB2795
Square Footage: 1,952

This three-bedroom design leaves no room for improvement. Any size family will find it difficult to surpass the fine qualities that this home offers. Begin with the exterior. This fine contemporary design has open trellis work above the front, covered private court. This area is sheltered by a privacy wall extending from the projecting garage. Inside, the floor plan will be just as breathtaking. Begin at the foyer and choose a direction. To the left is the sleeping wing equipped with three bedrooms and two baths. Straight ahead from the foyer is the gathering room with through-fireplace to the dining room. To the right is the work center. This area includes a breakfast room, a U-shaped kitchen and laundry.

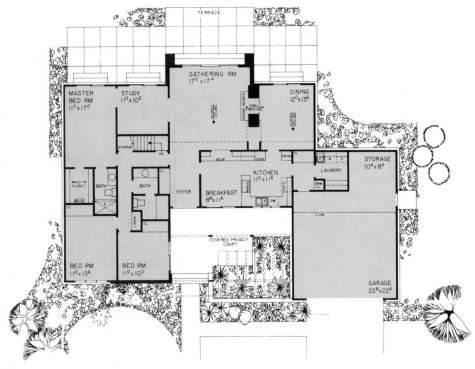

Width 73'-6"
Depth 52'-2"

Design BB2753

Square Footage: 1,539

D

● This three-bedroom home makes
use of full living patterns—a central
living room with a fireplace accommodates formal gatherings while a
family room takes care of everyday
situations. The kitchen enjoys direct
access to both the dining room and the
eating area. Or take your meals outside—a porch off the family room presents a pleasing atmosphere for dining
and relaxing. The front study may
convert to a bedroom if desired.
Access to a terrace surrounded by a
privacy wall is a prominent feature of
this room. Two other bedrooms
include a master bedroom. It utilizes a
walk-in closet in addition to another
set of closets, a private bath and outdoor access.

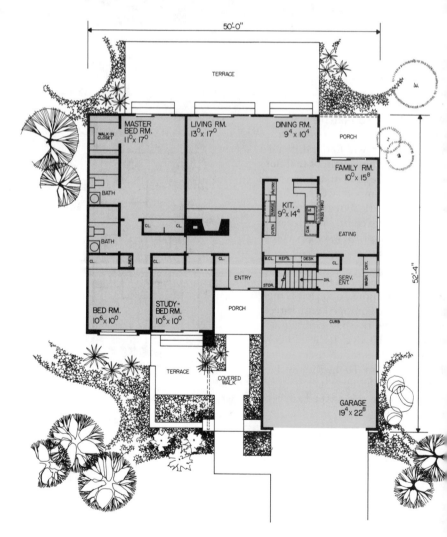

esign BB2528
quare Footage: 1,754

This inviting, U-shaped western ranch adaptation offers utstanding living potential behind its double front doors. A rmal living room/dining room combination serves as the cal point and pleases with its raised-hearth fireplace and rrace access. Adjacent is a breakfast nook and galley-style itchen. The nearby family room enjoys the convenience of a wash room. The family sleeping quarters are comprised of a master bedroom and two secondary bedrooms. In the master, a large walk-in closet, a dressing area with a bowl and vanity and a full bath provide full livability. Don't miss the sliding glass doors here, too, that lead out onto the back terrace.

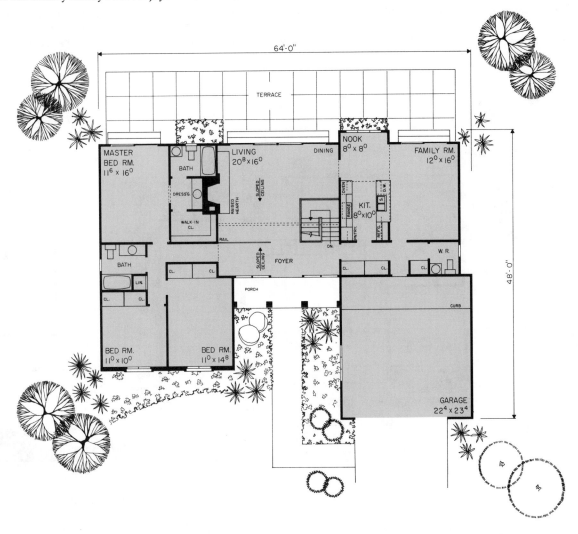

Design BB2818
Square Footage: 1,566

L **D**

● This is most certainly an outstanding contemporary design. Study the exterior carefully before your journey to inspect the floor plan. The vertical lines are carried from the siding to the paned windows to the garage door. The front entry is recessed so the overhanging roof creates a covered porch.

Note the planter court with privacy wall. The floor plan is just as outstanding. The rear gathering room has a sloped ceiling, raised hearth fireplace, sliding glass doors to the terrace and a snack bar with pass-thru to the kitchen. In addition to the gathering room, there is the living room/study. This

room could be utilized in a variety of ways depending on your family's choice. The formal dining room is convenient to the U-shaped kitchen. Three bedrooms and two closely located baths are in the sleeping wing. This plan includes details for the construction of an optional basement.

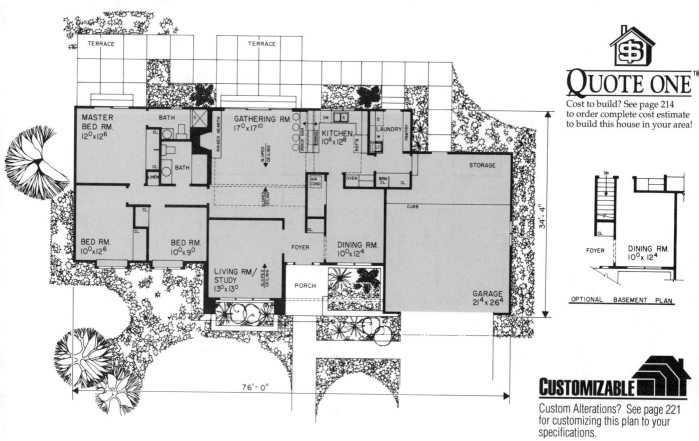

QUOTE ONE™
Cost to build? See page 214 to order complete cost estimate to build this house in your area!

CUSTOMIZABLE
Custom Alterations? See page 221 for customizing this plan to your specifications.

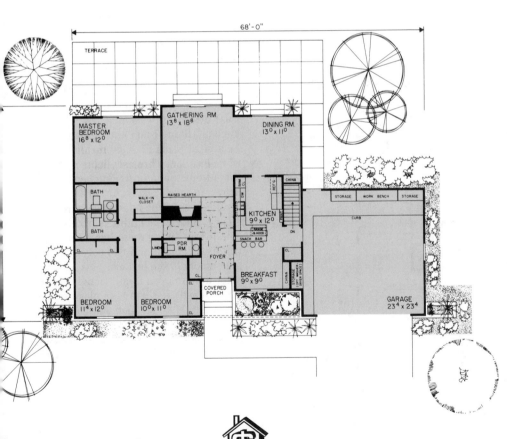

TERRACE

68'-0"

MASTER
BEDROOM
16⁸ x 12⁰

GATHERING RM.
13⁸ x 18⁸

DINING RM.
13⁰ x 11⁰

BATH

WALK-IN
CLOSET

RAISED HEARTH

CHINA

KITCHEN
9⁰ x 12⁰

BATH

SNACK BAR

CL   CL

LINEN

PDR.
RM.

FOYER

CL

BREAKFAST
9⁰ x 9⁰

CHINA

STORAGE   WORK BENCH   STORAGE

CURB

COVERED
PORCH

BEDROOM
11⁴ x 12⁰

BEDROOM
10⁰ x 11⁰

GARAGE
23⁴ x 23⁴

Design BB2671
Square Footage: 1,589

L **D**

● The rustic exterior of this one-story home features vertical wood siding. The entry foyer is floored with flagstone and leads to the three areas of the plan: sleeping, living, and work center. The sleeping area has three bedrooms. The master bedroom has sliding glass doors to the rear terrace. The living area, consisting of gathering and dining rooms, also has access to the terrace. The work center is efficiently planned. It houses the kitchen with snack bar, breakfast room with built-in china cabinet and stairs to the basement. This is a very livable plan. Special amenities include a raised-hearth fireplace and a walk-in closet in the master bedroom.

QUOTE ONE™
Cost to build? See page 214 to order complete cost estimate to build this house in your area!

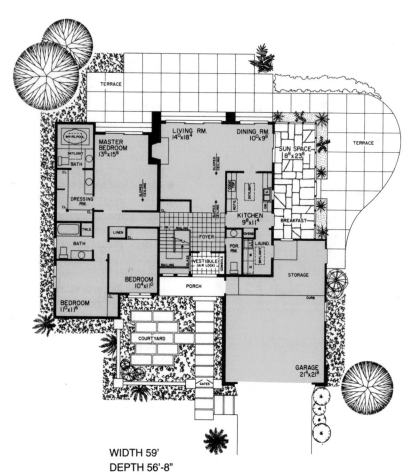

WIDTH 59'
DEPTH 56'-8"

Design BB2902
Square Footage: 1,632

● A sun space highlights this passive solar design. It has access from the kitchen, dining room and garage. It will be a great place to enjoy meals because of its location. Three skylights highlight the interior - one in the kitchen, laundrey and master bath. An air-locked vestibule helps this design's energy efficiency. Interior livability is excellent. The living/dining room has a sloping ceiling, fireplace and two sets of sliding glass doors to the terrace. This area will cater to numerous family activities. Additional activities can take place in the basement. Note its open staircase. Three bedrooms are in the sleeping wing. The square footage of the sun space is 216 and is not included in the above figure.

Cost to build? See page 214 to order complete cost estimate to build this house in your area!

Design BB2913
Square Footage: 1,835

D

● This smart design features multi-gabled ends, varied roof lines, and vertical windows. It also offers efficient zoning by room functions and plenty of modern comforts for Contemporary family lifestyle. A covered porch leads through a foyer to a large central gathering room with fireplace, sloped ceiling, and its own special view of a rear terrace. A modern kitchen with snack bar has a pass-thru to a breakfast room with view of the terrace. There's also an adjacent dining room. A media room isolated along with bedrooms from the rest of the house offers a quiet private area for listening to stereos or VCRs. A master bedroom suite includes its own whirlpool. A large garage includes extra storage.

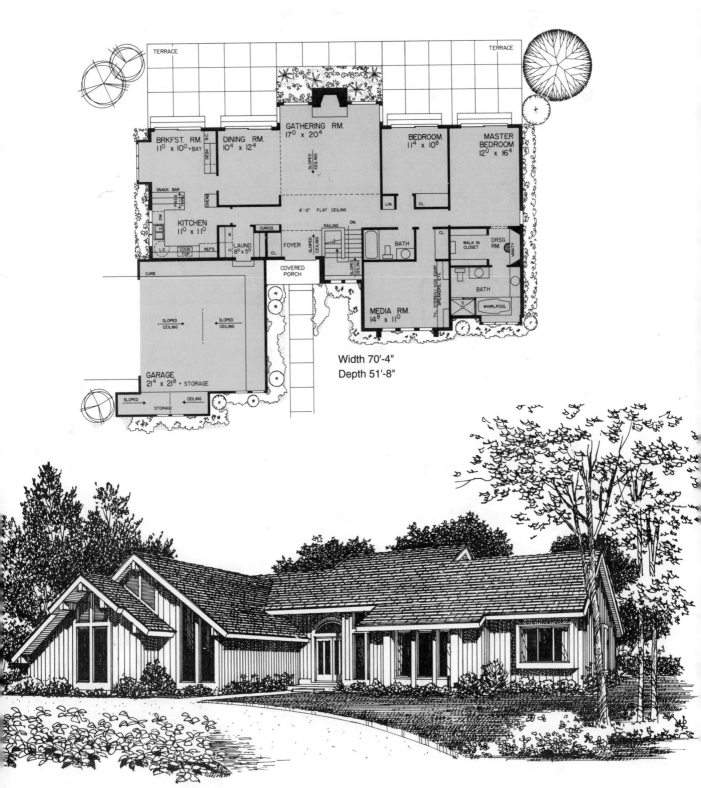

Width 70'-4"
Depth 51'-8"

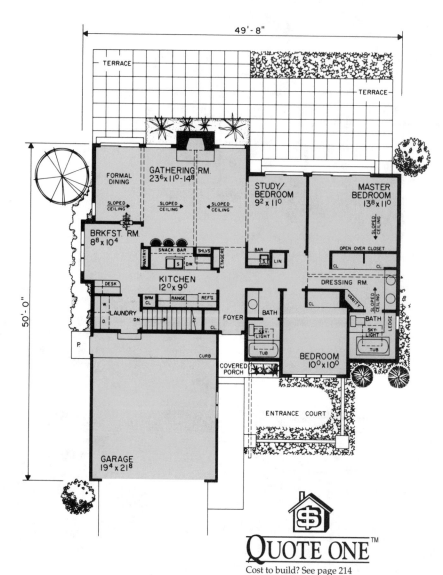

49'-8"

TERRACE

TERRACE

FORMAL DINING

GATHERING RM.
23⁶x11⁰-14⁸

STUDY/ BEDROOM
9²x11⁰

MASTER BEDROOM
13⁸x11⁰

SLOPED CEILING

SLOPED CEILING

SLOPED CEILING

SLOPED CEILING

BRKFST. RM.
8⁸x10⁴

SNACK BAR

SHLVS

BAR

LIN

OPEN OVER CLOSET

CL

CL

PANTRY

S DW

KITCHEN
12⁰x9⁰

ETAGERE

DRESSING RM.

DESK

W

LAUNDRY

D

BRM CL RANGE REF'G

DN

CL

FOYER

BATH

CL

VANITY

SLOPED CEILING

BATH

LEDGE

P

SKY-LIGHT

SKY-LIGHT

CURB

TUB

TUB

COVERED PORCH

BEDROOM
10⁰x10⁰

50'-0"

GARAGE
19⁴x21⁸

ENTRANCE COURT

Design BB2864

Square Footage: 1,387

L **D**

● Projecting the garage to the front of a house is very economical in two ways. One, it reduces the required lot size for building (in this case the overall width is under 50 feet). Two, it will protect the interior from street noise. Many other characteristics about this design deserve mention, too. Upon entering, the foyer will take you to the various areas. The interior kitchen has an adjacent breakfast room and a snack bar on the gathering room side. A study with a wet bar is adjacent. Sliding glass doors here and in the master bedroom open to the terrace.

California Engineered Plans and California Stock Plans are available for this home. Call 1-800-521-6797 for more information.

QUOTE ONE™

Cost to build? See page 214 to order complete cost estimate to build this house in your area!

CUSTOMIZABLE

Custom Alterations? See page 221 for customizing this plan to your specifications.

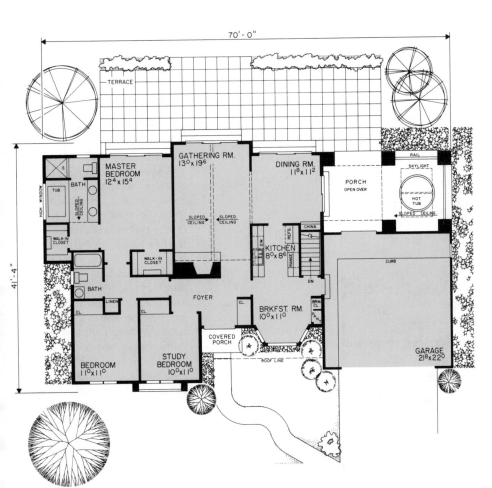

TERRACE

70'-0"

MASTER
BEDROOM
12⁴x15⁴

BATH

TUB

SLOPED
CEILING

WALK-IN
CLOSET

WALK-IN
CLOSET

BATH

LINEN

CL.

CL.

CL.

HIGH WINDOW

41'-4"

GATHERING RM.
13⁰x19⁶

SLOPED
CEILING

SLOPED
CEILING

FOYER

BEDROOM
11⁰x11⁰

STUDY
BEDROOM
10⁰x11⁰

COVERED
PORCH

ROOF LINE

DINING RM.
11⁸x11²

KITCHEN
8⁰x8⁶

REFS.

CHINA

DW

RANGE

BRKFST. RM.
10⁰x11⁰

BRM.
CL.

CL.

DN

PORCH
OPEN OVER

RAIL

SKYLIGHT

HOT
TUB

SLOPED CEILING

CURB

GARAGE
21⁸x22⁰

Design BB2809
Square Footage: 1,551

● This contemporary home
will delight all with its great
indoor/outdoor livability. A
front covered porch provides a
nice welcome to the inside
where a gathering room draws
attention. Here, a sloped ceiling
and raised-hearth fireplace
along with sliding glass doors to
a back terrace lend themselves
to the comfort of this room.
Attached is a dining room with
access to a porch and hot tub.
The kitchen, which easily serves
the dining room, also enjoys a
bayed breakfast room—perfect
for quiet conversations and
more. Three bedrooms include a
master suite with a walk-in closet and bath with dual lavatories,
a soaking tub and a compartmented stool and shower. If you
like, make one of the secondary
bedrooms into a study.

QUOTE ONE™

Cost to build? See page 214
to order complete cost estimate
to build this house in your area!

Design BB3453
Square Footage: 1,442

L

● This volume home impresses
with its stately rooflines and stucco
exterior. The front porch opens to
an eleven-foot ceiling in the foyer.
Straight ahead, an elegant living
room serves as a prelude to the
dramatic circular dining bay. Here,
family and guests alike will revel in
the fine views out the back of the
house. The kitchen, with its advan-
tageous snack bar, offers an abundance of counter and cabinet space.
The media room, with its closet
space and access to a full hall bath,
could easily convert to a bedroom.
In the master bedroom you'll find a
lengthy closet in addition to a stunning bath. Glass block provides
privacy to the toilet and shower
while the spa tub delights in its
well-illuminated nook. Dual lavatories complete the amenities in
this room.

TERRACE

TRAY CLG.

LIVING RM.
14⁰ X 15⁰

DINING RM.
11⁴ X 13⁰

SHLVS

MASTER BEDRM
13⁰ X 14⁰

W.I.C.

KITCHEN
9⁴ X 14⁴

SHWR

DN

REFG

CL.

LN

MASTER BATH

W D

LN

BATH

CL.

CL.

FOYER

LN

CL.

BEDRM
11⁶ X 11²

GARAGE
18⁴ X 18⁸

WIDTH 40'
DEPTH 57'-4"

90

52' - 8"

49' - 0"

TERRACE

TRAY CLG.

MASTER
BEDRM
18⁰ X 14⁰
9' CLG

BATH
SHWR

LIVING
RM.
15⁴ X 17⁴
9' CLG

DINING
RM.
10⁰ X 12²
9' CLG

W.I.C.

KITCHEN/
BRKFST.
12² X 16⁸

BATH
TWL
CL DR LIN DN

FOYER

OVN

REFG

BEDRM
11⁴ X 10⁴

BEDRM
11 X 11⁴

PORCH

GARAGE
19⁴ X 19⁸

Quote One™
Cost to build? See page 214
to order complete cost estimate
to build this house in your area!

Design BB3454

Square Footage: 1,699

L **D**

● Volume looks are achieved
through the use of a high-
pitched, hipped roof. The front
gable with lower projecting
brick pillars acts as a pleasing
architectural feature. Another
delightful architectural feature
is the radial window above the
front door; it brings an extra
measure of natural light to the
foyer. An efficient, spacious
interior comes through in this
compact floor plan. Through a
pair of columns, an open living
and dining room area creates a
warm space for all sorts of pursuits. Sliding glass doors guarantee a bright, cheerful interior
while providing easy access to
outdoor living. The L-shaped
kitchen has an island work
surface, a practical planning
desk and an informal eating
space. The breakfast area has
access to an outdoor living
area—perfect for enjoying a
morning cup of coffee. Sleeping
arrangements are defined by the
master suite with its tray ceiling
and sliding glass doors to the
yard as well as two family
bedrooms.

Design BB3569

Square Footage: 1,981

L **D**

● A graceful entry opens this impressive one-story design; the foyer introduces an open gathering room/dining room combination. A front-facing study could easily convert into a bedroom for guests—a full bath is directly accessible from the rear of the room. In the kitchen, such features as an island cooktop and a built-in desk add to livability. A corner bedroom takes advantage of front and side views. The master bedroom accesses the rear terrace and also sports a bath with dual lavatories and a whirlpool. Other special features of the house include multi-pane windows, a warming fireplace, a cozy covered dining porch and a two-car garage. Note the handy storage closet in the laundry area.

QUOTE ONE™

Cost to build? See page 214
to order complete cost estimate
to build this house in your area!

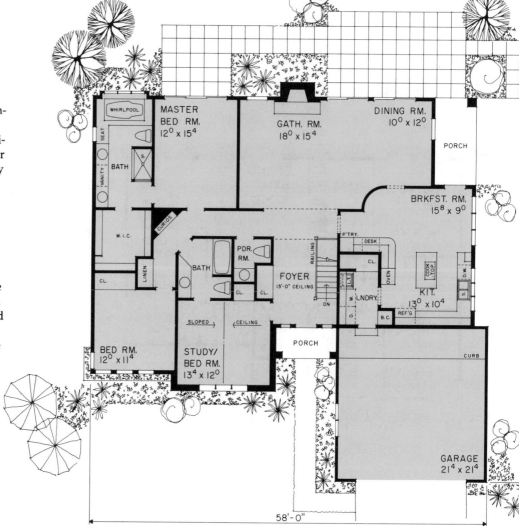

ONE-STORY HOMES
Over 2,000 Square Feet

*I*f you are like most empty-nesters, this is a time when you are really able to enjoy life. Your children are on their own and there's time and energy for doing all the things you never could before. Perhaps you'll want to pursue a new hobby. Maybe you'll investigate the possibility of working out of a home office. You might even make good on your resolutions to get in shape. Whatever pursuits you foresee, you'll want the space to make it happen. Larger one-story homes accommodate these changes in lifestyle easily. While allowing convenient access to every zone of the house, they also contain all of the spaces for an enhanced way of life. Formal living and dining spaces are offset nicely by more casual family and gathering rooms. You'll also find dens and studies, unique gourmet kitchens, plenty of terrace and patio space, and special areas for hobbies and exercise. Many plans include very special features, such as a greenhouse (see Design BB3357 on page 111) or His and Hers walk-in closets (see Design BB2880 on page 120).

Cost to build? See page 214 to order complete cost estimate to build this house in your area!

Design BB3440

Square Footage: 2,300

● Pack 'em in! There's plenty of room for everyone in this three-, or optional four-bedroom home. The expansive gathering room welcomes family and guests with a through-fireplace to the dining room, an audio/visual center, and a door to the outside. The kitchen includes a wide pantry, a snack bar, and a sep-arate eating area. Included in the master suite: two walk-in closets, shower, whirlpool tub and seat, dual vanities, and linen storage.

Custom Alterations? See page 221 for customizing this plan to your specifications.

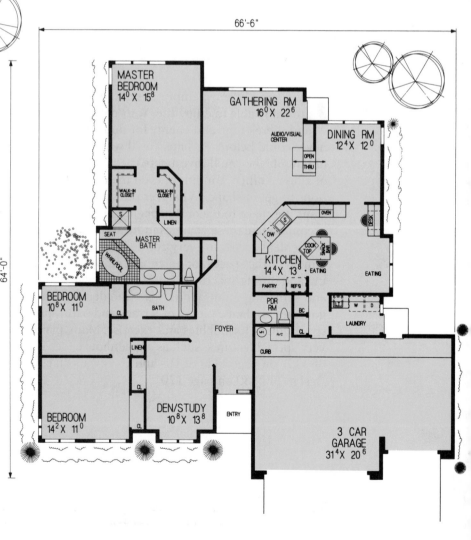

Design BB3408

Square Footage: 2,388

L

● Interesting angles make for interesting rooms. The sleeping zone features two large bedrooms with unique shapes and a master suite with spectacular bath. A laundry placed nearby is both convenient and economical, located adjacent to a full bath. The central kitchen offers a desk and built-in breakfast table. Meals can also be enjoyed in the adjacent eating area, formal dining room with stepped ceiling, or outside on the rear patio. A planter and glass block wall separate the living room and family room, which is warmed by a fireplace.

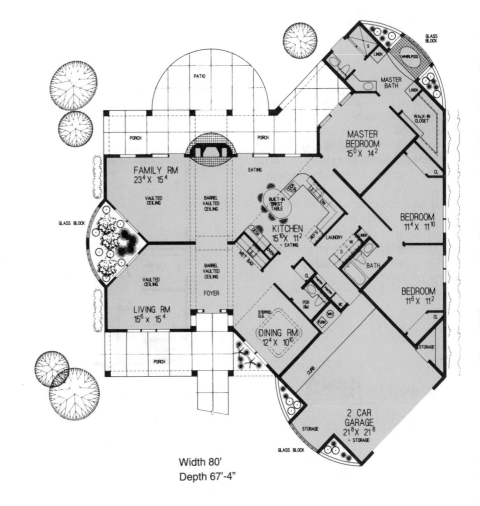

Width 80'
Depth 67'-4"

Quote One™

Cost to build? See page 214
to order complete cost estimate
to build this house in your area!

Design BB3319

Square Footage: 2,274

L **D**

● This attractive bungalow design
separates the master suite from family bedrooms and puts casual living
to the back in a family room. The
formal living and dining areas are
centrally located and have access to
a rear terrace, as does the master
suite. The kitchen sits between
formal and informal living areas.
The two family bedrooms are found
to the front of the plan. A home
office or study opens off the front
foyer and the master suite.

Customizable

Custom Alterations? See page 221
for customizing this plan to your
specifications.

Design BB3559

Square Footage: 2,916

● Intricate details make the most of
this lovely one-story: high, varied
rooflines, multi-pane windows and
a solid chimney stack. The floor plan
caters to comfortable living. Besides
the living room/dining room area to
the rear, there is a large conversation
area with a fireplace and plenty of
windows. The kitchen is separated
from living areas by an angled
snack-bar counter. A media room to
the front of the plan provides space
for more private activities. Three
bedrooms grace the right side of the
plan. The master suite features a
tray-vaulted ceiling and sliding
glass doors to the rear terrace. The
dressing area is graced by His and
Hers walk-in closets, a double-bowl
lavatory and a compartmented com-
mode. The shower area is highlighted with glass block and is sunken
down one step. A garden whirlpool
finishes off the area.

**California Engineered Plans and
California Stock Plans are available
for this home. Call 1-800-521-6797
for more information.**

Cost to build? See page 214
to order complete cost estimate
to build this house in your area!

Custom Alterations? See page 221
for customizing this plan to your
specifications.

97

Design BB2930

Square Footage: 2,032

● The clean lines of this L-shaped contemporary are enhanced by the interesting, wide overhanging roof planes. Horizontal and vertical siding compliment one another. The low privacy fence adds interest as it forms a delightful front courtyard adjacent to the covered walkway to the front door.

Here's a floor plan made to order for the active small family or empty-nesters. Sloping ceilings and fine glass areas foster a spacious interior. The master bedroom has an outstanding dressing room and bath layout. The guest room has its own full bath. Note how this bath can function as a handy

powder room. A favorite room will be the study with its fireplace and two sets of sliding glass doors. Don't miss the open-planned gathering and dining rooms, or the kitchen/laundry area. The breakfast room has its own terrace. Notice the rear covered porch. Fine indoor-outdoor relationships.

Design BB3560
Square Footage: 2,189

Simplicity is the key to the stylish good looks of this home's facade. A walled garden entry and large window areas appeal to outdoor enthusiasts. Inside, the kitchen forms the hub of the plan. It opens directly off the foyer and contains an island counter and a work counter with eating space on the living area side. A sloped ceiling, fireplace and sliding glass doors to a rear terrace are highlights of the living area. The master bedroom also sports sliding glass doors to the terrace. Its dressing area is enhanced with double walk-in closets and lavatories. A whirlpool tub and seated shower are additional amenities. Two family bedrooms are found on the opposite side of the house. They share a full bath with twin lavatories.

California Engineered Plans and California Stock Plans are available for this home. Call 1-800-521-6797 for more information.

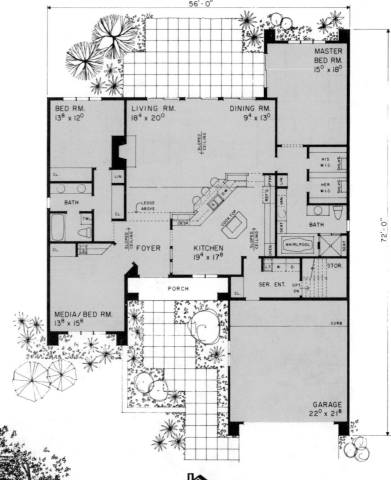

QUOTE ONE™
Cost to build? See page 214
to order complete cost estimate
to build this house in your area!

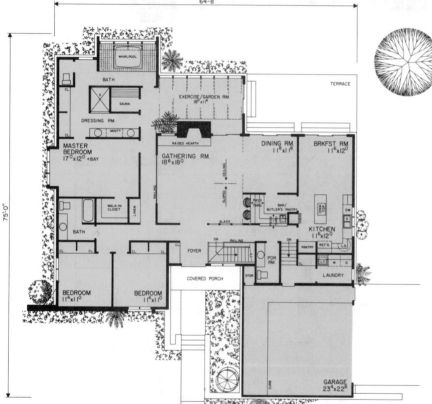

Design BB2873
Square Footage: 2,838

● This modern three-bedroom home incorporates many of the Contemporary features so popular today. A large gathering room with cozy raised-hearth fireplace and sloped ceiling is central focus and centrally located. Adjacent to the gathering room is a dining room that adjoins a bar or butler's pantry. This handy service area also has pass-thru entry to the central gathering room. Just off the pantry is a large modern kitchen with central cook-top island and adjoining breakfast room. The master bedroom suite is especially luxurious with its own sauna, whirlpool, dressing room, bay window, and adjoining exercise room. This adjacent exercise room could double as a lovely garden room. It's located just off the back terrace. There's even a powder room for guests in front, and a covered porch to keep visitors dry. A laundry is conveniently located off the spacious two-car garage. Note the large view glass off the rear exercise/garden room. This is a comfortable and modern home, indeed.

Design BB2858

Square Footage: 2,231

● This sun oriented design was created to face the south. By doing so, it has minimal northern exposure. It has been designed primarily for the more temperate U.S. latitudes using 2 x 6 wall construction. The morning sun will brighten the living and dining rooms along with the adjacent terrace. Sun enters the garden room by way of the glass roof and walls. In the winter, the solar heat gain from the garden room should provide relief from high energy bills. Solar shades allow you to adjust the amount of light that you want to enter in the warmer months. Interior planning deserves mention, too. The work center is efficient. The kitchen has a snack bar on the garden room side and a serving counter to the dining room. The breakfast room with laundry area is also convenient to the kitchen. Three bedrooms are on the northern wall. The master bedroom has a large tub and a separate shower with a four foot square skylight above. When this design is oriented toward the sun, it should prove to be energy efficient and a joy to live in.

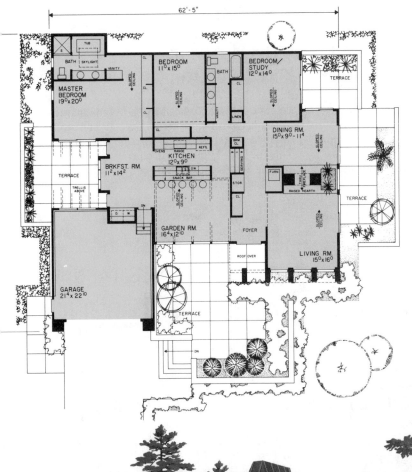

Design BB3368
Square Footage: 2,722

L **D**

QUOTE ONE™

Cost to build? See page 214
to order complete cost estimate
to build this house in your area!

● Roof lines are the key to the interesting exterior of this design. Their configuration allows for sloped ceilings in the gathering room and large foyer. The master bedroom suite has a huge walk-in closet, garden whirlpool and separate shower. Two family bedrooms share a full bath. One of these bedrooms could be used as a media room with pass-through wet bar. Note the large kitchen with conversation bay and the wide terrace to the rear.

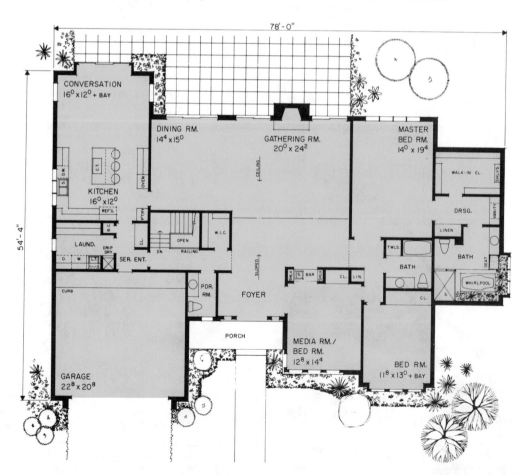

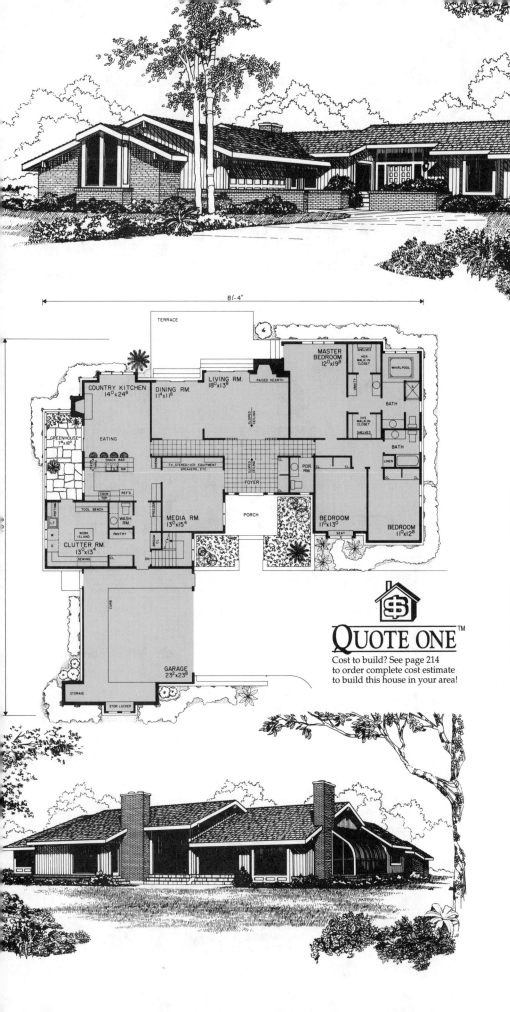

TERRACE

COUNTRY KITCHEN
14⁰x24⁸

DINING RM.
11⁴x11⁸

LIVING RM.
18⁰x13⁸

RAISED HEARTH

MASTER BEDROOM
12⁰x19⁸

SHELVES

HER WALK-IN CLOSET

WHIRLPOOL

VANITY

BATH

GREENHOUSE
7⁸x18⁰

EATING

SLOPED CEILING

HIS WALK-IN CLOSET

SHELVES

BATH

SNACK BAR

T.V., STEREO/ VCR EQUIPMENT
SPEAKERS, ETC.

PDR. RM.

LINEN

COOK TOP

REF'G.

SLOPED CEILING

FOYER

CL

POTTING

TOOL BENCH

WASH RM.

FREEZER

MEDIA RM.
13⁰x15⁴

PORCH

BEDROOM
11⁰x13⁰

SEAT

WORK ISLAND

PANTRY

BEDROOM
11⁰x12⁸

CLUTTER RM.
13⁰x13⁴

SEWING

CL

DN

GARAGE
23²x23⁸

STORAGE

STOR LOCKER

81'-4"

QUOTE ONE™

Cost to build? See page 214
to order complete cost estimate
to build this house in your area!

Design BB2915

Square Footage: 2,758

L **D**

● What a grand plan! This
well-zoned beauty has
nearly everything going
for it. Start with the 340-
square-foot country kitchen
which sports a fireplace,
snack bar and greenhouse
next door. Move to the
media room where there's
a wall of built-ins, and then
on to the combination living room/dining area (note
the sloped ceiling, raised-
hearth fireplace and doors
leading to the terrace in
back). Also check out both
the king-sized master suite
with His and Hers walk-in
closets and whirlpool made
for two, and all the extra
storage space. A clutter
room provides space for
the laundry and much
more.

**California Engineered
Plans and California Stock
Plans are available for this
home. Call 1-800-521-6797
for more information.**

Design BB3600

Square Footage: 2,258

L

 This unique one-story plan seems tailor-made for a small family or for empty-nesters. Formal areas are situated well for entertaining—living room to the right and formal dining room to the left. A large family room is found to the rear. It has access to a rear wood deck and is warmed in the cold months by a welcome hearth. The U-shaped kitchen features an attached morning room for casual meals. It is near the laundry and a washroom. Bedrooms are split. The master suite sits to the right of the plan and has a walk-in closet and fine bath. A nearby study has a private porch. One family bedroom is on the other side of the home and also has a private bath. If needed, the plan can also be built with a third bedroom sharing the bath.

Design BB1754
Square Footage: 2,080

D

● Boasting a traditional Western flavor, this rugged U-shaped ranch home has the features to assure grand living. The front flower court, inside the high brick wall, creates a delightfully dramatic atmosphere which carries inside. The floor plan is positively unique and exceptionally livable. Wonderfully zoned, the three bedrooms enjoy their full measure of privacy. The formal living and dining rooms function together in a most pleasing fashion. The laundry, kitchen, informal eating and family room fit together to guarantee efficient living patterns.

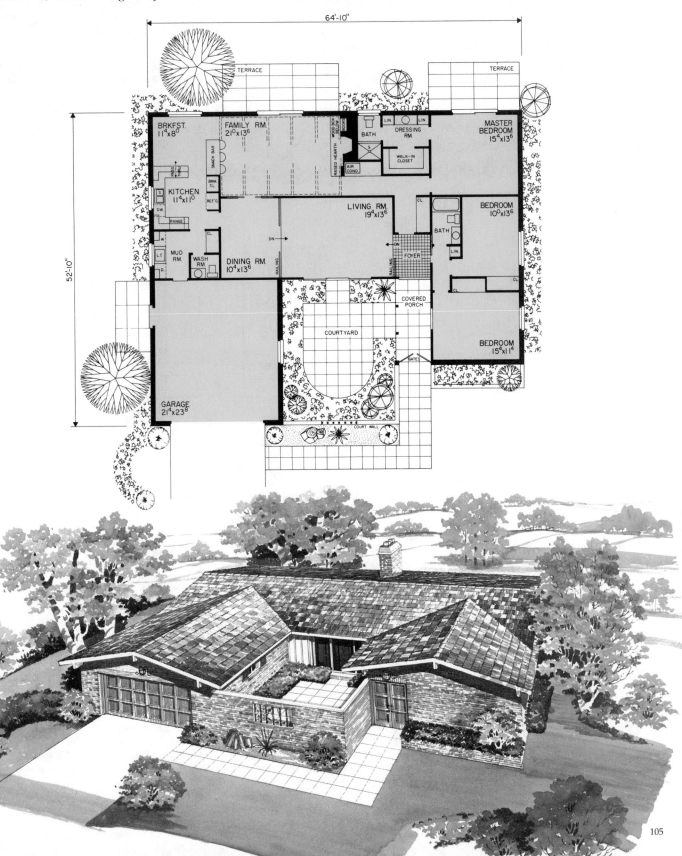

Design BB2789

Square Footage: 2,732

L D

● An attached three car garage! What a fantastic feature of this three bedroom contemporary design. And there's more. As one walks up the steps to the covered porch and through the double front doors the charm of this design will be overwhelming. Inside, a large foyer greets all visitors and leads them to each of the three areas, each down a few steps. The living area has a large gathering room with fireplace and a study adjacent on one side and the formal dining room on the other. The work center has an efficient kitchen with island range, breakfast room, laundry and built-in desk and bar. Then there is the sleeping area. Note the raised tub with sloped ceiling.

Design BB2778
Square Footage: 2,761

D

No matter what the occasion, family and friends alike will enjoy the sizable gathering room which is featured in this plan. A spacious 20' x 23', this room has a thru-fireplace to the study and two sets of sliding glass doors to the large rear terrace. Indoor-outdoor living can also be enjoyed from the dining room, study and master bedroom; all located to face the rear yard. There is a covered dining porch, too, accessible through sliding glass doors in the dining and breakfast rooms. A total of three bedrooms are planned for this design. Each has plenty of closet space. Notice the high lights of the master suite: large walk-in closet, tub plus stall shower and exercise area.

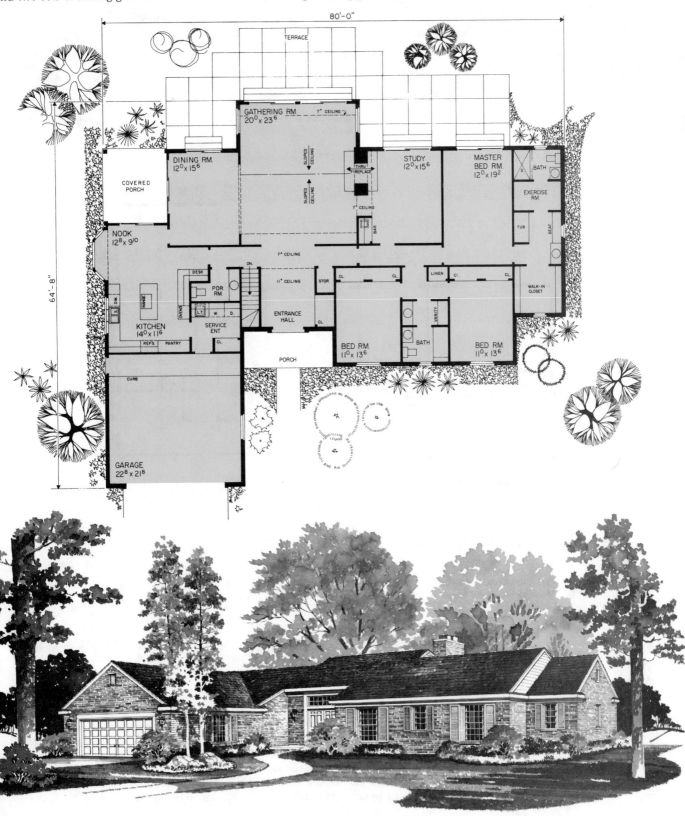

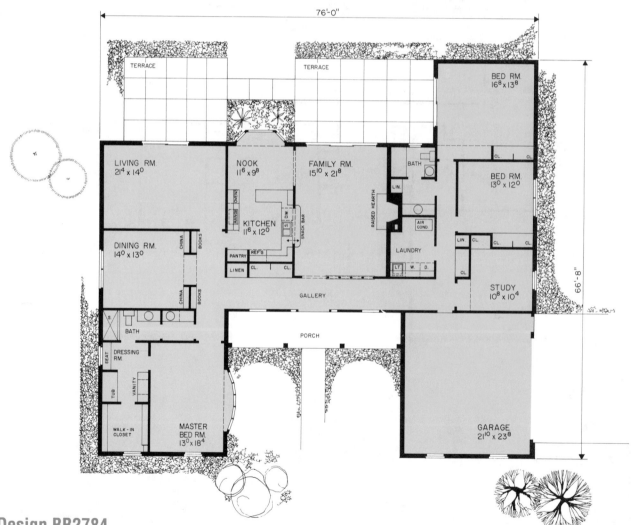

Design BB2784

Square Footage: 2,980

● The projection of the master bedroom and garage create an inviting U-shaped area leading to the covered porch of this delightful traditionally styled design. After entering through the double front doors, the gallery will lead to each of the three living areas:

the sleeping wing of two bedrooms, full bath and study; the informal area of the family room with raised hearth fireplace and sliding glass doors to the terrace and the kitchen/nook area (the kitchen has a pass-thru snack bar to the family room); and the formal area

consisting of a separate dining room with built-in china cabinets and the living room. The master bedroom suite, with its lovely bay window, has a large dressing area with a window seat and a walk-in closet. Notice the separate tub and shower in the master bath.

Design BB2594

Square Footage: 2,294

This handsome home offers a delightful plan for today's home owner. The tiled entry gives way to a spectacular gathering room. In it, a raised-hearth fireplace takes center stage. Two sets of sliding glass doors make up the back wall of the room and lead to an array of terraces out back. The dining room shares in the gathering room's grandness with its roomy interior and outdoor access. The kitchen provides a wealth of storage space and services a breakfast nook with a snack-bar pass-through.

A laundry room adds to everyday conveniences as well as offering passage to the two-car garage. The sleeping quarters are comprised of two secondary bedrooms—one could serve as a study, if desired—and an expansive master bedroom.

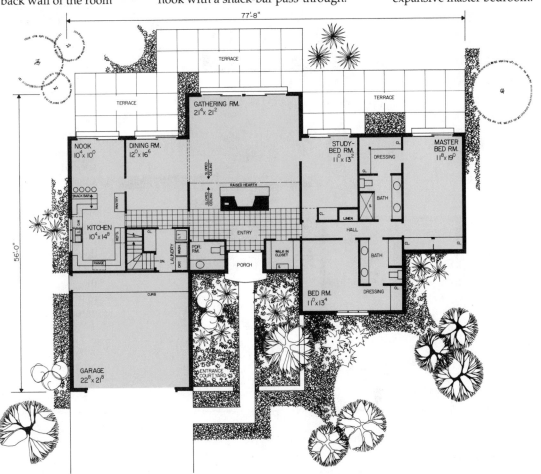

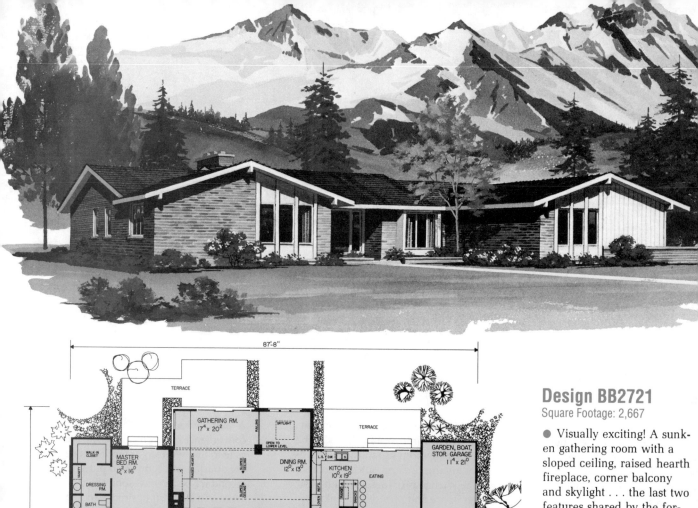

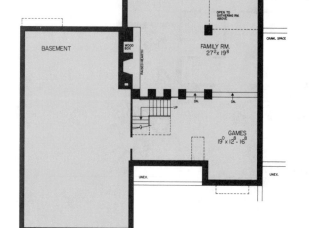

Design BB2721
Square Footage: 2,667

● Visually exciting! A sunken gathering room with a sloped ceiling, raised hearth fireplace, corner balcony and skylight . . . the last two features shared by the formal dining room. There's more. Two family rooms . . . one on the lower level (1,153 sq. ft.) with a raised hearth fireplace, another adjacent to the kitchen with a snack bar! Plus a study and game room. A lavish master suite and two large bedrooms. A first floor laundry and reams of storage space, including a special garage for a boat, sports equipment, garden tools etc. There's plenty of space for family activities in this home. From chic dinner parties for friends to birthday gatherings for kids, there's always the right setting . . . and so much room that adults and children can entertain at the same time.

Design BB3357
Square Footage: 2,913

[L] [D]

TERRACE

82'-8"

72'-0"

GREEN HOUSE

COUNRTY KITCHEN
14⁰ X 24⁸

EATING

SNACK BAR

LS · S · DW

LS · COOK TOP · REF'G

DINING RM
11⁰ X 11⁸

LIVING RM
18⁰ X 13⁸

RAISED HEARTH

LEDGE ABOVE

SLOPED CEILING

OVEN

LEDGE ABOVE

SLOPED CEILING

CLUTTER RM
14⁴ X 13⁴

D W LT

WASH RM

WORK ISLAND

PANTRY/STORAGE

SEWING

FREEZER

MEDIA RM/STUDY
13⁰ X 15⁴

FOYER

PDR RM

STORAGE · LINEN

PORCH

DN

CURB

GARAGE
23⁶ X 23⁸

MASTER BEDROOM
13⁰ X 19⁸

MASTER BATH

WALK-IN CLOSET

WHIRLPOOL

VANITY

BATH

LIN

BEDROOM
11⁰ X 15⁰

BEDROOM
11⁰ X 15⁰

● One-story living never had it so good! From the formal living and dining rooms to private media room, this home is designed to be enjoyed. The greenhouse off the kitchen adds 147 square feet to the plan. It offers access to the clutter room where gardening or hobby activities can take place. A the opposite end of the house are a master bedroom with generous bath and two family bedrooms. Notice the wealth of built-ins throughout the house.

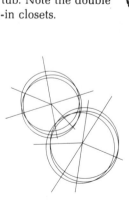

CUSTOMIZABLE

Custom Alterations? See page 221
for customizing this plan to your
specifications.

QUOTE ONE™

Cost to build? See page 214
to order complete cost estimate
to build this house in your area!

Design BB3346

Square Footage: 2,032

L

● This home boasts a de-
lightful Tudor exterior
with a terrific interior
floor plan. Though com-
pact, there's plenty of living space: large study
with fireplace, gathering
room, dining room, and
breakfast room. The mas-
ter bedroom has an at-
tached bath with whirl-
pool tub. Note the double
walk-in closets.

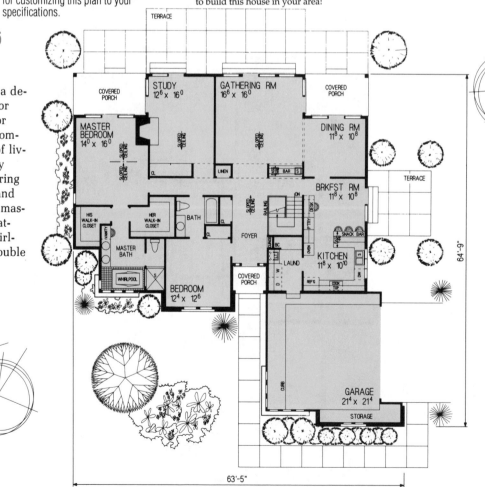

Quote One™

Cost to build? See page 214
to order complete cost estimate
to build this house in your area!

Design BB3336
Square Footage: 2,022

L

● Compact and comfort-
able! This three-bedroom
home is a good consideration
for a small family or empty-
nester retirees. Of special
note are the covered eating
porch and sloped ceilings in
the gathering room and master bedroom. The master bath
accommodates every need
with a whirlpool tub and
shower, closet space, vanity
and dual sinks. Stairs to the
basement and a well-placed
powder room are found at
the front entry.

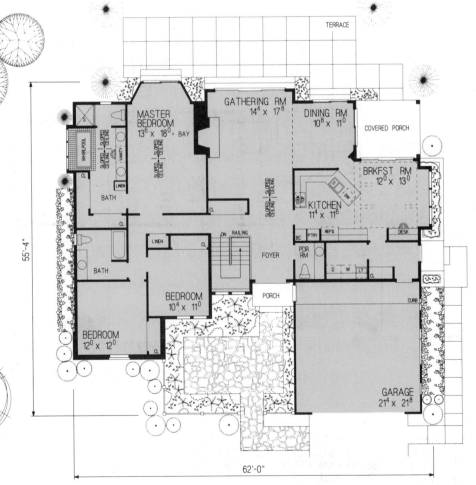

TERRACE

MASTER
BEDROOM
13^6 x 18^0 + BAY

GATHERING RM
14^4 x 17^8

DINING RM
10^8 x 11^0

COVERED PORCH

WHIRLPOOL

SLOPED CEILING

SLOPED CEILING

VANITY

LINEN

BATH

CL

SLOPED CEILING

SLOPED CEILING

CL

BRKFST RM
12^0 x 13^0

KITCHEN
11^4 x 11^6

COOK TOP

BC

P'TRY

REF'G

DESK

BATH

LINEN

CL

DN RAILING

FOYER

PDR RM

BEDROOM
10^4 x 11^0

D W LT

CL

BEDROOM
12^0 x 12^0

PORCH

GARAGE
21^4 x 21^8

CURB

55'-4"

62'-0"

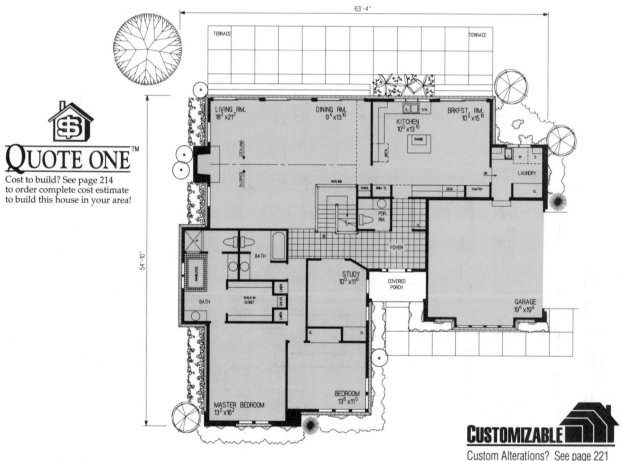

Cost to build? See page 214 to order complete cost estimate to build this house in your area!

QUOTE ONE™

CUSTOMIZABLE

Custom Alterations? See page 221 for customizing this plan to your specifications.

Design BB2962

Square Footage: 2,112

● A Tudor exterior with an efficient floor plan favored by many. Each of the three main living zones — the sleeping zone, living zone, and the working zone — are but a couple steps from the foyer. This spells easy, efficient traffic patterns. Open planning, sloping ceiling and plenty of glass create a nice environment for the living-dining area. Its appeal is further enhanced by the open staircase to the lower level recreation/hobby area. The L-shaped kitchen with its island range and work surface is delightfully opened to the large breakfast room. Again, plenty of glass area adds to the feeling of spaciousness. Nearby is the step-saving first floor laundry. The sleeping zone has the flexibility of functioning as a two or three bedroom area. Notice the economical back-to-back plumbing.

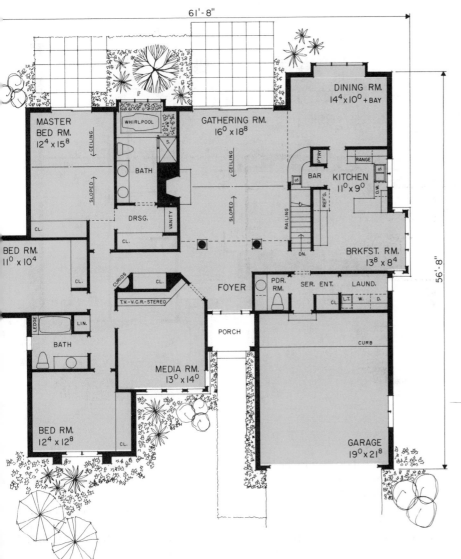

Design BB3377

Square Footage: 2,217

L **D**

● This Tudor design provides a handsome exterior complemented by a spacious and modern floor plan. The sleeping area is positioned to the left side of the home. The master bedroom features an elegant bath with whirlpool, shower, dual lavs and a separate vanity area. Two family bedrooms share a full bath. A media room exhibits the TV, VCR and stereo. The enormous gathering room is set off by columns and contains a fireplace and sliding doors to the rear terrace. The dining room and breakfast room each feature a bay window.

Quote One™

Cost to build? See page 214 to order complete cost estimate to build this house in your area!

115

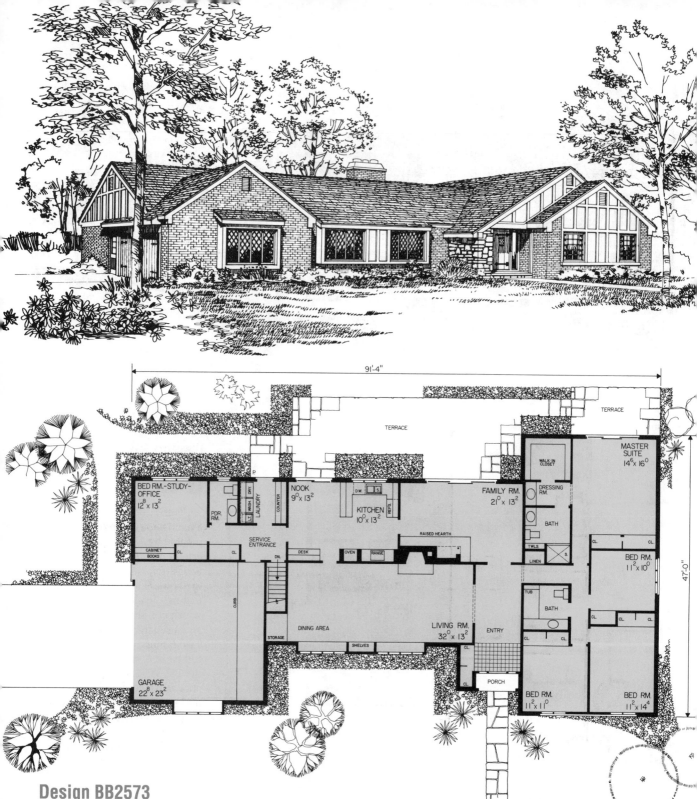

Design BB2573
Square Footage: 2,747

● Combining brick and wood gives this Tudor ranch an elegant look. It has a living/dining room measuring 32' by 13'. It is fully appointed with a traditional fireplace and built-in shelves flanked by diagonally paned windows. There's a family room with a raised-hearth fireplace and sliding glass doors that open onto the terrace. A U-shaped kitchen has lots of built-ins including a planning desk. A separate breakfast nook makes casual dining easy. The sleeping facilities consist of three family bedrooms plus an elegant master bedroom suite. A conveniently located laundry with a folding counter is in the service entrance. Adjacent to the laundry is a wash room.

California Engineered Plans and California Stock Plans are available for this home. Call 1-800-521-6797 for more information.

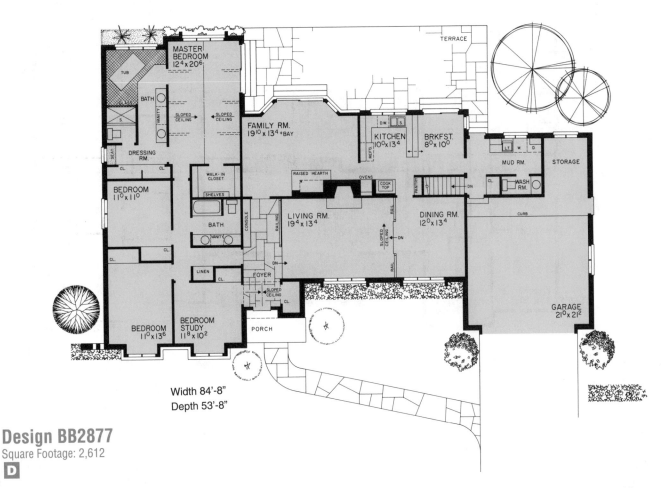

Width 84'-8"
Depth 53'-8"

Design BB2877
Square Footage: 2,612

D

● Here's a dramatic, Post-Modern exterior with a popular plan featuring an outstanding master bedroom suite. The bedroom itself is spacious, has a sloped ceiling, a large walk-in closet and sliding glass doors to the terrace. Now examine the bath and dressing area. Two large closets, twin vanities, built-in seat and a dramatically presented corner tub are present. The tub will be a great place to spend the evening hours after a long, hard day. Along with this bedroom, there are three more served by a full bath. The living area of this plan has the formal areas in the front and the informal areas in the rear. Both have a fireplace. The spacious work center is efficiently planned.

WIDTH 88'-8"
DEPTH 53'-6"

Design BB3348
Square Footage: 2,549

L

● Covered porches front and rear will be the envy of the neighborhood when this house is built. The interior plan meets family needs perfectly in well-zoned areas: a sleeping wing with four bedrooms and two baths, a living zone with formal and informal gathering space and a work zone with a U-shaped kitchen and a laundry with a wash room.

The master bedroom with a deluxe bath is noteworthy. Open planning and fireplaces enhance the living areas. Extra storage space is provided in the two-car garage.

California Engineered Plans and California Stock Plans are available for this home. Call 1-800-521-6797 for more information.

Design BB3332
Square Footage: 2,168

L

● Nothing completes a tra-
ditional-style home quite as
well as a country kitchen
with a fireplace. Notice also
the sloped-ceiling living
room and well-appointed
master suite. A handy wash
room is near the laundry, just
off the garage.

**California Engineered
Plans and California Stock
Plans are available for this
home. Call 1-800-521-6797
for more information.**

QUOTE ONE™
Cost to build? See page 214
to order complete cost estimate
to build this house in your area!

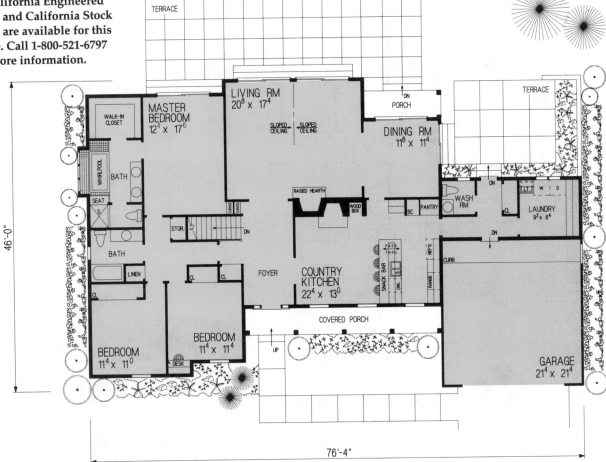

TERRACE

MASTER BEDROOM
12⁰x19⁸

SHLV'S

HER WALK-IN CLOSET

WHIRLPOOL

VANITY

BATH

COUNTRY KITCHEN
14⁰x24⁸

DINING RM.
11⁴x11⁸

LIVING RM.
18⁰x13⁸

HIS WALK-IN CLOSET

SHLV'S

BATH

GREENHOUSE
7⁸x18⁰

EATING

SLOPED CEILING

LINEN

SNACK BAR

COOK TOP

REF'G

TV, STEREO/VCR EQUIPMENT SPEAKERS, ECT.

SLOPED CEILING

POR. RM.

CL

CL

FOYER

TOOL BENCH

WASH RM.

FREEZER

WORK ISLAND

PANTRY

MEDIA RM.
13⁰x15⁴

COVERED PORCH

BEDROOM
11⁰x13⁰

BEDROOM
11⁰x12⁸

CLUTTER RM.
13⁰x13⁴

SEWING

CL

DN

SEAT

CURB

GARAGE
23²x23⁸

STORAGE

FLOWER BOX

81'-4"

76'-0"

Design BB2880
Square Footage: 2,758

L **D**

● This comfortable traditional home offers plenty of modern livability. A clutter room off the two-car garage is the perfect space for workbench, sewing, and hobbies. It includes a work island and bench space. Across the hall one finds a modern media room, the perfect place for stereo speakers, videos, and more. A spacious country kitchen off the greenhouse is a cozy gathering place for family and friends, as well as convenient work area. The 149-foot greenhouse itself easily could be the focal point of this home filled with modern amenities. The house also features a formal dining room, living room with fireplace, covered porch, and three bedrooms including a master bedroom suite.

QUOTE ONE™
Cost to build? See page 214 to order complete cost estimate to build this house in your area!

CUSTOMIZABLE
Custom Alterations? See page 221 for customizing this plan to your specifications.

PLANS WITH TWO OR MORE LEVELS

Sometimes a one-story home just isn't enough or doesn't provide the kind of livability you're looking for. Though not specifically designed for the empty-nester lifestyle, many two-story, split-level and hillside homes prove to be the perfect solution to a new way of living. The collection presented in this section allows empty-nesters to live essentially on one floor for most daily situations. On additional floors are secondary bedrooms, play rooms, summer kitchens, lounges, hobby rooms, guest apartments, studios and other optional spaces. Smaller in square footage than most plans with more than one story, these homes will allow empty-nesters who appreciate the space and style of more than one level to enjoy single-level convenience and livability. Represented are styles from ultra-contemporaries to elegant traditionals and farmhouses. Some plans even have unfinished space that can be developed later on as needed. (See Design BB2828 on page 124 and Design BB2887 on page 127.)

Design BB4115

Entry Level: 1,494 square feet
Upper Level: 597 square feet
Total: 2,091 square feet

● Interior spaces are dramatically proportioned because of the long and varied roof lines of this contemporary. The two-story living area has a sloped ceiling as does the master bedroom and two upper-level bedrooms. Two fireplaces, a huge rear wooden deck, a small upstairs sitting room, and a liberal number of windows make this a most comfortable vacation residence.

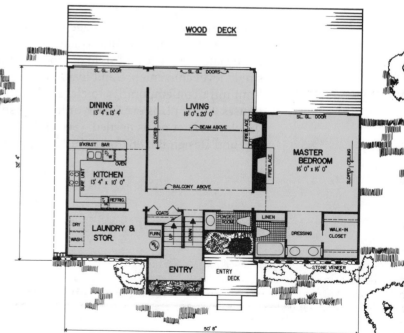

Design BB4308

First Floor: 1,494 square feet
Second Floor: 597 square feet
Basement Level: 1,035 square feet
Total: 3,126 square feet

L

● You can't help but feel spoiled by this design. Behind the handsome facade lies a spacious, amenity-filled plan. Downstairs from the entry is the large living room with sloped ceiling and fireplace. Nearby is the U-shaped kitchen with a pass-through to the din-ing room — a convenient step-saver. Also on this level, the master suite boasts a fireplace and a sliding glass door onto the deck. The living and din-ing rooms also feature deck access. Upstairs are two bedrooms and shared bath. A balcony sitting area overlooks the living room. The enormous lower-level playroom includes a fireplace, a large bar, and sliding glass doors to the patio. Also notice the storage room with built-in workbench.

Design BB2828

First Floor: 1,078 square feet
Second Floor: 1,066 square feet
Total: 2,144 square feet

● The first floor of this contemporary home features an interior kitchen with a snack bar, a living room with raised-hearth fireplace, and a dining room. The first-floor bedroom will make a great guest suite with nearby full bath and terrace access. Upstairs, a large master bedroom is joined by two family bedrooms, one of which

could easily serve as a nursery, office or media room. Also notice the two balconies, three skylights and sewing/hobbies room upstairs. Storage space is available everywhere you look—hall closets on the second floor, in the first floor laundry room and garage, and in the basement plan.

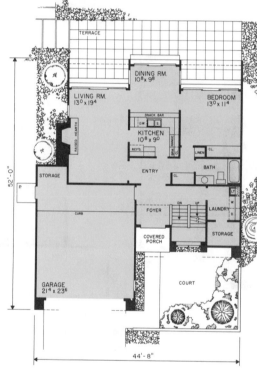

Design BB2827

Upper Level: 1,618 square feet
Lower Level: 1,170 square feet
Total: 2,788 square feet

L

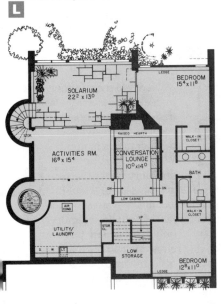

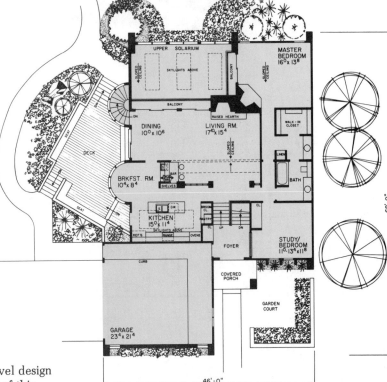

● The towering, two-story solarium in this bi-level design is its key to energy savings. Study the efficiency of this floor plan. The conversation lounge on the lower level is a unique focal point.

Design BB2822

First Floor: 1,363 square feet
Second Floor: 351 square feet
Total: 1,714 square feet

L

● Here is a truly unique house whose interior was designed with modern economics, lifestyles and demographics in mind. While functioning as a one-story home, the second floor provides an extra measure of livability when required. In addition, this two-story section adds to the dramatic appeal of both the exterior and the interior. Within only 1,363 square feet, this contemporary delivers refreshing and outstanding living patterns for those who are buying their first home, those who have raised their family and are looking for a smaller home and those in search of a retirement home.

California Engineered Plans and California Stock Plans are available for this home. Call 1-800-521-6797 for more information.

QUOTE ONE™

Cost to build? See page 214 to order complete cost estimate to build this house in your area!

Width 54'-8"
Depth 54'

ALTERNATE SECOND FLOOR

Design BB2887

First Floor: 1,338 square feet
Second Floor: 661 square feet
Total: 1,999 square feet

● This attractive, contemporary 1½-story will be the envy of many. First, examine the efficient kitchen. Not only does it offer a snack bar for those quick meals but also a large dining room. Notice the adjacent dining porch. The laundry and garage access are also adjacent to the kitchen. An exciting feature is the gathering room with fireplace. The first floor also offers a study with a wet bar and sliding glass doors that open to a private porch. This will make those quiet times cherishable. Adjacent to the study is a full bath followed by a bedroom. Upstairs a large master bedroom suite occupies the entire floor. It features a bath with an oversized tub and shower, a large walk-in closet with built-ins and an open lounge with fireplace. Both the lounge and master bedroom, along with the gathering room, have sloped ceilings. Develop the lower level for additional space.

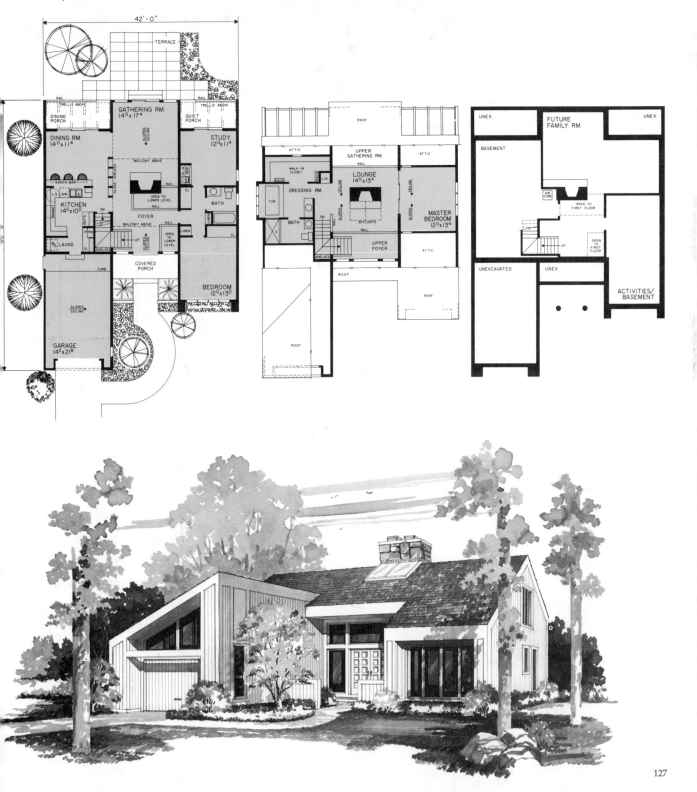

Design BB3450

First Floor: 1,801 square feet
Second Floor: 1,086 square feet
Total: 2,887 square feet

L **D**

● A striking facade includes a covered front porch with four columns. To the left of the foyer is a large gathering room with a fireplace and bay window. The adjoining dining room leads to a covered side porch. The kitchen includes a snack bar, pantry, desk, and eating area. The first-floor master suite provides a spacious bath with walk-in closet, whirlpool and shower. Also on the first floor: a study and a garage workshop. Two bedrooms and a lavish guest suite share the second floor.

Quote One™

Cost to build? See page 214 to order complete cost estimate to build this house in your area!

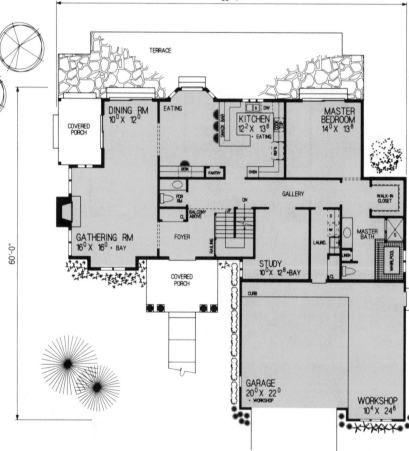

CUSTOMIZABLE

Custom Alterations? See page 221 for customizing this plan to your specifications.

128

esign BB3323

rst Floor: 1,923 square feet
cond Floor: 838 square feet
tal: 2,751 square feet

This two-story southwestern home was
esigned to make living patterns as pleasant
s they can be. Take a step down from the
yer and go where your mood takes you: a
athering room with fireplace and an alcove
r reading or quiet conversations, a media
om for enjoying the latest technology, or to
e dining room with sliding glass doors to
e terrace. The kitchen has an island range
nd eating space. Also on the first floor is a
rge master suite including a sitting area
ith terrace access, walk-in closet and
hirlpool. An elegant spiral staircase leads to
wo family bedrooms sharing a full bath and
guest bedroom with private bath.

QUOTE ONE™

Cost to build? See page 214
to order complete cost estimate
to build this house in your area!

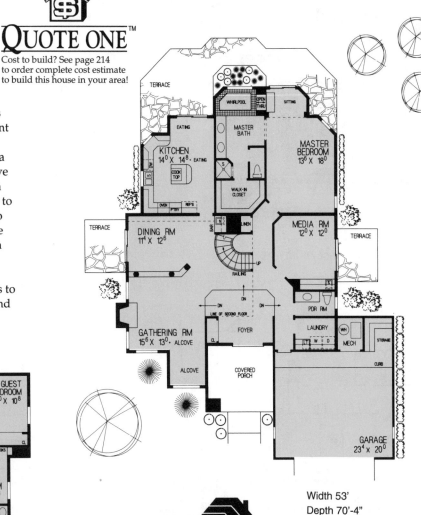

Width 53'
Depth 70'-4"

CUSTOMIZABLE

Custom Alterations? See page 221
for customizing this plan to your
specifications.

Design BB3573

First Floor: 1,650 square feet
Second Floor: 1,508 square feet
Total: 3,158 square feet
Bonus Room: 275 square feet
Bedroom Option: 176 square feet

L D

QUOTE ONE™

Cost to build? See page 214
to order complete cost estimate
to build this house in your area!

● A design for the times, this beautiful transitional home may be built with a fourth bedroom and/or a first-floor bonus room. The entrance court introduces a covered porch. Inside, the tiled foyer offers a dramatic space comprised of a dining room on the left and, separated by a staircase, a living room on the right. Both rooms enjoy their own terrace. Casual living takes off in the family room with its terrace. An expansive kitchen backs up the plan and includes a walk-in pantry and an island countertop. Upstairs, overlooking the dining room, a hallway branches off into three bedrooms, including a delightful master suite. Here, highlights range from two balconies to a bath with a whirlpool tub.

ENTRANCE COURT

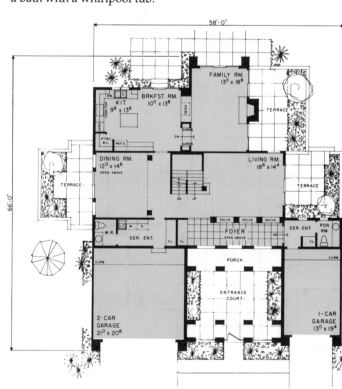

Design BB2493

First Floor: 1,387 square feet
Second Floor: 929 square feet
Total: 2,316 square feet

● Perfect for a narrow lot, this shingle-and stone-sided Nantucket Cape caters to the casual lifestyle. The side entrance gives direct access to the wonderfully open living areas: gathering room with fireplace, kitchen with angled, pass-through snack bar, dining area with sliding glass doors to a covered eating area. Note also the large deck that further extends the living potential. Also on this floor is a large master suite. Upstairs is a convenient guest suite with private balcony. It is complemented by two smaller bedrooms.

CUSTOMIZABLE

Custom Alterations? See page 221 for customizing this plan to your specifications.

Design BB8898

First Floor: 1,075 square feet
Second Floor: 816 square feet
Total: 1,891 square feet

● The vaulted entry area of this home will impress visitors. The great room features a vaulted ceiling shared with the dining room. The U-shaped kitchen serves the family room with a pass-through. A bay window and deck access make the family room extra special, as does a warming hearth. A utility room and a powder room lead to the two-car garage. Upstairs, three bedrooms include a master bedroom suite with an efficient, private bath and two closets. The secondary bedrooms share a full hall bath.

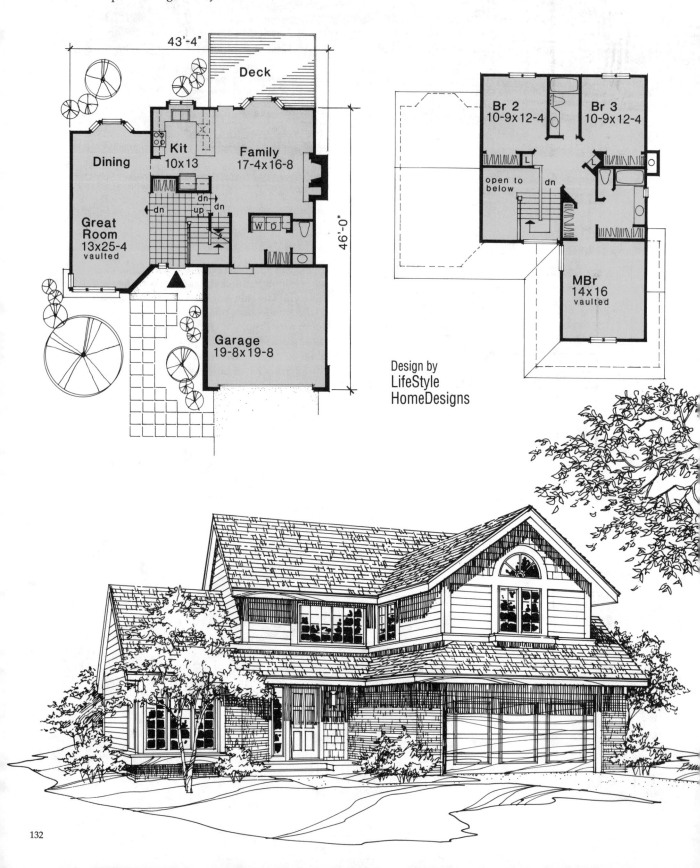

43'-4"

Deck

Kit
10x13

Family
17-4x16-8

Dining

Great
Room
13x25-4
vaulted

dn

up

dn

dn

w   o

46'-0"

Garage
19-8x19-8

Br 2
10-9x12-4

Br 3
10-9x12-4

open to
below

L

dn

L

MBr
14x16
vaulted

Design by
LifeStyle
HomeDesigns

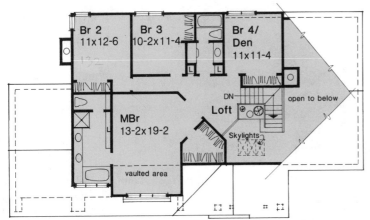

Br 2
11x12-6

Br 3
10-2x11-4

Br 4/
Den
11x11-4

DN

open to below

MBr
13-2x19-2

Loft

Skylights

vaulted area

Design by
LifeStyle
HomeDesigns

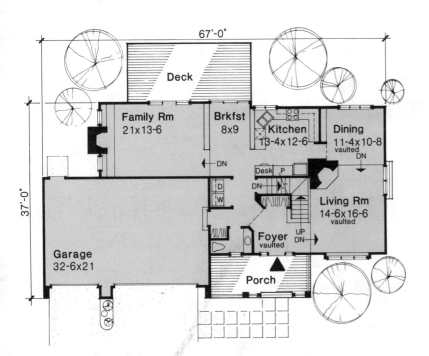

67'-0"

Deck

37'-0"

Family Rm
21x13-6

Brkfst
8x9

Kitchen
13-4x12-6

Dining
11-4x10-8
vaulted

DN

Desk   P

DN

DN

D
W

Living Rm
14-6x16-6
vaulted

UP
DN

Foyer
vaulted

Garage
32-6x21

Porch

Design BB8899

First Floor: 1,290 square feet
Second Floor: 1,155 square feet
Total: 2,445 square feet

● A vaulted, skylit foyer with a
dramatic staircase opens this plan.
To the right, a gracious living room
with a fireplace opens to a dining
room. The full kitchen is conveniently located between the dining
room and the breakfast room. The
family room features a central
hearth and built-in cabinets. A rear
deck enhances outdoor livability.
On the second floor, four bedrooms–or three and a den–include
a spacious master suite. Its bath
extends a separate shower and tub
and dual lavatories.

133

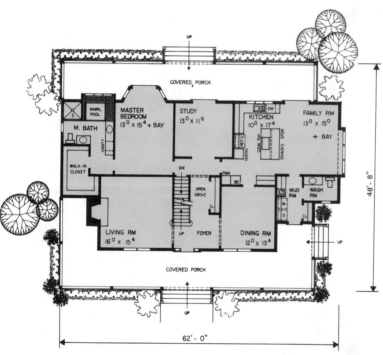

UP

COVERED PORCH

WHIRL POOL

MASTER BEDROOM
13⁰ x 15⁴ + BAY

STUDY
13⁰ x 11⁶

KITCHEN
10⁰ x 17⁴

FAMILY RM
13⁰ x 15⁰
+ BAY

M. BATH

VANITY

OVENS

COOK TOP

SNACK'S

STOR

WALK-IN CLOSET

DN

OPEN ABOVE

PAN

BC

MUD RM

WASH RM

W

LIVING RM
16⁰ x 15⁴

UP

FOYER

DINING RM
12⁰ x 13⁴

UP

COVERED PORCH

UP

48' - 8"

62' - 0"

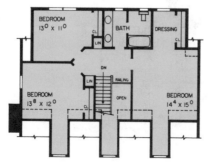

BEDROOM
13⁰ x 11⁰

BATH

DRESSING

LIN

CL

CL

DN

LIN

RAILING

BEDROOM
13⁸ x 12⁰

OPEN

CL

BEDROOM
14⁴ x 15⁰

Design BB3396

First Floor: 1,829 square feet
Second Floor: 947 square feet
Total: 2,776 square feet

L **D**

● Rustic charm abounds in this pleasant farm-house rendition. Covered porches to the front and rear enclose living potential for the whole family. Flanking the entrance foyer are the living and dining rooms. To the rear is the L-shaped kitchen with island cook top and snack bar. A small family room/breakfast nook is attached. A private study is tucked away on this floor next to the master suite. On the second floor are three bedrooms and a full bath. Two of the bedrooms have charming dormer windows.

QUOTE ONE™

Cost to build? See page 214
to order complete cost estimate
to build this house in your area!

LUXURY HOMES
Over 3,000 Square Feet

For the homes in this section, luxury is not just a state of mind, it's a reality. Each is imbued with an attention to amenities and stylish flair that sets it apart from the average home. However, all maintain the same uncomplicated livability that empty-nest couples are looking for. In mostly two- and three-bedroom models, these luxury homes satisfy contemporary and traditional tastes. The floor plans include uniquely configured rooms; spacious, well-appointed master suites; specialty areas for hobbies, work or exercise; three-car garages; and hearth-warmed conversation areas. The homes include many design points—such as angled rooms, volume ceilings and elaborate entry foyers—that give them a special touch. Be sure to notice the split-bedroom personality of many of these homes. (Design BB2920 on page 139 and Design BB3557 on page 140 are good examples.)

Width 110'-7"
Depth 66'-11"

Design BB2922
Square Footage: 3,505

● Loaded with custom features, this plan seems to have everything imaginable. There's an enormous sunken gathering room and a cozy study. The country-style kitchen contains an efficient work area, as well as space for relaxing in the morning. Two nice-sized bedrooms and a luxurious master suite round out the plan.

California Engineered Plans and California Stock Plans are available for this home. Call 1-800-521-6797 for more information.

Design BB3475

Square Footage: 3,286

L

● Transcend the ordinary with this dazzling Floridian house. A covered porch serves as a friendly introduction to a truly pampering design. Inside, the foyer gives way to a sunken living room which features a corner fireplace and double doors that lead to a covered terrace in back. The dining room exhibits elegance with its views overlooking a front garden. The kitchen will delight with its fully efficient layout that incorporates an island work station and a round counter separating the breakfast nook. Here you'll also find a family room for more casual living. Two bedrooms on this side of the house enjoy abundant closet space. On the other side of the house, the master suite provides a true escape from the hustle and bustle of the day. A terrace offers outside livability while, inside, the amenities include a private bath with a corner whirlpool tub and a walk-in closet. Down the hall, a den with a wet bar leads to a privacy patio and garden area.

Width 77'-4"
Depth 74'-8"

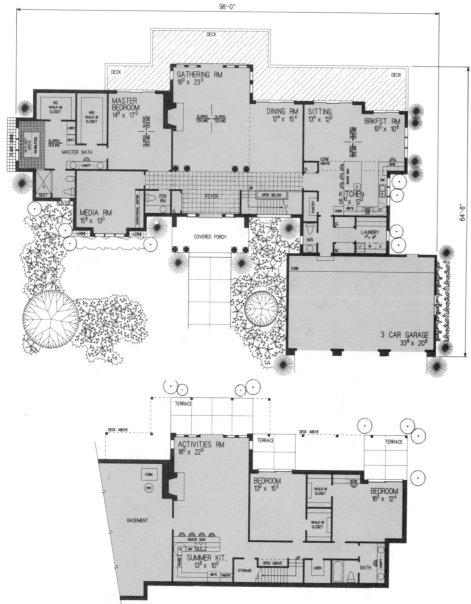

Design BB3311

Main Level: 2,662 square feet
Lower Level: 1,548 square feet
Total: 4,210 square feet

L D

● Here's a hillside haven for family living with plenty of room to entertain in style. Enter the main level from a dramatic columned portico that leads to a large entry hall. The gathering room is straight back and adjoins a formal dining area. A true gourmet kitchen with plenty of room for casual eating and conversation is nearby. The abundantly appointed master suite on this level is complemented by a luxurious bath. Note the media room to the front of the house. On the lower level are two more bedrooms, a full bath, a large activity area with fireplace and a convenient summer kitchen.

QUOTE ONE™

Cost to build? See page 214 to order complete cost estimate to build this house in your area!

CUSTOMIZABLE

Custom Alterations? See page 221
for customizing this plan to your
specifications.

Design BB2920

First Floor: 3,067 square feet
Second Floor: 648 square feet;Total: 3,715 square feet

L **D**

● This contemporary design also has a
great deal to offer. Study the living areas. A
fireplace opens up to both the living room
and country kitchen. Privacy is the key
word when describing the sleeping areas.
The first-floor master bedroom is away from
the traffic of the house and features a dress-
ing/exercise room, whirlpool tub and shower and a spacious walk-in closet. Two more
bedrooms and a full bath are on the second
floor. The three-car garage is arranged so
that the owners have use of a double-garage
with an attached single on reserve for
guests. The sun room adds 296 square feet
to the total.

**California Engineered Plans and
California Stock Plans are available for
this home. Call 1-800-521-6797 for more
information.**

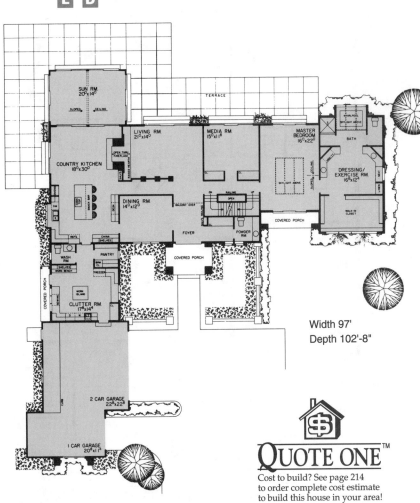

Width 97'
Depth 102'-8"

QUOTE ONE™

Cost to build? See page 214
to order complete cost estimate
to build this house in your area!

139

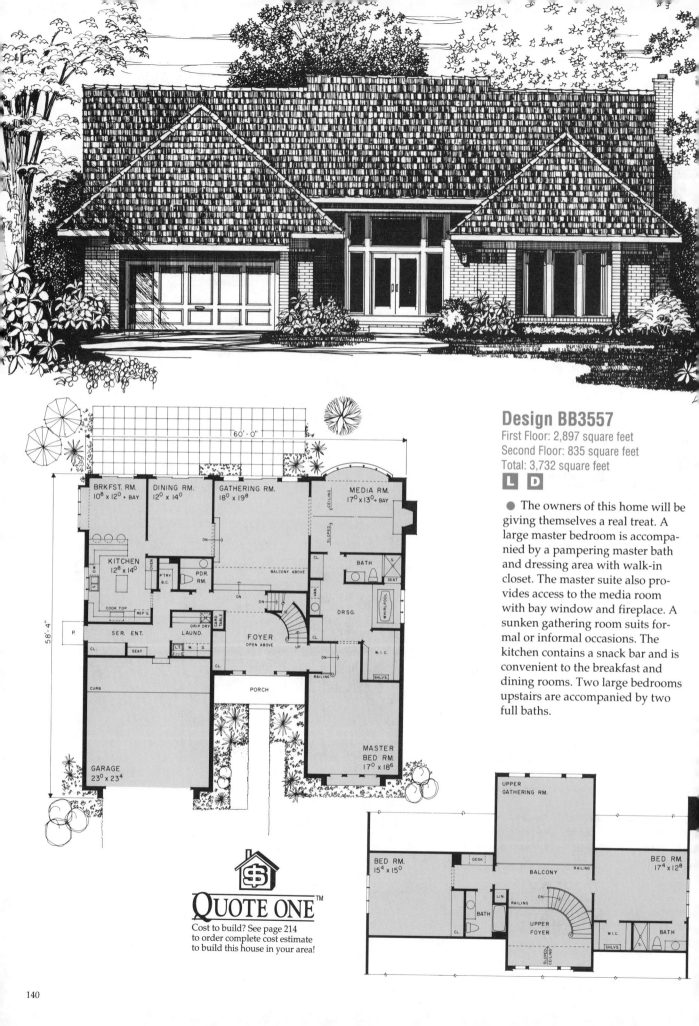

Design BB3557

First Floor: 2,897 square feet
Second Floor: 835 square feet
Total: 3,732 square feet

L **D**

● The owners of this home will be giving themselves a real treat. A large master bedroom is accompanied by a pampering master bath and dressing area with walk-in closet. The master suite also provides access to the media room with bay window and fireplace. A sunken gathering room suits formal or informal occasions. The kitchen contains a snack bar and is convenient to the breakfast and dining rooms. Two large bedrooms upstairs are accompanied by two full baths.

QUOTE ONE™

Cost to build? See page 214 to order complete cost estimate to build this house in your area!

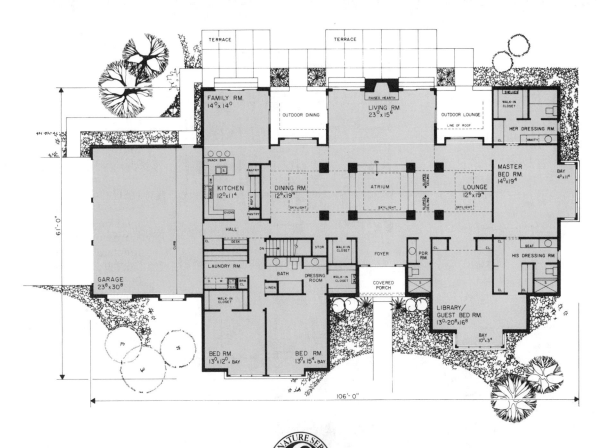

Design BB2791
Square Footage: 3,809

● The use of vertical paned windows and the hipped roof highlight the exterior of this unique design. Upon entrance one will view a charming sunken atrium with skylight above plus a skylight in the dining room and one in the lounge. Formal living will be graciously accommodated in the living room. It features a raised-hearth fireplace, two sets of sliding glass doors to the rear terrace plus two more sliding doors, one to an outdoor dining terrace and the other to an outdoor lounge. Informal living will be enjoyed in the family room with snack bar and in the large library. All will praise the fine planning of the master suite. It features a bay window, His and Hers dressing room with private baths and an abundance of closet space.

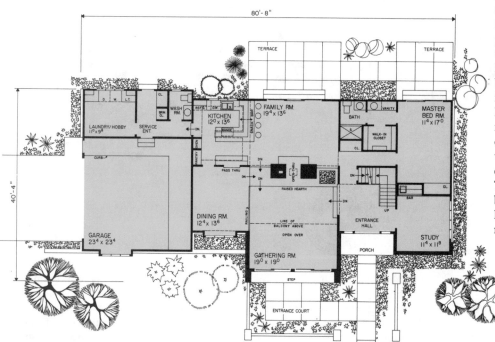

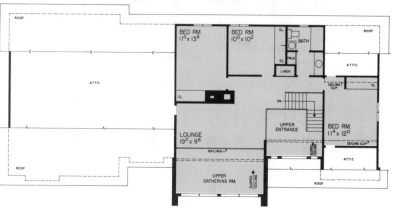

Design BB2782

First Floor: 2,060 square feet
Second Floor: 897 square feet
Total: 2,957 square feet

D

● What makes this such a distinctive four-bedroom design? This plan includes great formal and informal living for the family at home or when entertaining guests. The formal gathering room and informal family room share a dramatic raised-hearth fireplace. Other features of the sunken gathering room include high, sloped ceilings, built-in planter and sliding glass doors to the front entrance court. The kitchen has a snack bar, many built-ins, a pass-through to dining room and easy access to the large laundry/washroom. The master bedroom suite is located on the main level for added privacy and convenience. There's even a study with a built-in bar. The upper level has three more bedrooms, a bath and a lounge looking down into the gathering room.

Design BB2857
Square Footage: 2,982

L

● You'll applaud the many outstanding features of this home. Notice first the master bedroom. It has His and Hers baths, each with a large walk-in closet, sliding glass doors to a private terrace, and an adjacent study. Two family bedrooms are separate from the master for total privacy. The gathering room is designed for entertaining. It has its own balcony and a fireplace as a focal point. The U-shaped kitchen is efficient and has an attached breakfast room and snack bar pass-through to the dining room.

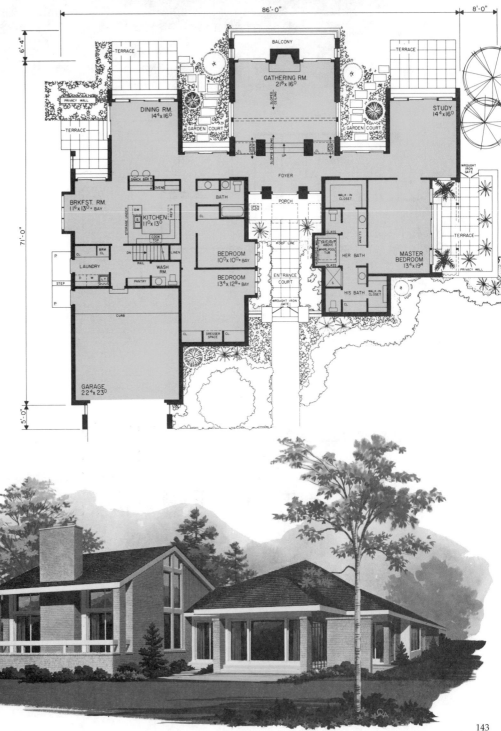

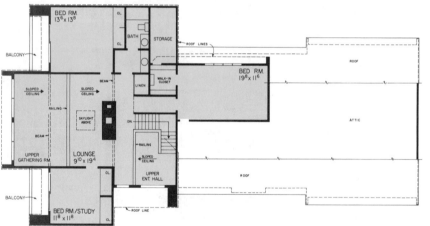

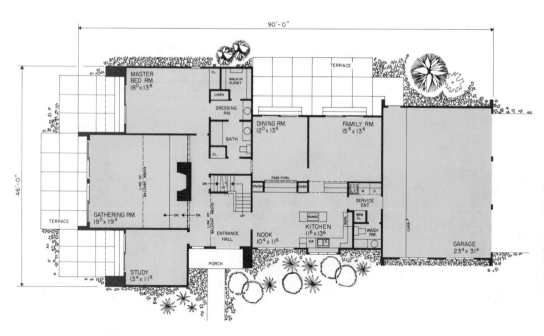

Design BB2781

First Floor: 2,132 square feet
Second Floor: 1,156 square feet
Total: 3,288 square feet

L **D**

● This beautifully designed two-story could be con-
sidered a dream house of a
lifetime. The exterior is
sure to catch the eye of
anyone who takes sight of
its unique construction.
The front kitchen features
an island range, adjacent
breakfast nook and pass-
thru to formal dining room.
The master bedroom suite
with its privacy and con-
venience on the first floor
has a spacious walk-in
closet and dressing room.
The side terrace is accessible through sliding glass
doors from the master bedroom, gathering room and
study. The second floor has
three bedrooms and storage
space galore. Also notice
the lounge which has a
sloped ceiling and a sky-
light above. This delightful
area looks down into the
gathering room. The out-
door balconies overlook the
wrap-around terrace. Surely an outstanding trend
house for decades to come.

144

Design BB3404

First Floor: 3,358 square feet
Second Floor: 868 square feet
Total: 4,226 square feet

L **D**

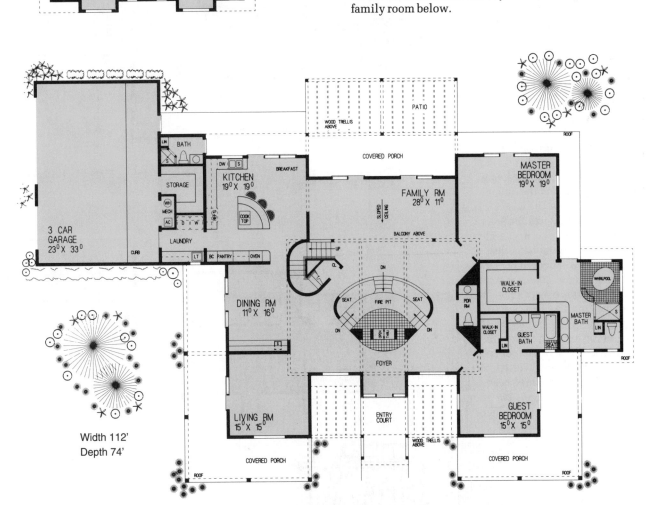

QUOTE ONE™

Cost to build? See page 214
to order complete cost estimate
to build this house in your area!

● Farmhouse design does a double take in this
unusual and elegant rendition. Notice that
most of the living takes place on the first floor:
formal living room and dining room, gigantic
family room with enormous firepit and porch
access, guest bedroom or den and master bedroom suite. Upstairs there are two smaller bedrooms and a dramatic balcony overlook to the
family room below.

Width 112'
Depth 74'

Design BB3505

First Floor: 2,899 square feet
Second Floor: 1,519 square feet
Total: 4,418 square feet
Bonus Room: 540 square feet

L

● A sweeping veranda with tapered columns supports the low-pitched roof and its delicately detailed cornice work. The wood railing effectively complements the lattice-work below. Horizontal siding and double-hung windows with muntins and shutters enhance the historic appeal of this 1½-story home. Inside, the spacious central foyer has a high ceiling and a dramatic, curving staircase to the second floor. Two formal areas flank the foyer and include the living room to the left and the dining room to the right. The U-shaped kitchen easily services the latter through a butler's pantry. A library and gathering room flank the kitchen and will delight the family. Sleeping accommodations excel with a spacious master suite. Here, a private bath and two closets—one a walk-in—guarantee satisfaction. At the top of the dramatic staircase to the second floor is a generous sitting area which looks down on the foyer. Three bedrooms are directly accessible from this area. A bonus room further enhances this fabulous family home.

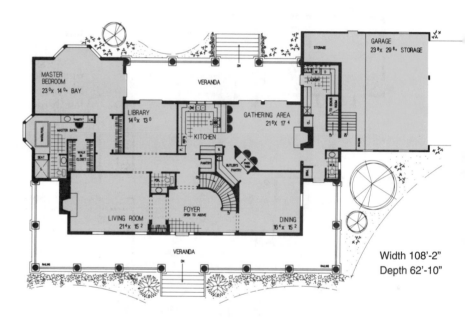

Width 108'-2"
Depth 62'-10"

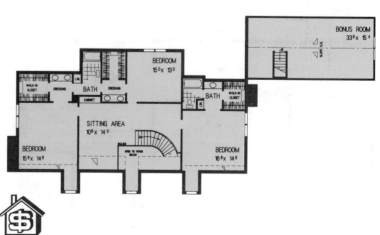

Cost to build? See page 214 to order complete cost estimate to build this house in your area!

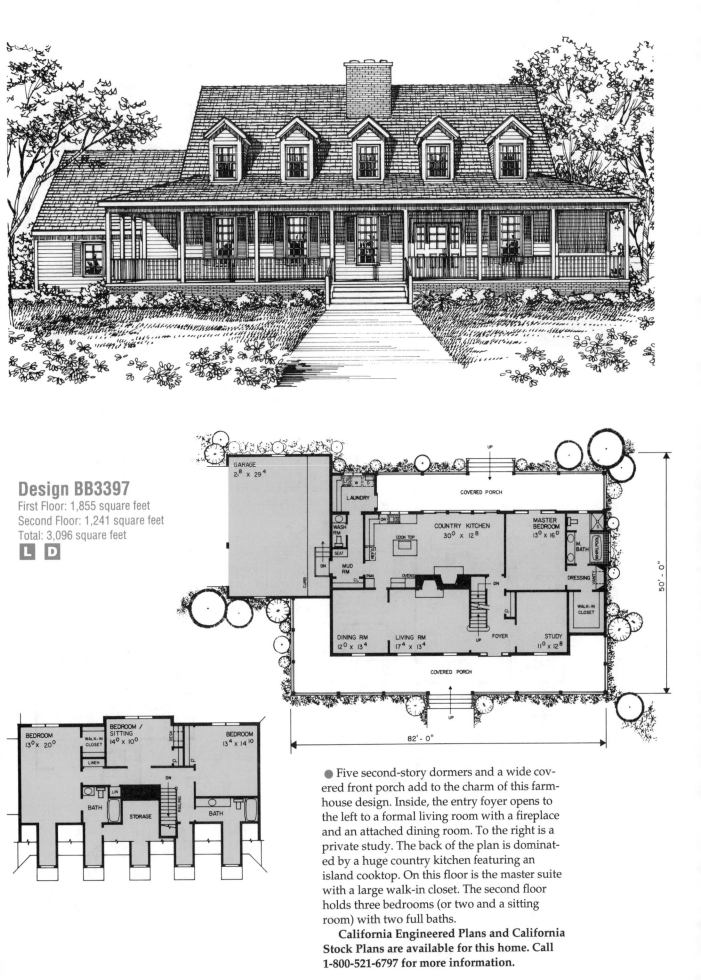

Design BB3397

First Floor: 1,855 square feet
Second Floor: 1,241 square feet
Total: 3,096 square feet

L **D**

● Five second-story dormers and a wide covered front porch add to the charm of this farmhouse design. Inside, the entry foyer opens to the left to a formal living room with a fireplace and an attached dining room. To the right is a private study. The back of the plan is dominated by a huge country kitchen featuring an island cooktop. On this floor is the master suite with a large walk-in closet. The second floor holds three bedrooms (or two and a sitting room) with two full baths.

California Engineered Plans and California Stock Plans are available for this home. Call 1-800-521-6797 for more information.

Design BB3550

First Floor: 2,328 square feet
Second Floor: 712 square feet
Total: 3,040 square feet

L D

● A transitional 1½-story home combines the best of contemporary and traditional elements. This one uses vertical wood siding, stone and multi-paned windows to beautiful advantage. The floor plan makes great use of space with first-floor living and dining areas and a first-floor master suite. Two secondary bedrooms, a full bath and an open lounge area are found on the second floor. The garage is accessed from the island kitchen through the laundry.

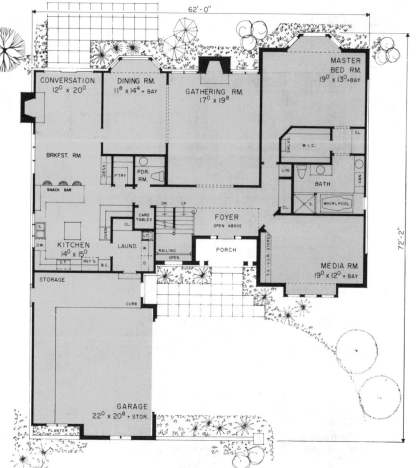

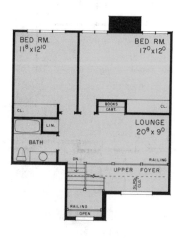

Cost to build? See page 214
to order complete cost estimate
to build this house in your area!

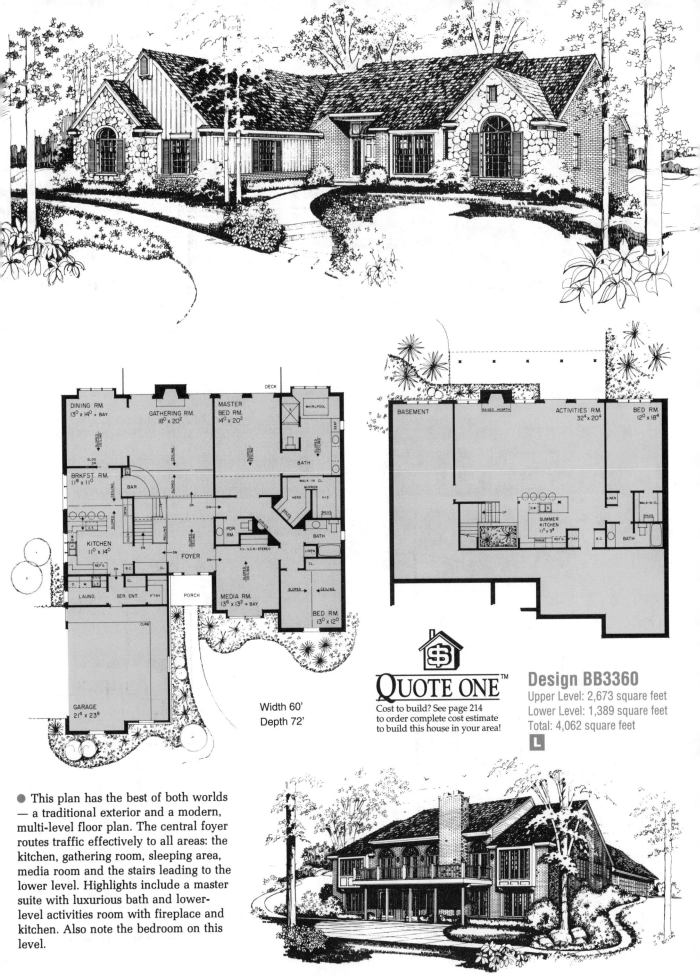

DINING RM.
13⁰ x 14⁰ + BAY

GATHERING RM.
18⁰ x 20²

MASTER
BED RM.
14⁰ x 20²

DECK

WHIRLPOOL

SEAT

BATH

BRKFST. RM.
11⁸ x 11⁰

SLDG. DR.

BAR

SLOPED CEILING

WALK-IN CL.

MIRROR

HERS

HIS

SHLVS.

KITCHEN
11⁰ x 14⁰

DN

OVEN

FOYER

DN

PDR. RM.

T.V.·V.C.R.·STEREO

BATH

LINEN

REF'G.

B.C.

CL.

CL.

DN

D.

W.

CL.

SLOPED CEILING

SLOPED

CEILING

LAUND.

SER. ENT.

P'TRY

PORCH

MEDIA RM.
13⁶ x 13² + BAY

BED RM.
13⁰ x 12⁰

GARAGE
21⁴ x 23⁸

CURB

Width 60'
Depth 72'

BASEMENT

RAISED HEARTH

ACTIVITIES RM.
32⁴ x 20⁴

BED RM.
12⁰ x 18⁴

UP

SUMMER
KITCHEN
11⁰ x 9⁰

RANGE

REF'G.

P'TRY

B.C.

LINEN

WALK-IN CL.

SHLVS.

BATH

QUOTE ONE™

Cost to build? See page 214
to order complete cost estimate
to build this house in your area!

Design BB3360

Upper Level: 2,673 square feet
Lower Level: 1,389 square feet
Total: 4,062 square feet

L

● This plan has the best of both worlds
— a traditional exterior and a modern,
multi-level floor plan. The central foyer
routes traffic effectively to all areas: the
kitchen, gathering room, sleeping area,
media room and the stairs leading to the
lower level. Highlights include a master
suite with luxurious bath and lower-
level activities room with fireplace and
kitchen. Also note the bedroom on this
level.

Design BB3575

Main Level: 1,650 square feet
Upper Level: 628 square feet
Lower Level: 977 square feet
Total: 3,255 square feet

L

QUOTE C

Cost to build? See page
to order complete cost e
to build this house in yc

● This contemporary design accommodates hillside lots well with its lower-level living areas. The guest bedroom located here accesses a full bath with an exercise room nearby. Also notable about this area is the activities room with its raised-hearth fireplace. A spacious, two-story gathering room with a large fireplace and a balcony defines the main floor. A formal dining room, also with a balcony, connects to the breakfast room with outside access and the modern kitchen. A laundry room facilitates ease in everyday living and sits on the other side of the two-car garage. The master bedroom, with its private bath with whirlpool tub, finishes off this floor. Upstairs, two family bedrooms—each with their own balcony—share a full hall bath.

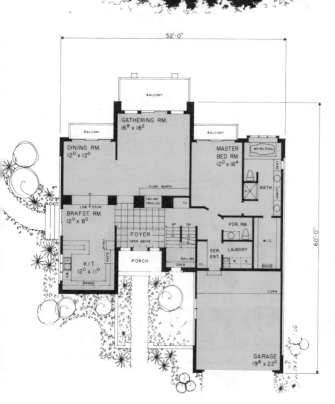

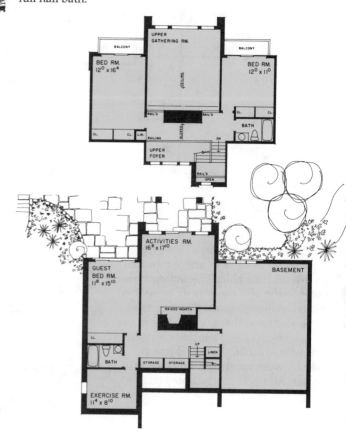

Design BB3366

Main Level: 1,638 square feet
Upper Level: 650 square feet; Lower Level: 934 square feet
Total: 3,222 square feet

L

● There is much more to this design than meets the eye. While it may look like a 1½-story plan, bonus recreation and hobby space in the walk-out basement adds almost 1,000 square feet. The first floor holds living and dining areas as well as the master bedroom suite. Two family bedrooms on the second floor are connected by a balcony area that overlooks the gathering room below. Notice the covered porch beyond the breakfast and dining rooms.

QUOTE ONE™

Cost to build? See page 214 to order complete cost estimate to build this house in your area!

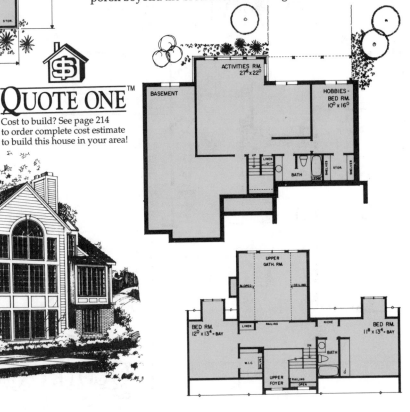

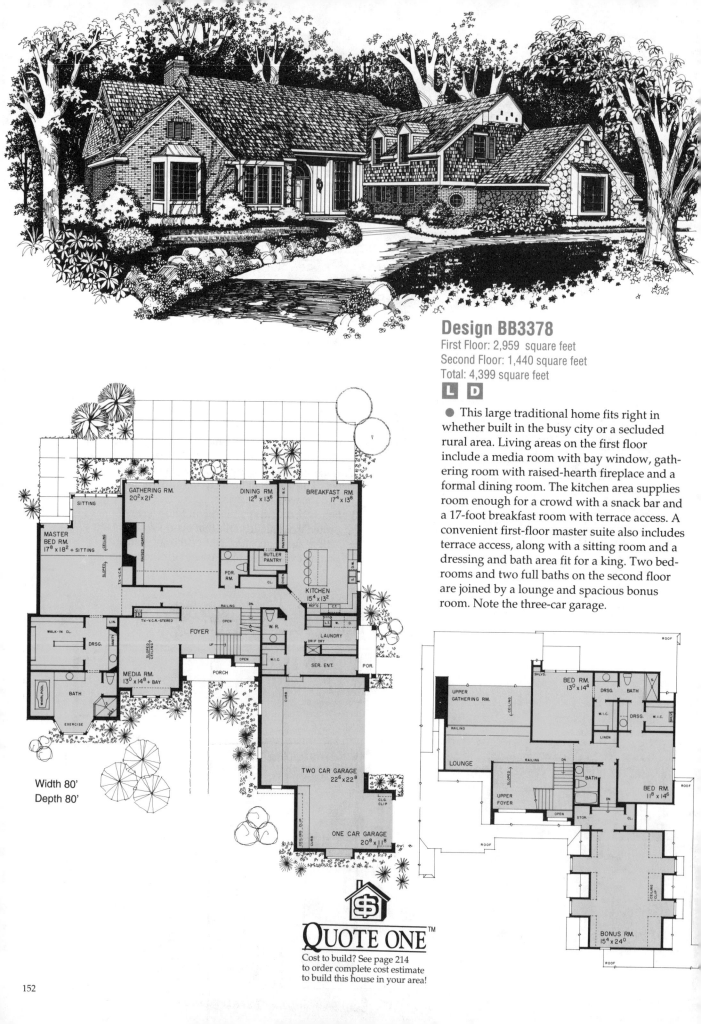

Design BB3378

First Floor: 2,959 square feet
Second Floor: 1,440 square feet
Total: 4,399 square feet

L **D**

● This large traditional home fits right in whether built in the busy city or a secluded rural area. Living areas on the first floor include a media room with bay window, gathering room with raised-hearth fireplace and a formal dining room. The kitchen area supplies room enough for a crowd with a snack bar and a 17-foot breakfast room with terrace access. A convenient first-floor master suite also includes terrace access, along with a sitting room and a dressing and bath area fit for a king. Two bedrooms and two full baths on the second floor are joined by a lounge and spacious bonus room. Note the three-car garage.

Width 80'
Depth 80'

QUOTE ONE™

Cost to build? See page 214
to order complete cost estimate
to build this house in your area!

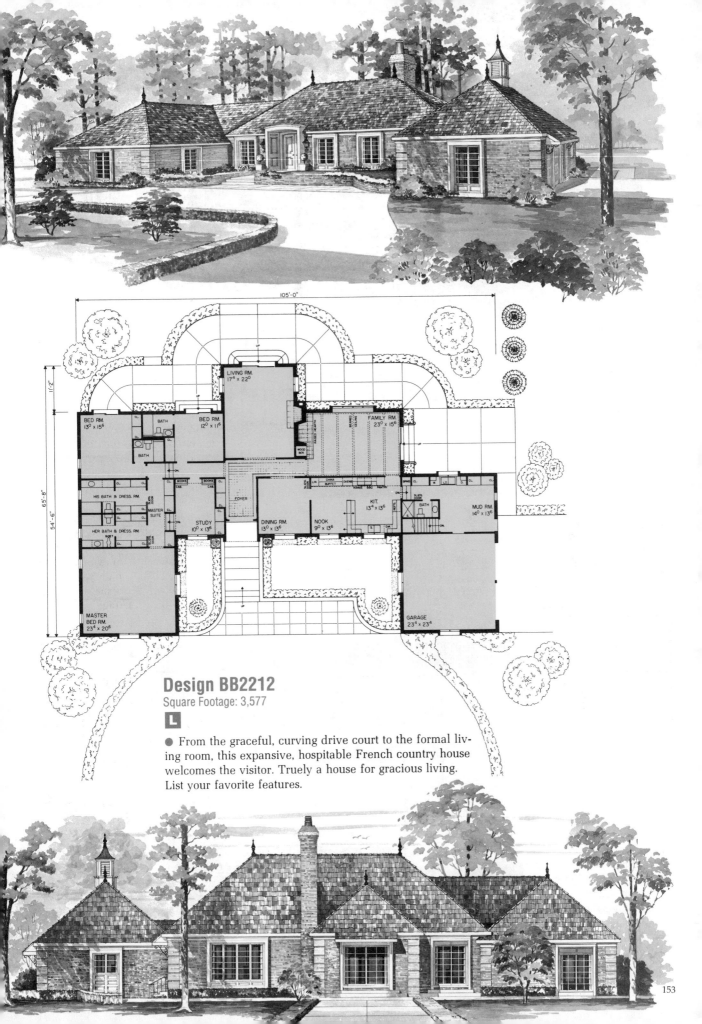

Design BB2212

Square Footage: 3,577

L

● From the graceful, curving drive court to the formal living room, this expansive, hospitable French country house welcomes the visitor. Truely a house for gracious living. List your favorite features.

Design BB3353

First Floor: 2,191 square feet
Second Floor: 874 square feet
Total: 3,065 square feet

QUOTE ONE™

Cost to build? See page 214
to order complete cost estimate
to build this house in your area!

● This captivating 1½ story Southern
Colonial provides the best in livability.
On the first floor are the living room, dining room and private media room. A
country kitchen with fireplace offers casual living space. The master suite is also
located on this floor and has a lavish master bath with whirlpool spa. Upstairs are
two family bedrooms, each with its own
bath, and a central lounge overlooking
the living room.

Design BB3334

First Floor: 2,193 square feet
Second Floor: 831 square feet
Total: 3,024 square feet

L

● A traditional favorite, this home combines classic style with progressive floor planning. Four bedrooms are split — master suite and one bedroom on the first floor, two more bedrooms upstairs. The second-floor lounge overlooks a large, sunken gathering room near the formal dining area. A handy butler's pantry connects the dining room and kitchen.

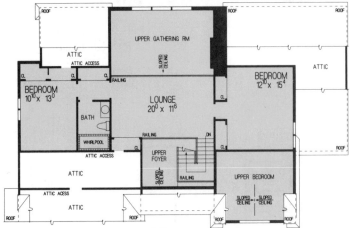

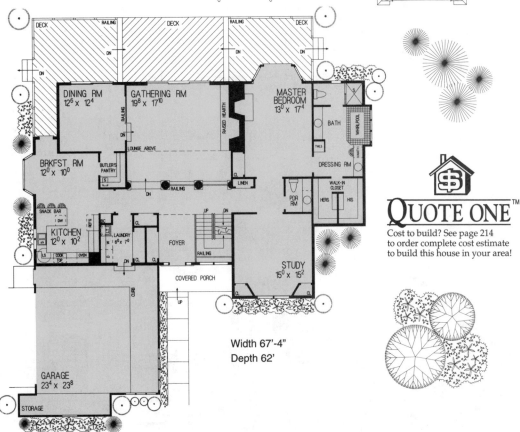

Width 67'-4"
Depth 62'

QUOTE ONE™

Cost to build? See page 214 to order complete cost estimate to build this house in your area!

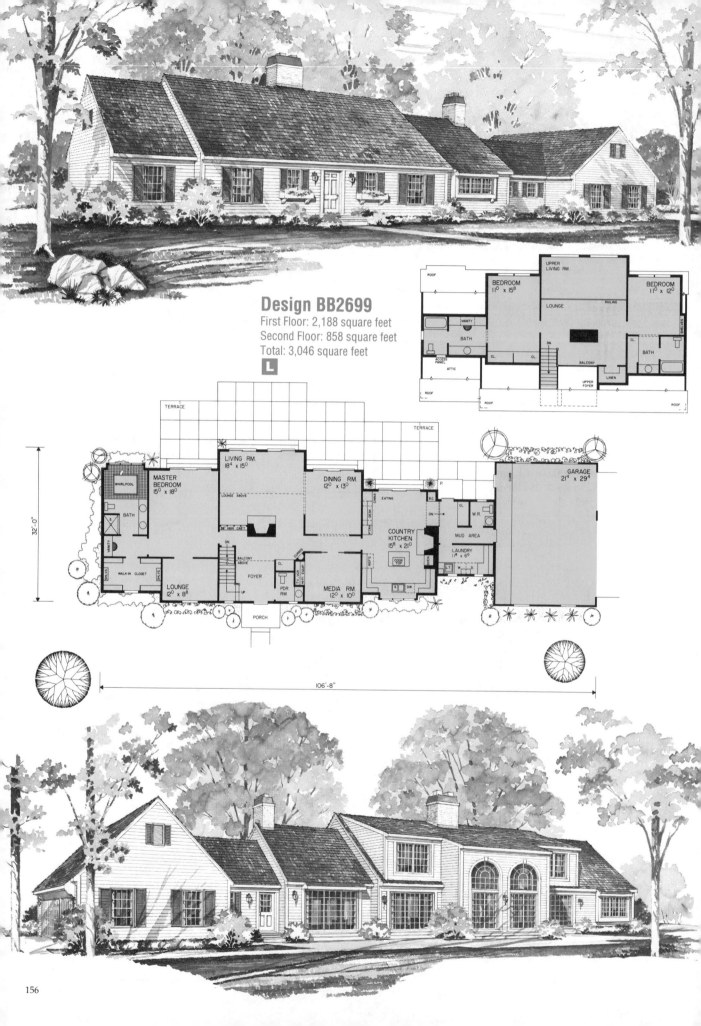

Design BB2699

First Floor: 2,188 square feet
Second Floor: 858 square feet
Total: 3,046 square feet

L

Second Floor Plan labels:
ROOF
BEDROOM 11⁰ x 15⁸
UPPER LIVING RM.
BEDROOM 11⁰ x 12⁰
VANITY
BATH
LOUNGE
RAILING
SHELVES
ACCESS PANEL
ATTIC
CL.
CL.
DN.
BALCONY
CL.
BATH
LINEN
UPPER FOYER
ROOF
ROOF
ROOF

First Floor Plan labels:
TERRACE
TERRACE
LIVING RM. 18⁴ x 15⁰
DINING RM. 12⁰ x 13⁰
GARAGE 21⁴ x 29⁴
MASTER BEDROOM 15 x 18⁰
WHIRLPOOL
BATH
LOUNGE ABOVE
CHINA
EATING
DESK
B.C.
CL.
W.R.
COUNTRY KITCHEN 15⁸ x 21⁰
MUD AREA
DN.
36" HIGH CAB'T
COOK TOP
OVEN
VANITY
SHLVS.
WALK-IN CLOSET
SHLVS.
DN.
BALCONY ABOVE
CL.
T.V. VCR
HI-FI EQUIP.
PTR.
REF'G.
LAUNDRY 11⁸ x 6⁰
LOUNGE 12⁰ x 8⁸
FOYER
PDR. RM.
MEDIA RM. 12⁰ x 10⁰
S
DW
UP
PORCH

32'-0"

106'-8"

156

Design BB2888
Square Footage: 3,018

L

● This is an outstanding Early American design for the 20th-Century. The exterior detailing with narrow clapboards, multi-paned windows and cupola are the features of yesteryear. Interior planning, though, is for today's active family. Formal living room, informal family room plus a study are present. Every activity will have its place in this home. Picture yourself working in the kitchen. There's enough counter space for two or three helpers. Four bedrooms are in the private area. Stop and imagine your daily routine if you occupied the master bedroom. Both you and your spouse would have plenty of space and privacy. The flower porch, accessible from the master bedroom, living and dining rooms, is a very delightful "plus" feature. Study this design's every detail.

Design BB2995

First Floor: 2,465 square feet
Second Floor: 617 square feet
Total: 3,082 square feet

L **D**

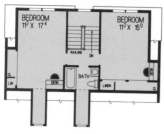

● This New England Colonial delivers beautiful proportions and great livability on 1½ levels. The main area of the house, the first floor, holds a living room, library, family room, dining room and gourmet kitchen. The master bedroom, also on this floor, features a whirlpool tub and a sloped ceiling. A long rear terrace stretches the full width of the house. Two bedrooms on the second floor share a full bath; each has a built-in desk.

California Engineered Plans and California Stock Plans are available for this home. Call 1-800-521-6797 for more information.

Quote One™

Cost to build? See page 214 to order complete cost estimate to build this house in your area!

Width 120'-11"
Depth 52'-6"

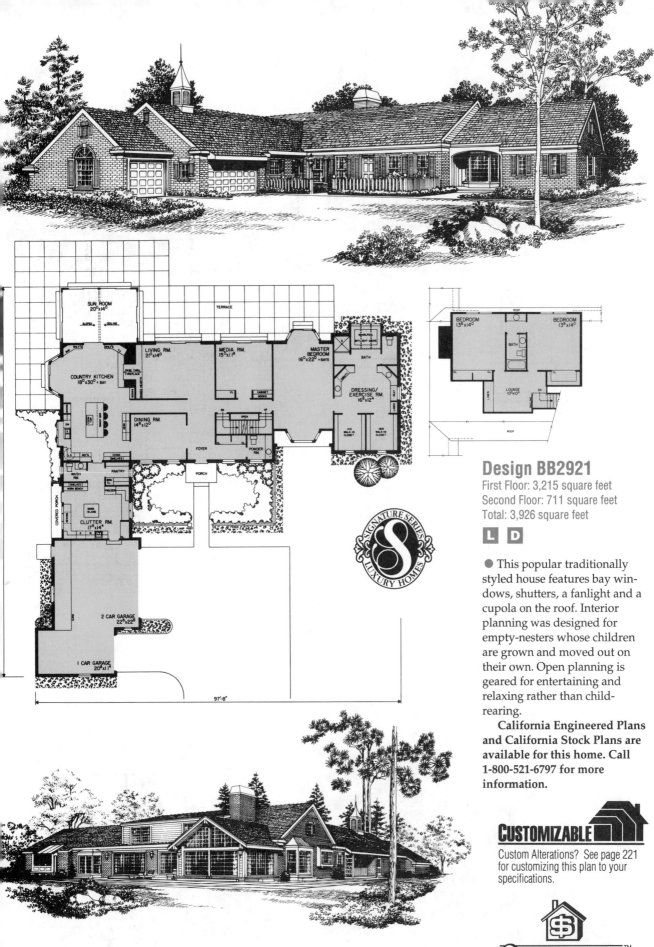

Design BB2921

First Floor: 3,215 square feet
Second Floor: 711 square feet
Total: 3,926 square feet

L D

● This popular traditionally styled house features bay windows, shutters, a fanlight and a cupola on the roof. Interior planning was designed for empty-nesters whose children are grown and moved out on their own. Open planning is geared for entertaining and relaxing rather than child-rearing.

California Engineered Plans and California Stock Plans are available for this home. Call 1-800-521-6797 for more information.

CUSTOMIZABLE

Custom Alterations? See page 221 for customizing this plan to your specifications.

QUOTE ONE™

Cost to build? See page 214 to order complete cost estimate to build this house in your area!

Design BB2615

First Floor: 2,563 square feet
Second Floor: 552 square feet
Total: 3,115 square feet

L **D**

● Here are two more examples of the rambling Cape Cod house that illustrate just how delightful the appearance of those added dependents can be. The appealing result is houses with varying roof planes, projecting and recessed exterior walls and interesting, irregular configurations. In addition to charm, these two houses deliver exceptional country-estate livability for the growing, active family. Each one has a central entrance leading to a foyer, but from there the many features are distinct.

QUOTE ONE™

Cost to build? See page 214 to order complete cost estimate to build this house in your area!

SPANISH AND SOUTHWESTERN HOMES

*W*arm-weather climates have always attracted more mature homeowners and the style of homes native to these climates has long been popular. The classic Southwestern or Spanish-style home lends itself well to empty-nester living. Rooms are open, light-filled and casual with large window areas to capture grand views. Outdoor living is essential and manifests itself in all varieties of porches, patios, terraces, balconies and other fresh-air spots. Exteriors allow all the well-known features of Spanish and Southwestern design: stucco siding, tile roofs, graceful arches and curves, and simplistic ornamentation. Among the homes in this section are Floridian homes, Mission-style, Spanish Eclectic, Spanish Colonial and some unique Pueblo-style plans. Empty-nesters will appreciate some of the more outstanding features in these designs: the media room with built-ins in Design BB2949 and the angled kitchen area in Design BB2948

Design BB3428 First Floor: 2,623 square feet
Second Floor: 551 square feet; Total: 3,174 square feet
L

● High sloping ceilings and plenty of windows lend a light, airy feel to this Southwestern design. Flanking the two-story foyer are the sleeping areas, the regal master suite to the left and three more bedrooms (or two plus study) to the right. Overlooking the back yard are the dining room and living room with raised-hearth fireplace. The U-shaped kitchen has a pass-through to the family room which also has a fireplace. Doors here and in the dining room open onto the covered porch. Notice the pot shelves scattered throughout the plan.

QUOTE ONE™
Cost to build? See page 214 to order complete cost estimate to build this house in your area!

CUSTOMIZABLE
Custom Alterations? See page 221 for customizing this plan to your specifications.

Width 64'
Depth 65'

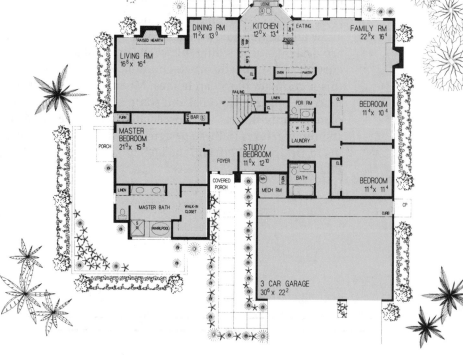

This design is carefully zoned for utmost livability. The entry foyer routes traffic to all areas of the house. To the rear is the living room/dining room combination with built-in china cabinet. To the left, the kitchen is open to the breakfast room and family room with fireplace. The master bedroom is on the right and features a whirlpool and a private porch. Upstairs are three more bedrooms and an outdoor balcony.

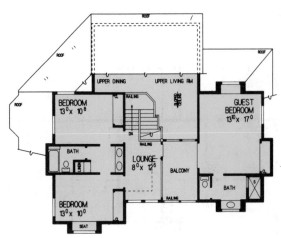

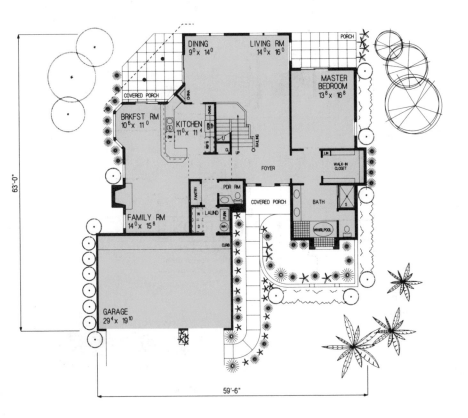

Design BB3426

First Floor: 1,859 square feet
Second Floor: 969 square feet
Total: 2,828 square feet

L

QUOTE ONE™

Cost to build? See page 214 to order complete cost estimate to build this house in your area!

CUSTOMIZABLE

Custom Alterations? See page 221 for customizing this plan to your specifications.

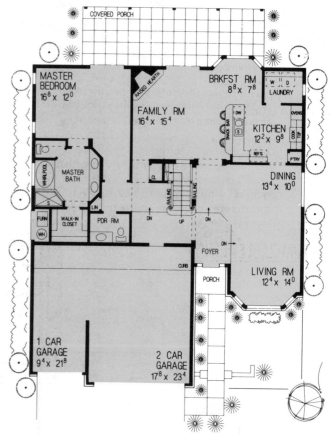

Width 48'
Depth 64'-4"

Design BB3420

First Floor: 1,617 square feet
Second Floor: 658 square feet
Total: 2,275 square feet

 L

● Here is a moderate-sized house with a wealth of amenities typical of much larger homes. Interesting window treatments include two bay windows, one in the living room and one in the breakfast room. In the kitchen there's a snack-bar pass-through to the family room which boasts a corner raised-hearth fireplace. Also on this level, the master suite features a large bath with a whirlpool and access to the rear covered porch. Upstairs are three more bedrooms and a shared bath.
California Engineered Plans and California Stock Plans are available for this home. Call 1-800-521-6797 for more information.

Quote One™

Cost to build? See page 214
to order complete cost estimate
to build this house in your area!

Customizable

Custom Alterations? See page 221
for customizing this plan to your
specifications.

Design BB3418

First Floor: 1,283 square feet
Second Floor: 552 square feet
Total: 1,835 square feet

● This home is ideal for the economically minded who don't want to sacrifice livability. The entry foyer opens directly into the two-story living room with fireplace. To the right, the kitchen with peninsula cooktop and snack bar conveniently serves both the breakfast room and the formal dining room. Also on this level, the master bedroom boasts an enormous bath with a whirlpool and His and Hers walk-in-closets. Three other bedrooms are located upstairs to ensure peace and quiet. Also notice the abundant storage space in the attic.

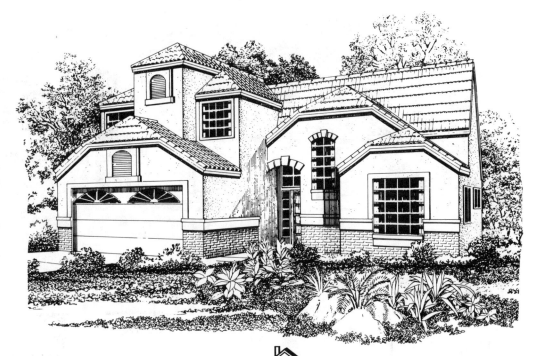

QUOTE ONE™

Cost to build? See page 214 to order complete cost estimate to build this house in your area!

CUSTOMIZABLE

Custom Alterations? See page 221 for customizing this plan to your specifications.

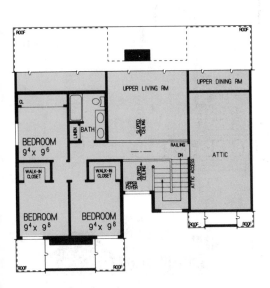

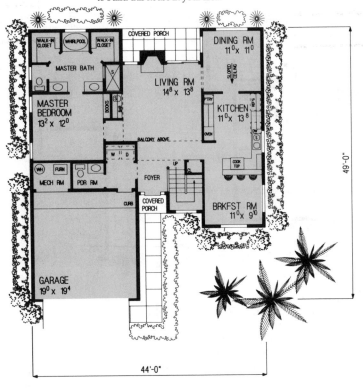

GUEST BEDROOM
14⁰ x 17⁴

RAILING

DECK

UPPER FAMILY ROOM

BATH

CL

BEDROOM
10⁴ x 12⁰

RAILING

DN

MECH
WH
FURN

LINEN

CL

BATH

WALK-IN CLOSET

UPPER FOYER

CL

BEDROOM
12⁴ x 11⁸

BEDROOM
12⁴ x 10⁵

Design BB3414

First Floor: 2,024 square feet
Second Floor: 1,144 square feet
Total: 3,168 square feet

L

WHIRLPOOL   S

MASTER BATH

COVERED PORCH

HER WALK-IN CLOSET

HIS WALK-IN CLOSET

FAMILY RM
19⁸ x 18⁶

BREAKFAST
12⁰ x 9⁶

MASTER BEDROOM
14² x 20⁴

SLOPED CEILING

SNACK BAR   DW

KITCHEN
11⁸ x 12⁶

PANTRY   REF'G

CL

DN

RAILING

DINING
16⁴ x 8⁸

WH   FURN   D   W

MECH RM   **LAUNDRY**

PDR RM

UP

DN

SLOPED CEILING

CURB

FOYER

GARAGE
29⁰ x 19⁶

COVERED PORCH

LIVING RM
16⁰ x 13¹⁰

● Though seemingly compact from the exterior, this home allows for "wide-open-spaces" living. The two-story entry connects directly to a formal living/dining area, a fitting complement to the more casual family room and cozy breakfast room. Split-bedroom planning puts the master suite on the first floor for utmost privacy. Up the curved staircase are three family bedrooms, a guest room with deck and two full baths.

Width 57'
Depth 64'

CUSTOMIZABLE

Custom Alterations? See page 221 for customizing this plan to your specifications.

Quote One

Cost to build? See page 214 to order complete cost estimate to build this house in your area!

Design BB3435

First Floor: 1,946 square feet
Second Floor: 986 square feet
Total: 2,932 square feet

● Here's a grand Spanish Mission home designed for family living. Enter at the angled foyer which contains a curved staircase to the second floor. Family bedrooms are here along with a spacious guest suite. The master bedroom is found on the first floor and has a private patio and whirlpool overlooking an enclosed garden area. Besides a living room and dining room connected by a through-fireplace, there is a family room with casual eating space. There is also a library with large closet. You'll appreciate the abundant built-ins and interesting shapes throughout this home.

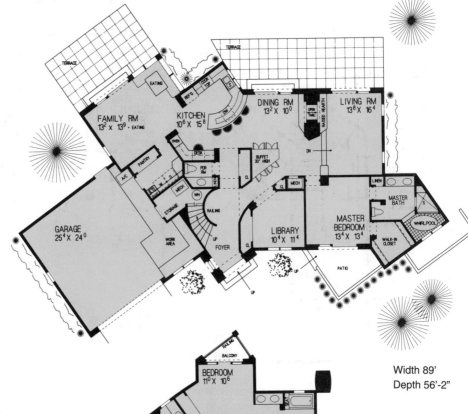

Width 89'
Depth 56'-2"

Custom Alterations? See page 221 for customizing this plan to your specifications.

Cost to build? See page 214 to order complete cost estimate to build this house in your area!

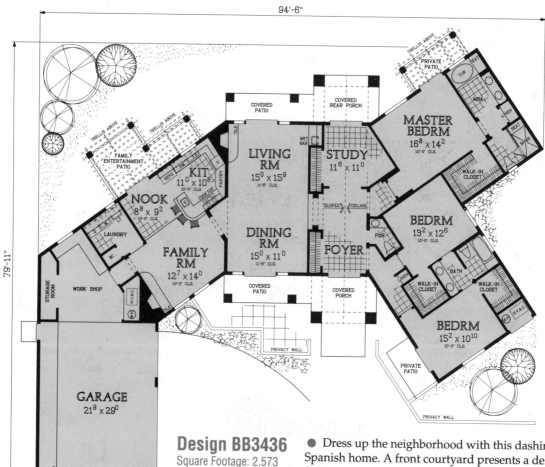

94'-6"

79'-11"

TRELLIS ABOVE
PRIVATE PATIO

COVERED PATIO

COVERED REAR PORCH

MASTER BEDRM
16⁸ x 14²
10'-0" CLG.

MBA
TUB
LINEN
SEAT
SHWR

TRELLIS ABOVE
TRELLIS ABOVE
FAMILY ENTERTAINMENT PATIO

KIT
11⁰ x 10⁸
10'-0" CLG.

REFG.
CK.

COOK TOP

PANTRY

WET BAR

LIVING RM
15⁰ x 15⁹
11'-6" CLG.

STUDY
11⁶ x 11⁰

WALK-IN CLOSET

NOOK
8⁸ x 9²
10'-0" CLG.

SLOPED CEILING

BEDRM
13² x 12⁶
10'-0" CLG.

LAUNDRY

BC

DINING RM
15⁰ x 11⁰
11'-6" CLG.

FOYER

PDR.

LINEN

STORAGE ROOM

WORK SHOP

FAMILY RM
12⁷ x 14⁰
10'-0" CLG.

H.V.A.C.

TILE

COVERED PATIO

COVERED PORCH

WALK-IN CLOSET

BATH

WALK-IN CLOSET

LINEN

BEDRM
15² x 10¹⁰
10'-0" CLG.

H.V.A.C.

GARAGE
21⁹ x 29⁰

PRIVACY WALL

PRIVATE PATIO

PRIVACY WALL

CURB

Design BB3436
Square Footage: 2,573

L

● Dress up the neighborhood with this dashing Spanish home. A front courtyard presents a delightful introduction to the inside living spaces. These excel with a central living room/dining room combination. A wet bar here makes entertaining easy. In the kitchen, a huge pantry and interesting angles are sure to please the house gourmet. A breakfast nook with a corner fireplace further enhances this area. Notice the laundry room nearby as well as the expansive work shop just off the three-car garage. The master bedroom makes room for a private bath with a whirlpool tub and dual lavatories. Two additional bedrooms make use of a Hollywood bath. Each bedroom is highlighted by a spacious walk-in closet.

California Engineered Plans and California Stock Plans are available for this home. Call 1-800-521-6797 for more information.

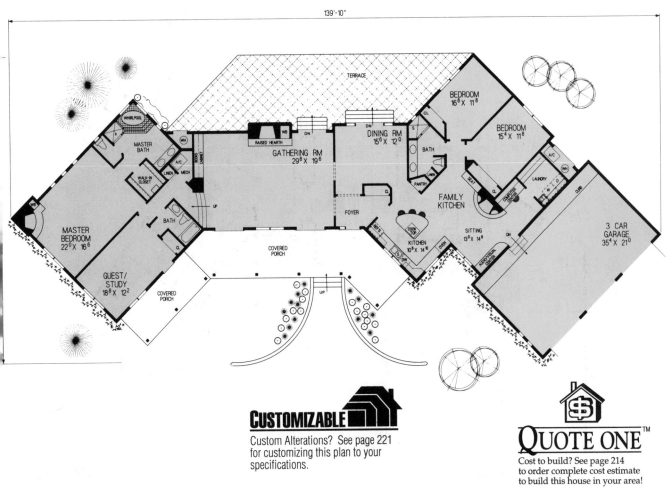

139'-10"

TERRACE

BEDROOM
16⁶ X 11⁸

BEDROOM
15⁴ X 11⁸

WHIRLPOOL

MASTER
BATH

RAISED HEARTH

GATHERING RM
29⁸ X 19⁶

DINING RM
15⁶ X 12⁰

BATH

CL

A/C

WH

LAUNDRY

WALK-IN
CLOSET

LINEN MECH

PANTRY

FAMILY
KITCHEN

SEAT

CL

W D

CL/S

A/C

WH

3 CAR
GARAGE
35⁴ X 21⁰

UP

BATH

FOYER

CL

COOK
TOP

REF/S

KITCHEN
10⁸ X 14¹⁰

SITTING
13⁰ X 14⁸

AUDIO/VISUAL
CENTER

DN

MASTER
BEDROOM
22⁰ X 16⁶

CL

COVERED
PORCH

DW

GUEST/
STUDY
18⁸ X 12²

COVERED
PORCH

UP

CUSTOMIZABLE

Custom Alterations? See page 221 for customizing this plan to your specifications.

QUOTE ONE™

Cost to build? See page 214 to order complete cost estimate to build this house in your area!

Design BB3405

Square Footage: 3,144

● In classic Santa Fe style, this home strikes a beautiful combination of historic exterior detailing and open floor planning. A covered porch running the width of the facade leads to an entry foyer that connects to a huge gathering room with a fireplace and formal dining room. The family kitchen allows special space for casual gatherings. The right wing of the home holds two family bedrooms and a full bath. The left wing is devoted to the master suite and guest room or study.

California Engineered Plans and California Stock Plans are available for this home. Call 1-800-521-6797 for more information.

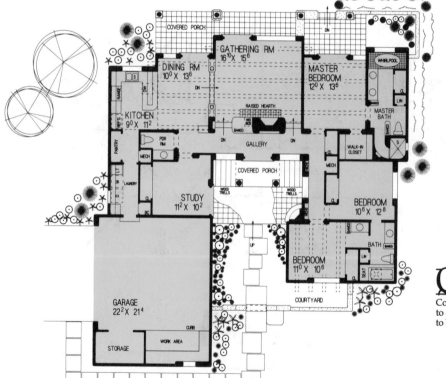

COVERED PORCH

GATHERING RM
16¹⁰ X 15⁶

DINING RM
10⁰ X 13⁶

MASTER
BEDROOM
12⁰ X 13⁶

WHIRLPOOL

RANGE

RAISED HEARTH

MASTER
BATH

LIN

KITCHEN
9⁰ X 11²

PANTRY

PDR
RM

GALLERY

WALK-IN
CLOSET

MECH

LAUNDRY

COVERED PORCH

MECH

STUDY
11² X 10²

WOOD
TRELLIS

WOOD
TRELLIS

BEDROOM
10⁶ X 12⁸

BATH

UP

BEDROOM
11⁰ X 10⁶

LIN

SEAT

GARAGE
22² X 21⁴

COURTYARD

CURB

STORAGE

WORK AREA

Width 61'-6"
Depth 67'-4"

QUOTE ONE™
Cost to build? See page 214
to order complete cost estimate
to build this house in your area!

CUSTOMIZABLE
Custom Alterations? See page 221
for customizing this plan to your
specifications.

Design BB3431
Square Footage: 1,907

● Graceful curves welcome you into
the courtyard of this Santa Fe home.
Inside, a gallery directs traffic to the
work zone on the left or the sleeping
zone on the right. Straight ahead lies a
sunken gathering room with a

fireplace. A large pantry offers extra
storage space for kitchen items. The
covered rear porch is accessible from
the dining room, gathering room and
master bedroom. Luxury describes the
feeling in the master bath with its

whirlpool tub, separate shower, double vanity and closet space.

**California Engineered Plans and
California Stock Plans are available
for this home. Call 1-800-521-6797 for
more information.**

Width 92'-7"
Depth 79'

Design BB3433
Square Footage: 2,350

● Santa Fe styling creates interesting angles in this one-story home. A grand entrance leads through a courtyard into the foyer with circular skylight, closet space and niches, and convenient powder room. Turn right to the master suite with deluxe bath and a bedroom close at hand, perfect for a nursery, home office or exercise room. Two more family bedrooms are placed quietly in the far wing of the house. Fireplaces in the living room, dining room and covered porch create various shapes. Make note of the island range in the kitchen, extra storage in the garage, and covered porches on two sides.

Design BB3402

Square Footage: 3,212

L

● This one-story pairs the customary tile and stucco of Spanish design with a livable floor plan. The sunken living room with its open-hearth fireplace promises to be a cozy gathering place. For more casual occasions, there's a family room with fireplace off the entry foyer. Also noteworthy: a sizable kitchen and a sumptuous master suite.

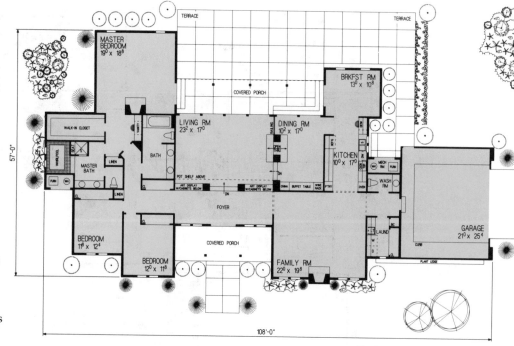

CUSTOMIZABLE

Custom Alterations? See page 221 for customizing this plan to your specifications.

QUOTE ONE™

Cost to build? See page 214 to order complete cost estimate to build this house in your area!

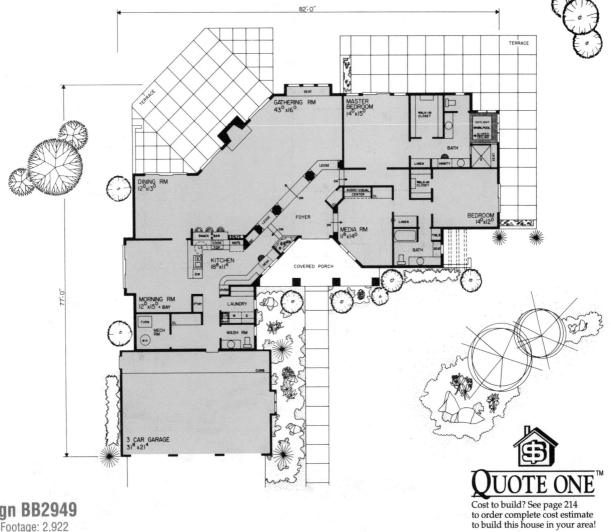

82'-0"

77'-0"

TERRACE

TERRACE

SEAT

GATHERING RM
43⁰x16⁰

MASTER
BEDROOM
14⁰x15⁰

WALK-IN
CLOSET

SKYLIGHT

WHIRLPOOL

BATH

DINING RM
12⁰x13⁰

LINEN

VANITY

WALK-IN
CLOSET

SEAT

LEDGE

DN

AUDIO/VISUAL
CENTER

CL

FOYER

DN

LINEN

BEDROOM
14⁰x12⁰

SNACK BAR

COOK TOP

REFG

DN

MEDIA RM
11⁸x14⁰

BATH

SEAT

KITCHEN
18⁸x11⁴

DW

COVERED PORCH

OVEN

MORNING RM
12⁰x15⁰ + BAY

P'TRY

LAUNDRY

FURN

CL

MECH
RM

WH

WASH RM

CURB

3 CAR GARAGE
31⁸x21⁴

Design BB2949
Square Footage: 2,922

● Spanish and western influences take center stage in a long, low stucco design. You'll enjoy the Texas-sized gathering room that opens to a formal dining area and has a snack bar to the kitchen. More casual dining is accommodated in the nook. A luxurious master suite is graced by plenty of closet space. Besides another bedroom and full bath, there is a media room that could easily double as a third bedroom or guest room.

California Engineered Plans and California Stock Plans are available for this home. Call 1-800-521-6797 for more information.

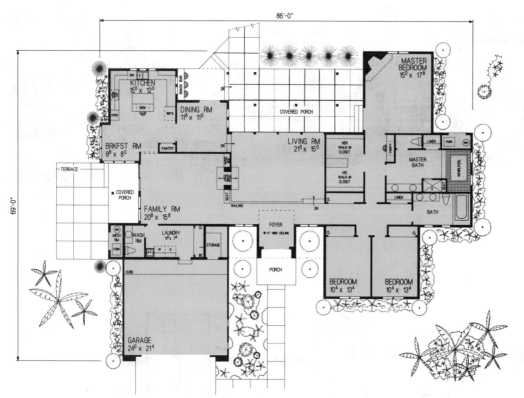

86'-0"

69'-0"

KITCHEN
15⁰ x 12⁰

DINING RM
11⁶ x 11⁰

BRKFST RM
8⁸ x 8⁰

PANTRY

TERRACE

COVERED PORCH

MASTER
BEDROOM
15⁰ x 17⁸

LIVING RM
21⁶ x 15⁰

HER WALK-IN CLOSET

HIS WALK-IN CLOSET

MASTER BATH

WHIRLPOOL

LINEN

FURN

VANITY

LINEN

BATH

COVERED PORCH

FAMILY RM
20⁸ x 15⁸

RAILING

SEAT

FOYER
9'-4" HIGH CEILING

MECH RM

FURN

WASH RM

LAUNDRY
11⁶ x 7⁰

STORAGE

W D

CURB

PORCH

BEDROOM
10⁴ x 13⁴

BEDROOM
10⁴ x 13⁴

GARAGE
24⁰ x 21⁴

Design BB3401
Square Footage: 2,850

L

● This Southwestern design caters to families who enjoy outdoor living and entertaining. Doors open onto a shaded terrace from the master bedroom and living room, while a sliding glass door in the family room accesses a smaller terrace. Also notice the outdoor bar with pass-through window to the kitchen.

CUSTOMIZABLE

Custom Alterations? See page 22 for customizing this plan to your specifications.

QUOTE ONE

Cost to build? See page 214 to order complete cost estimate to build this house in your area!

CUSTOMIZABLE

Custom Alterations? See page 221 for customizing this plan to your specifications.

Design BB3400

Square Footage: 2,784

L

● Abundant terrace space favors an outdoor lifestyle in this charming one-story. Each room has access to a porch or terrace; think of the added entertainment possibilities! Interior highlights include corner fireplaces in the master suite and family room, a dining room with bay window, and a regal master bath. Note the dramatic two-story foyer.

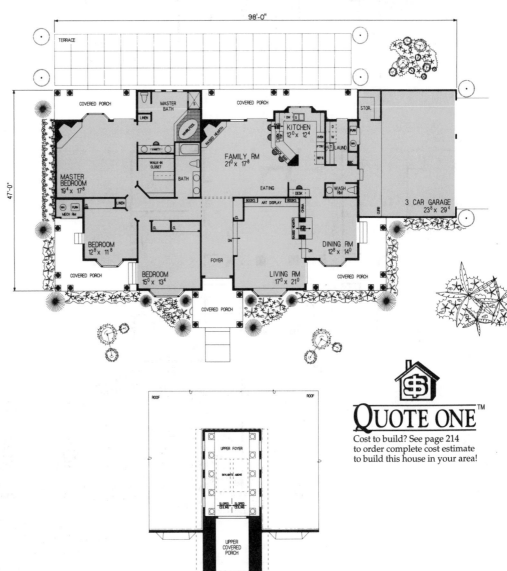

QUOTE ONE™

Cost to build? See page 214 to order complete cost estimate to build this house in your area!

Design BB2950
Square Footage: 2,559

● A natural desert dweller, this stucco, tile-roofed beauty is equally comfortable in any clime. Inside, there's a well-planned design. Common living areas—gathering room, formal dining room and breakfast room—are offset by a quiet study that could be used as a bedroom or guest room. A master suite features two walk-in closets, a double vanity and a whirlpool spa. The two-car garage has a service entrance. Close by is an adequate laundry area and a pantry. Notice the warming hearth in the gathering room and the snack bar area for casual dining.

California Engineered Plans and California Stock Plans are available for this home. Call 1-800-521-6797 for more information.

Cost to build? See page 214 to order complete cost estimate to build this house in your area!

Design BB2948

Square Footage: 1,830

● Styled for Southwest living, this home is a good choice in any region. All on one story, look for three bedrooms, one a master suite with a deluxe bath and one an optional study. The large gathering room/dining room combination contains a fireplace, sliding glass doors to the terrace and a snack bar served by the uniquely shaped kitchen. Notice the covered porch with open skylights and the extra storage space in the garage.

California Engineered Plans and California Stock Plans are available for this home. Call 1-800-521-6797 for more information.

TERRACE

WHIRLPOOL

MASTER BEDROOM
11¹⁰ x 17⁸

GATHERING RM.
15⁰ x 17⁸

DINING RM
12⁰ x 9⁸

SLOPED CEILING

BATH

SEAT

VANITY

DRESS RM

CL

LINEN

SHELVES

SNACK BAR

REF'G

PANTRY

GARAGE
21⁴ x 22⁴ + STOR

BC

CL

SHELVES

KIT.
14² x 12⁰

DESK

DN

BATH

LEDGE

CL

BOOKS CAB'T

FOYER

BRKFST RM
8⁸ x 10⁴

LAUNDRY

CL

BEDROOM
10⁶ x 11⁶

STUDY/ BEDROOM
11² x 11⁶

COVERED PORCH
OPEN SKYLIGHTS

STORAGE

43'-5"

75'-0"

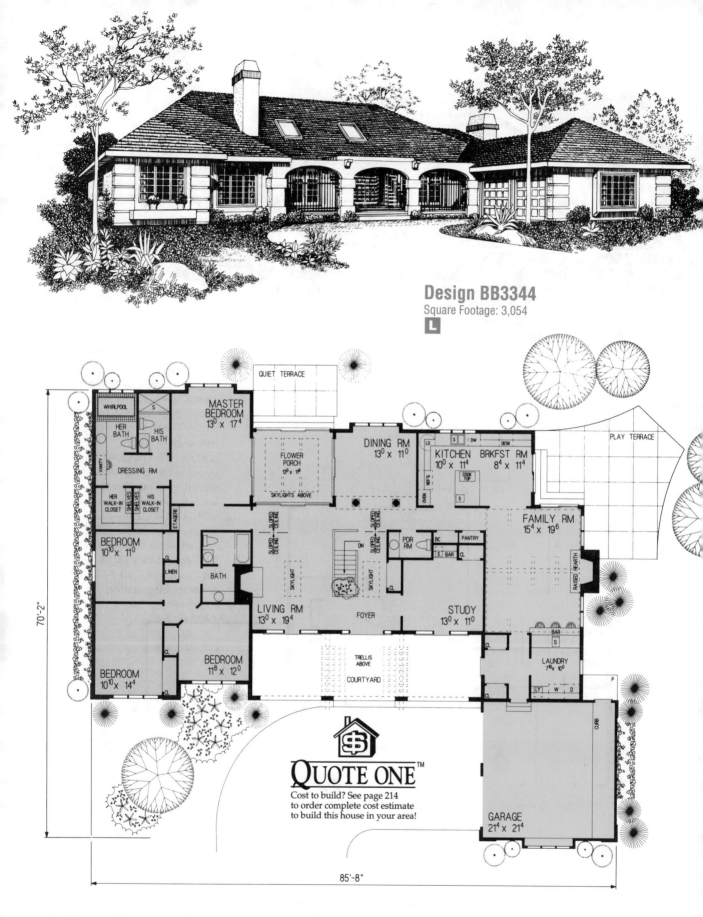

Design BB3344
Square Footage: 3,054

L

Quote One™

Cost to build? See page 214
to order complete cost estimate
to build this house in your area!

● This home features interior planning for today's active family. Living areas include a living room with fireplace, a cozy study and family room with wet bar. Convenient to the kitchen is the formal dining room with attractive bay window overlooking the back yard. The four-bedroom sleeping area contains a sumptuous master suite. Also notice the cheerful flower porch with access from the master suite, living room and dining room.

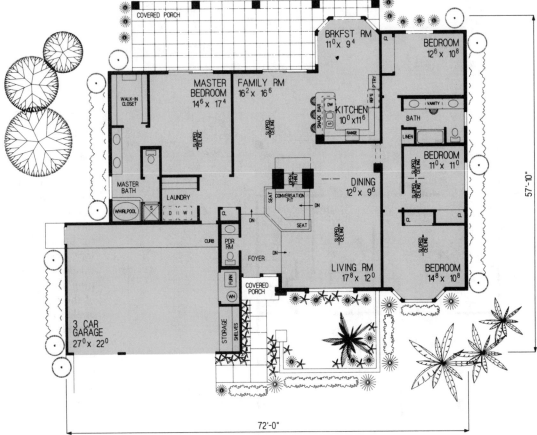

COVERED PORCH

BRKFST RM
11⁰ x 9⁴

BEDROOM
12⁶ x 10⁸

MASTER
BEDROOM
14⁶ x 17⁴

FAMILY RM
16² x 16⁶

WALK-IN
CLOSET

SLOPED
CEILING

SLOPED
CEILING

KITCHEN
10⁰ x 11⁶

SNACK BAR

DW

PTRY

REF'S

RANGE

VANITY

BATH

LINEN

BEDROOM
11⁰ x 11⁰

SLOPED
CEILING

MASTER
BATH

LAUNDRY

WHIRLPOOL

S

D   W

DINING
12⁰ x 9⁶

CONVERSATION
PIT

SEAT

DN

SEAT

SLOPED
CEILING

SLOPED
CEILING

CURB

CL

DN

FOYER

LIVING RM
17⁸ x 12⁰

BEDROOM
14⁸ x 10⁸

PDR
RM

FURN

COVERED
PORCH

DN

3 CAR
GARAGE
27⁰ x 22⁰

STORAGE

SHELVES

WH

57'-10"

72'-0"

Design BB3430
Square Footage: 2,394

L

● This dramatic design benefits from open planning. The centerpiece of the living area is a
sunken conversation pit which shares a through-
fireplace with the family room. The living room
and dining room share space beneath a sloped
ceiling. The open kitchen features a snack bar
and breakfast room and conveniently serves all
living areas. Split zoning in the sleeping area
places the private master suite to the left of the
plan and three more bedrooms, including one
with a bay window, to the right.

CUSTOMIZABLE
Custom Alterations? See page 221
for customizing this plan to your
specifications.

QUOTE ONE™
Cost to build? See page 214
to order complete cost estimate
to build this house in your area!

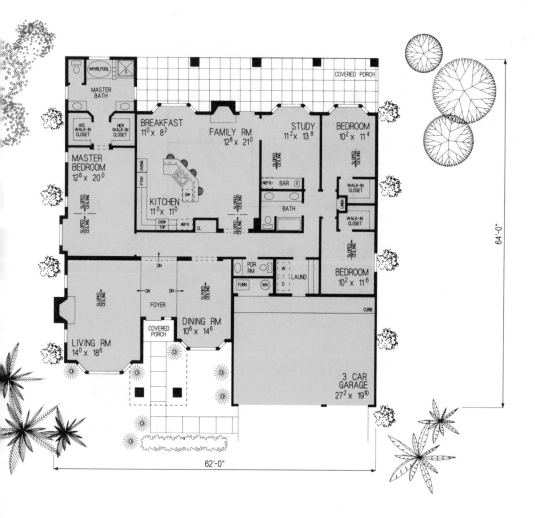

Design BB3413
Square Footage: 2,517

 L

● Though distinctly Southwest in design, this home
has some features that are
universally appealing. Note,
for instance, the central gallery, perpendicular to the
raised entry hall, and running almost the entire width
of the house. An L-shaped,
angled kitchen serves the
breakfast room and family
room in equal fashion.
Sleeping areas are found in
four bedrooms including an
optional study and exquisite
master suite.

Quote One™

Cost to build? See page 214
to order complete cost estimate
to build this house in your area!

Customizable

Custom Alterations? See page 221
for customizing this plan to your
specifications.

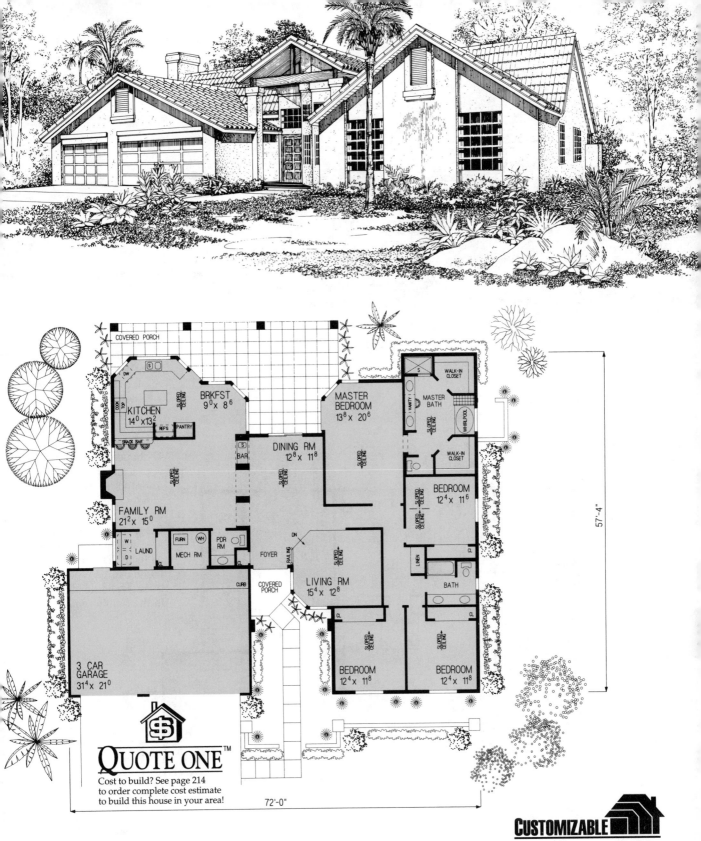

COVERED PORCH

KITCHEN
14⁰ x 13²

BRKFST
9⁰ x 8⁶

PANTRY

SNACK BAR

FAMILY RM
21² x 15⁰

LAUND

FURN WH

MECH RM

PDR RM

FOYER

BAR

DINING RM
12⁸ x 11⁸

MASTER BEDROOM
13⁸ x 20⁶

WALK-IN CLOSET

MASTER BATH

WHIRLPOOL

VANITY

WALK-IN CLOSET

BEDROOM
12⁴ x 11⁶

LINEN

BATH

CURB

COVERED PORCH

RAILING

DN

LIVING RM
15⁴ x 12⁸

3 CAR GARAGE
31⁴ x 21⁰

BEDROOM
12⁴ x 11⁸

BEDROOM
12⁴ x 11⁸

57'-4"

72'-0"

QUOTE ONE™
Cost to build? See page 214
to order complete cost estimate
to build this house in your area!

CUSTOMIZABLE
Custom Alterations? See page 221
for customizing this plan to your
specifications.

Design BB3423
Square Footage: 2,577

● This spacious Southwestern home
will be a pleasure to come home to.
Immediately off the foyer are the dining room and step-down living room
with bay window. The highlight of the
four-bedroom sleeping area is the
master suite with porch access and a
whirlpool for soaking away the day's
worries. The informal living area features an enormous family room with
fireplace and bay-windowed kitchen
and breakfast room. Notice the snack
bar pass-through to the family room.

Design BB3421
Square Footage: 2,145

L

● Split-bedroom planning makes the most of a one-story design. In this case the master suite is on the opposite side of the house from two family bedrooms. Gourmets can rejoice at the abundant work space in the U-shaped kitchen and will appreciate the natural light afforded by the large bay window in the breakfast room. A formal living room has a sunken conversation area with a cozy fireplace as its focus. The rear covered porch can be reached through sliding glass doors in the family room.

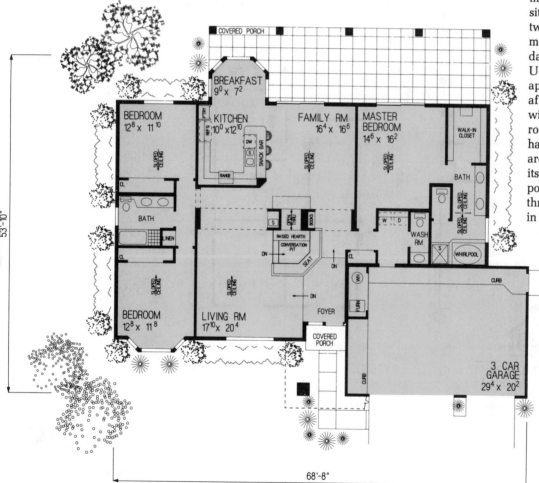

COVERED PORCH

BREAKFAST
9⁰ x 7²

BEDROOM
12⁸ x 11¹⁰
SLOPED CEILING

KITCHEN
10⁰ x 12¹⁰
PTRY
REFS
DW
S
SNACK BAR
RANGE

FAMILY RM
16⁴ x 16⁶
SLOPED CEILING

MASTER BEDROOM
14⁶ x 16²
SLOPED CEILING

WALK-IN CLOSET

BATH

CL.
BATH
LINEN
CL.

OPEN RAIL
BOOKS
RAISED HEARTH
CONVERSATION PIT
SEAT
DN

W D
WASH RM
S
WHIRLPOOL
SLOPED CEILING

BEDROOM
12⁸ x 11⁸
SLOPED CEILING

LIVING RM
17¹⁰ x 20⁴
SLOPED CEILING

DN
FOYER
CL.
WH
FURN

COVERED PORCH

CURB

3 CAR GARAGE
29⁴ x 20²

CURB

53'-10"

68'-8"

CUSTOMIZABLE
Custom Alterations? See page 221 for customizing this plan to your specifications.

QUOTE ONE™
Cost to build? See page 214 to order complete cost estimate to build this house in your area!

Design BB3415
Square Footage: 2,406

L

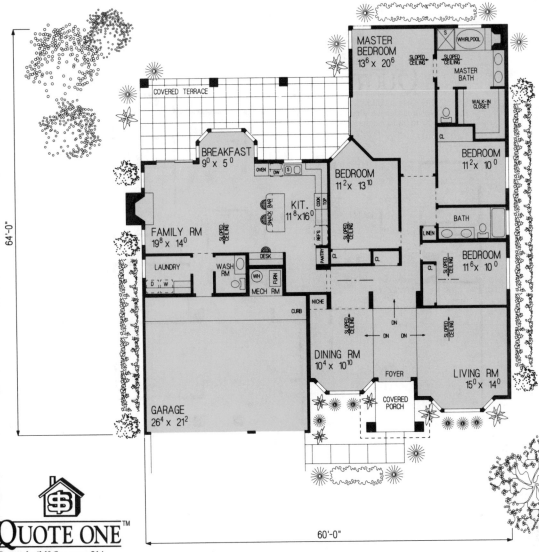

COVERED TERRACE

MASTER BEDROOM
13⁶ x 20⁶

SLOPED CEILING

S — WHIRLPOOL
SLOPED CEILING
MASTER BATH

WALK-IN CLOSET

CL

BREAKFAST
9⁰ x 5⁰

OVEN   DW   S

BEDROOM
11² x 13¹⁰

SLOPED CEILING

BEDROOM
11² x 10⁰

BATH

LINEN

KIT.
11⁸ x 16⁰

SNACK BAR

COOK TOP

REF.

FAMILY RM
19⁸ x 14⁰

SLOPED CEILING

DESK

PANTRY   CL

CL

BEDROOM
11⁶ x 10⁰

SLOPED CEILING

LAUNDRY

WASH RM

WH   FURN

D   W   MECH RM

NICHE

SLOPED CEILING

DN
DN   DN

SLOPED CEILING

GARAGE
26⁴ x 21²

CURB

DINING RM
10⁴ x 10¹⁰

FOYER

COVERED PORCH

LIVING RM
15⁰ x 14⁰

64'-0"

60'-0"

● Relax and enjoy the open floor plan of this lovely one-story. Its family room with fireplace and space for eating are a suitable complement to the formal living and dining rooms to the front of the house. There are four bedrooms, or three if you choose to make one a den, and 2½ baths. Don't miss the large pantry and convenient laundry area.

CUSTOMIZABLE

Custom Alterations? See page 221 for customizing this plan to your specifications.

Design BB3411
Square Footage: 2,441

 L

● You'll love the entry to this Southwestern home — it creates a dramatic first impression and leads beautifully to the formal living and dining rooms. Beyond, look for an open family room and dining area in the same proximity as the kitchen. Sliding glass doors here open to a backyard patio. Take your choice of four bedrooms or five, depending on how you wish to use the optional room. The huge master suite is not to be missed.

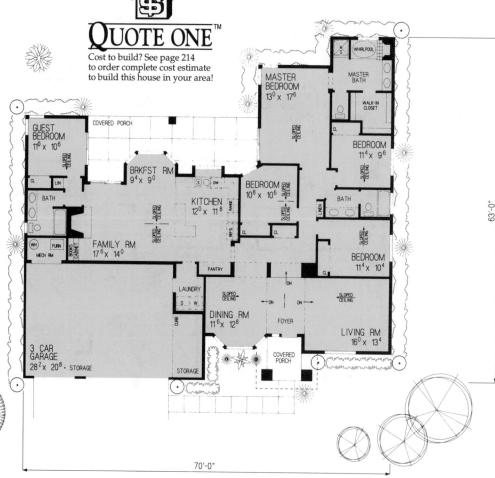

QUOTE ONE™
Cost to build? See page 214
to order complete cost estimate
to build this house in your area!

CUSTOMIZABLE

Custom Alterations? See page 221
for customizing this plan to your
specifications.

QUOTE ONE™

Cost to build? See page 214
to order complete cost estimate
to build this house in your area!

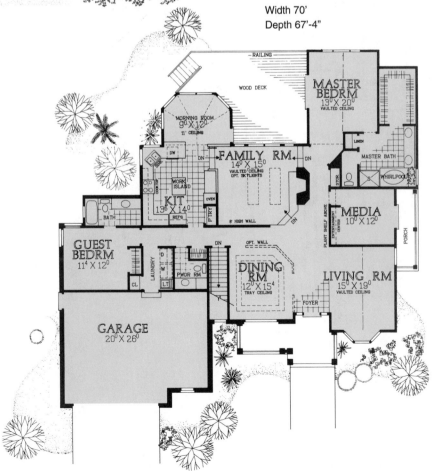

Width 70'
Depth 67'-4"

Design BB3602
Square Footage: 2,195

L

● This lovely one-story home fits
right into sunny regions—or any
area of the country for that matter.
Its stucco exterior and easily
accessed outdoor living areas make
it an all-time favorite. Inside, the
floor plan accommodates empty-
nester lifestyles. There is plenty of
room for both formal and informal
entertaining: living room, dining
room, family room and morning
room. A quiet study or media room
provides a getaway for more inti-
mate occasions. Sleeping areas are
split with the master bedroom and
bath on one side and a secondary
bedroom and bath on the other. A
third bedroom can be built if the
extra room is needed. Other special
features include a warming hearth
in the family room, a private porch
off the study and a grand rear deck.

Design BB3422
Square Footage: 1,932

L

● An enclosed entry garden greets visitors to this charming Southwestern home. Inside, the foyer is flanked by formal and informal living areas — a living room and dining room to the right and a cozy study to the left. To the rear, a large family room, breakfast room and open kitchen have access to a covered porch and overlook the back yard. Notice the fireplace and bay window. The three-bedroom sleeping area includes a master with a spacious bath with whirlpool.

CUSTOMIZABLE

Custom Alterations? See page 221 for customizing this plan to your specifications.

QUOTE ONE™

Cost to build? See page 214 to order complete cost estimate to build this house in your area!

Width 50'
Depth 68'

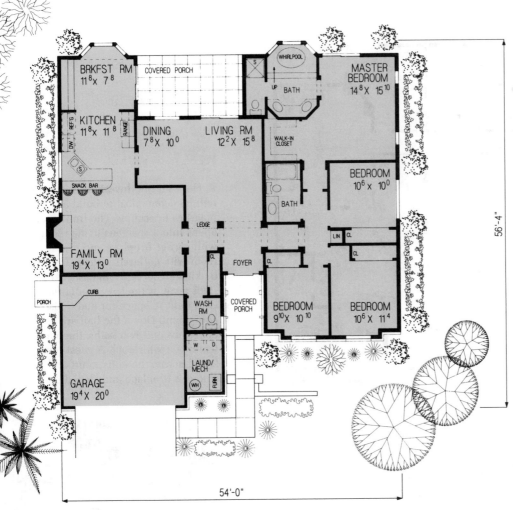

Design BB3419
Square Footage: 1,965

L

● This attractive, multi-gabled exterior houses a compact, livable interior. The entry foyer effectively routes traffic to all areas: left to the family room and kitchen, straight back to the dining room and living room, and right to the four-bedroom sleeping area. The spacious family room provides an informal gathering space while the living and dining rooms are perfect for formal occasions. The highlight of the sleeping area is the master bedroom with its whirlpool, walk-in closet and view of the back yard.

Quote One™

Cost to build? See page 214 to order complete cost estimate to build this house in your area!

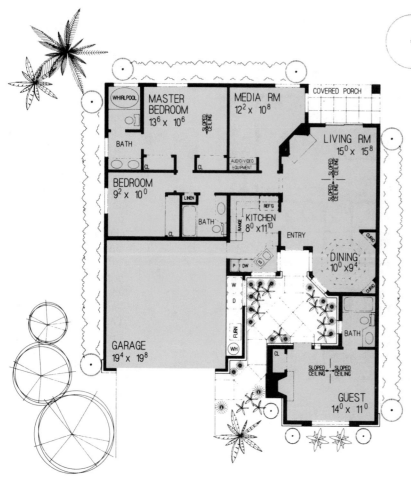

WHIRLPOOL

MASTER
BEDROOM
13⁶ x 10⁶

SLOPED
CEILING

MEDIA RM
12² x 10⁸

COVERED PORCH

BATH

CL

CL

AUDIO/VIDEO
EQUIPMENT

LIVING RM
15⁰ x 15⁸

SLOPED
CEILING

SLOPED
CEILING

BEDROOM
9² x 10⁰

LINEN

BATH

CL

REF'G

RANGE

KITCHEN
8⁰ x 11¹⁰

ENTRY

DINING
10⁰ x 9⁴

P DW

W

D

FURN

WH

BATH

CL

GARAGE
19⁴ x 19⁸

SLOPED
CEILING

SLOPED
CEILING

GUEST
14⁰ x 11⁰

Width 44'
Depth 52'-4"

Design BB3416
Square Footage: 1,375

L

● Here's a Southwestern design that
will be economical to build and a
pleasure to occupy. The front door
opens into a spacious living room
with corner fireplace and dining
room with coffered ceiling. The nearby kitchen serves both easily. A few
steps away is the cozy media room
with built-in space for audio-visual
equipment. Down the hall are two
bedrooms and two baths; the master
features a whirlpool. A guest room is
found across the entry court and includes a fireplace and sloped ceiling.

CUSTOMIZABLE
Custom Alterations? See page 221
for customizing this plan to your
specifications.

QUOTE ON
Cost to build? See page 214
to order complete cost estima
to build this house in your a.

VACATION AND RETIREMENT HOMES

*L*eisure and recreation are a big part of the empty-nester lifestyle. And what better way to relax than in your own cozy getaway! In this section is a splendid group of homes for vacation living, whether it be mountain retreat or seaside cottage. Casual living is the order of the day in these homes. Large living areas, most with warming fireplaces and huge windows for views, make up the gathering areas of these homes. Dining rooms and kitchens usually overlook the gathering spots so that the cook misses none of the fun. Sleeping accommodations vary from elaborate master suites with accompanying secondary bedrooms, to simple two-bedroom/one-bath plans. Many have large upstairs lofts or bunk rooms where grandchildren can pile in together for an indoor camping adventure. All plans cater to outdoor lifestyles with decks and terraces (see Designs BB4061 and BB2488), covered terraces (see Design BB1499), and second-floor balconies (see Design BB2427).

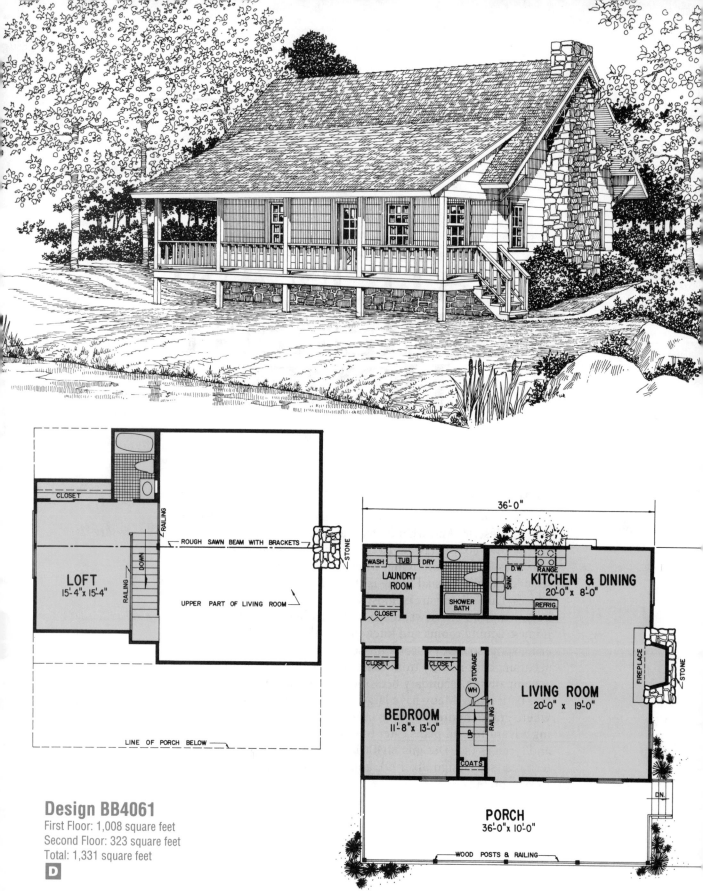

LOFT
15'-4" x 15'-4"

CLOSET

RAILING

DOWN

RAILING

ROUGH SAWN BEAM WITH BRACKETS

STONE

UPPER PART OF LIVING ROOM →

LINE OF PORCH BELOW

36'-0"

WASH | TUB | DRY

LAUNDRY ROOM

D.W. | RANGE

SINK

KITCHEN & DINING
20'-0" x 8'-0"

CLOSET

SHOWER BATH

REFRIG.

CLOSET | CLOSET

STORAGE

WH

RAILING

LIVING ROOM
20'-0" x 19'-0"

FIREPLACE

STONE

BEDROOM
11'-8" x 13'-0"

UP

COATS

DN.

PORCH
36'-0"x 10'-0"

WOOD POSTS & RAILING

Design BB4061

First Floor: 1,008 square feet
Second Floor: 323 square feet
Total: 1,331 square feet

D

● This charming farmhouse design will be economical to build and a pleasure to occupy. Like most vacation homes, this design features an open plan. The large living area includes a living room and dining room and a massive stone fireplace. A partition separates the kitchen from the living room. Also downstairs are a bedroom, full bath and laundry room. Upstairs is a spacious sleeping loft overlooking the living room.

California Engineered Plans and California Stock Plans are available for this home. Call 1-800-521-6797 for more information.

Design BB2488

First Floor: 1,113 square feet
Second Floor: 543 square feet
Total: 1,656 square feet

D

QUOTE ONE™

Cost to build? See page 214
to order complete cost estimate
to build this house in your area!

CUSTOMIZABLE

Custom Alterations? See page 221
for customizing this plan to your
specifications.

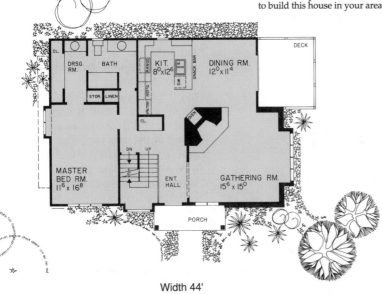

Width 44'
Depth 32'

● A cozy cottage for the young at heart! Whether called upon to serve the young active family as a leisure-time retreat at the lake, or the retired couple as a quiet haven in later years, this charming design will perform well. This year-round second home, has two sizable bedrooms upstairs,

and a full bath and lounge area looking down into the gathering room below. It will ideally accommodate the younger generation. When called upon to function as a retirement home, the second floor will cater to visiting family members and friends. Also, it will be available for use as a

home office, study, sewing room or music room.

California Engineered Plans and California Stock Plans are available for this home. Call 1-800-521-6797 for more information.

Floor Plan (Main Level)

44'-0"

DECK

GREAT ROOM
15'-0" X 27'-4"

SLOPED CLG.
GLASS SLI. DOORS
SLOPED CLG.

DN.

DOWN

OPEN RAIL

CLOSET

CLOSET

KITCHEN
15'-8" X 8'-2"

B/C

RANGE

PANTRY

CLOS

REF'G

D/W

CLOSET

BEDROOM
12'-4" X 13'-6"
SLOPED CLG.

BEDROOM
12'-4" X 13'-6"
SLOPED CLG.

DN.

28'-0"

Design BB4027

Square Footage: 1,232

● Good things come in small packages, too! The size and shape of this design will help hold down construction costs without sacrificing livability. The enormous great room is a multi-purpose living space with room for a dining area and several seating areas. Also notice the sloped ceilings. Sliding glass doors provide access to the wraparound deck and sweeping views of the outdoors. The well-equipped kitchen includes a pass-through and pantry. Two bedrooms, each with sloped ceilings, and compartmented bath round out the plan.

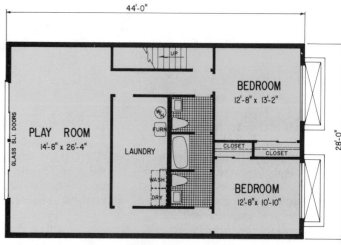

44'-0"

PLAY ROOM
14'-8" x 26'-4"

GLASS SLI. DOORS

UP

W.H.

FURN

LAUNDRY

WASH

DRY

CLOSET

CLOSET

BEDROOM
12'-8" x 13'-2"

BEDROOM
12'-8" x 10'-10"

28'-0"

Optional Basement

Design BB2485

Main Level: 1,108 square feet
Lower Level: 983 square feet
Total: 2,091 square feet

● This hillside vacation home gives the appearance of being a one-story from the road. However, since it is built off the edge of a slope, the rear exterior is a full two-story structure. Notice the projecting deck and how it shelters the terrace. Each of the generous glass areas is protected from the summer sun by the overhangs and the extended walls. The clerestory windows of the front exterior provide natural light to the center of the plan.

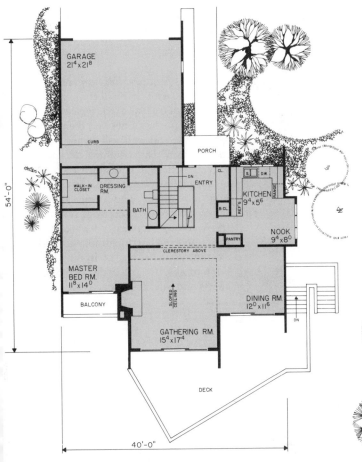

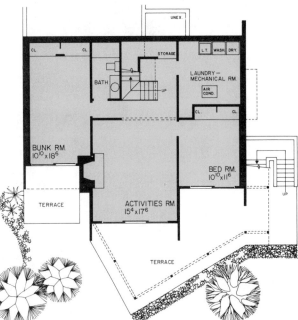

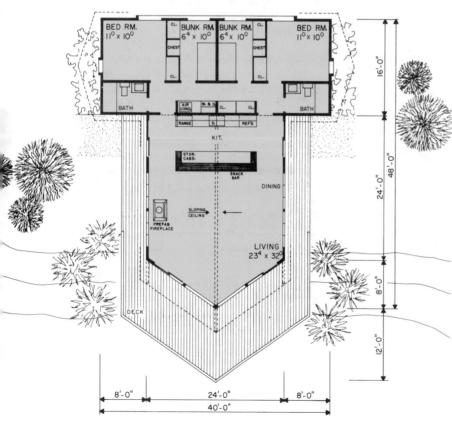

Design BB2439
Square Footage: 1,312

● Here is a wonderfully organized plan with an exterior that will command the attention of each and every passerby. Certainly the roof lines and the pointed glass gable-end wall will be noticed immediately. The delightful deck will be quickly noticed, too. Inside a visitor will be thrilled by the spaciousness of the huge living room. The ceilings slope upward to the exposed ridge beam. A free-standing fireplace will make its contribution to a cheerful atmosphere. The sleeping zone has two bedrooms, two bunk rooms, two full baths, two built-in chests and fine closet space.

Design BB4293
Square Footage: 1,873

D

● This spacious layout
has a big, big advan-
tage–a country kitchen
with all the trimmings:
300 square feet, a large
island counter and
breakfast bar, plenty of
space for more formal
dining, and a laundry
room close at hand.
The great room is also
a center of attention,
showing off clerestory
windows and a large
fireplace. What's more,
the entrance is grand
indeed, with a raised
bridge leading into a
large foyer. The master
bedroom is long on liv-
ing and storage space,
and the rear deck ties
everything together,
connecting with the
kitchen, great room,
and master bedroom.

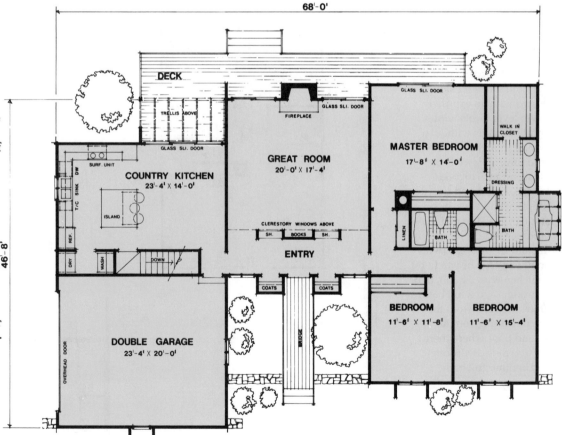

Design BB1475

First Floor: 1,120 square feet
Second Floor: 522 square feet
Lower Level: 616 square feet
Total: 2,258 square feet

● Built to accommodate the slopes, this hillside design with an exposed lower level meets winter vacation needs without a second thought. The covered lower terrace is the ideal entrance to a ski lounge with raised-hearth fireplace and walk-in ski storage area. The main floor holds sloped-ceilinged dining and living areas (with another raised hearth here), a kitchen with a patio, two bedrooms and a full bath. Enjoy the view from the balcony lounge on the second floor where there are two more bedrooms and another full bath.

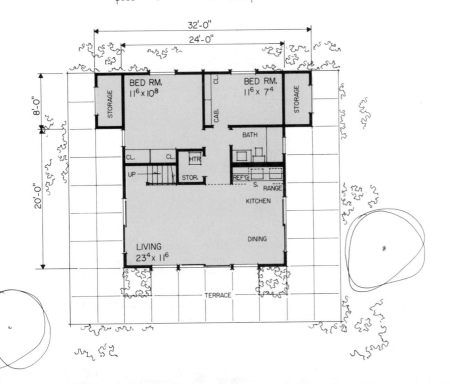

DORMITORY
15⁸ x 15⁸

STOR.

STORAGE

CL.

CL.

DN.

UPPER LIVING

SLOPED CEILING →

← SLOPED CEILING

32'-0"

24'-0"

8'-0"

20'-0"

STORAGE

BED RM.
11⁶ x 10⁸

CL.

CAB.

BED RM.
11⁶ x 7⁴

STORAGE

BATH

CL.

CL.

HTR

UP

STOR.

REF'G

S.

RANGE

KITCHEN

DINING

LIVING
23⁴ x 11⁶

TERRACE

Design BB1424

First Floor: 672 square feet
Second Floor: 256 square feet
Total: 928 square feet

● This chalet-type vacation home with its steep, overhanging roof, will catch the eye of even the most casual onlooker. It is designed to be completely livable whether the season be for swimming or skiing. The dormitory on the upper level will sleep many vacationers, while the two bedrooms of the first floor provide the more convenient and conventional sleeping facilities. The upper level overlooks the living and dining area with its beamed ceiling. The lower level provides everything that one would want for vacation living.

Design BB1499

Main Level: 896 square feet; Upper Level: 298 square feet
Lower Level: 896 square feet; Total: 2,090 square feet

● Three level living results in family living patterns which will foster a delightful feeling of informality. Upon arrival at this charming second home, each family member will enthusiastically welcome the change in environment – both indoors and out. Whether looking down into the living room from the dormitory balcony, or walking through the sliding doors onto the huge deck, or participating in some family activity in the game room, everyone will count the hours spent here as relaxing ones. Study the plan carefully. Note the sleeping facilities on each of the three levels. Two bedrooms and a dormitory in all to sleep the family and friends comfortably. There are two full baths, a separate laundry room and plenty of storage. Don't miss the efficient U-shaped kitchen.

Design BB2431

First Floor: 1,057 square feet
Second Floor: 406 square feet
Total: 1,463 square feet

● Dramatic use of glass and sweeping lines characterize a classic favorite—the A-frame. The sloped ceiling and exposed beams in the living room are gorgeous touches complemented by a wide deck for enjoying fresh air. The convenience of the central bath with attached powder room is accentuated by space here for a washer and dryer. The truly outstanding feature of this plan, however, is its magnificent master suite. There's a private balcony outside and a balcony lounge inside—the scenery is splendid from every angle.

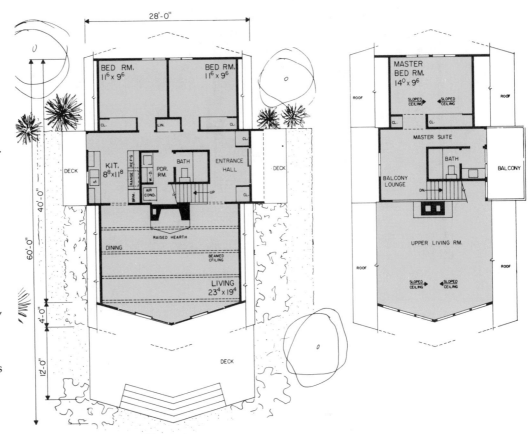

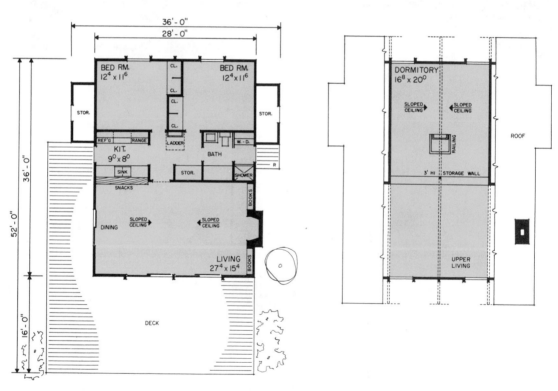

BED RM.
12⁴ x 11⁶

BED RM.
12⁴ x 11⁶

CL.

CL.

CL.

CL.

STOR.

STOR.

REF'G

RANGE

LADDER

W. - D.

KIT.
9⁰ x 8⁰

BATH

SINK

SNACKS

STOR.

SHOWER

R

DINING

SLOPED
CEILING

SLOPED
CEILING

BOOKS

LIVING
27⁴ x 15⁴

BOOKS

DECK

36' - 0"

28' - 0"

36' - 0"

52' - 0"

16' - 0"

DORMITORY
16⁸ x 20⁰

SLOPED
CEILING

SLOPED
CEILING

RAILING

ROOF

3' HI STORAGE WALL

UPPER
LIVING

Design BB1472

First Floor: 1,008 square feet; Second Floor: 546 square feet; Total: 1,554 square feet

● Wherever perched, this smart leisure-time home will surely make your visits memorable ones. The large living area with its sloped ceiling, dramatic expanses of glass and attractive fireplace will certainly offer the proper atmosphere for quiet relaxation. Keeping house will be no chore for the weekend homemaker. The kitchen is compact and efficient. There is plenty of storage space for all the necessary recreational equipment. There is a full bath and even a stall shower accessible from the outside for use by the swimmers. A ladder leads to the second floor sloped ceiling dormitory which overlooks the living/dining area. Ideal for the younger generation.

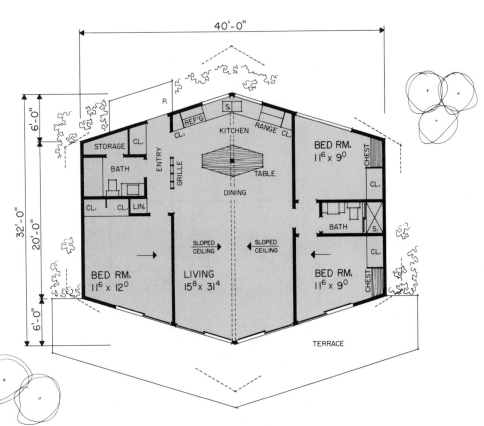

40'-0"

6'-0"

32'-0"

20'-0"

6'-0"

STORAGE

CL.

P.

REF'G

KITCHEN

RANGE

CL.

S.

BED RM.
11⁶ x 9⁰

CHEST

BATH

ENTRY

GRILLE

TABLE

DINING

CL.

CL.

CL.

LIN.

CL.

BATH

S.

CHEST

BED RM.
11⁶ x 12⁰

SLOPED CEILING

SLOPED CEILING

LIVING
15⁸ x 31⁴

BED RM.
11⁶ x 9⁰

CHEST

TERRACE

Design BB1438
Square Footage: 1,040

● Vacations begin with this
unique house. The angled terrace is
echoed throughout the floor plan—
with this orientation, no view is
missed. The living room features a
sloped ceiling and large dimensions. In the kitchen, a built-in table
accommodates a feast. Three bedrooms sleep all. Two of these
include built-in chests and well-
balanced proportions. Another
bedroom located on the other side
of the house will make a nice master retreat. Two full baths and storage space round out the amenities.

Design BB1482

First Floor: 1,008 square feet
Second Floor: 637 square feet
Total: 1,645 square feet

● Five bedrooms and a 27-foot living area! This darling chalet will take on the whole gang. A fireplace provides a warm glow and a snack bar in the kitchen means carefree dining. This plan also offers two full baths (one with access from outside and with a laundry area) and a second-floor master bedroom with a balcony overlooking the wood deck below.

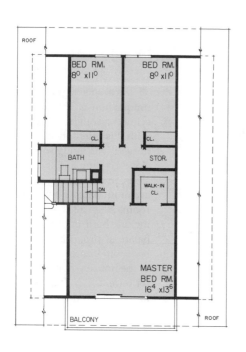

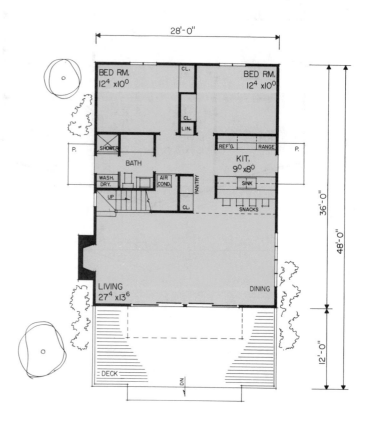

Design BB2427

First Floor: 784 square feet
Second Floor: 504 square feet
Total: 1,288 square feet

● Make your vacation dreams a reality with this fabulous chalet. A wood deck stretches the width of the house and finds the living room nearby. The kitchen utilizes a dining area and an efficient layout. A first-floor bedroom enjoys the use of a full hall bath. Upstairs, focus your attention on the master bedroom with its wall of closets and balcony. A dormitory sits across the hall from the master bedroom and leaves room for all the kids. Storage space abounds in this design—perfect for all of your seasonal storage needs.

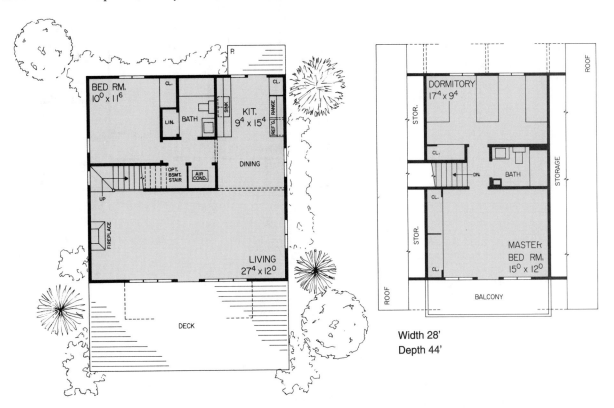

Width 28'
Depth 44'

Design BB1440
Square Footage: 1,248

● Take time off and escape to this accommodating house. Livability centers around a large living room with a fireplace in its center. A kitchen stretches along one wall, thus economizing space. With two decks to enjoy—be sure to orient one with maximum sun exposure in mind—a range of activities is possible. This plan incorporates four bedrooms cleverly designed with two on either side of the house. Identical dimensions create pleasing symmetry.

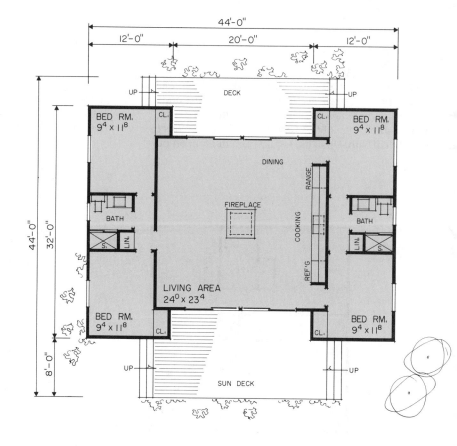

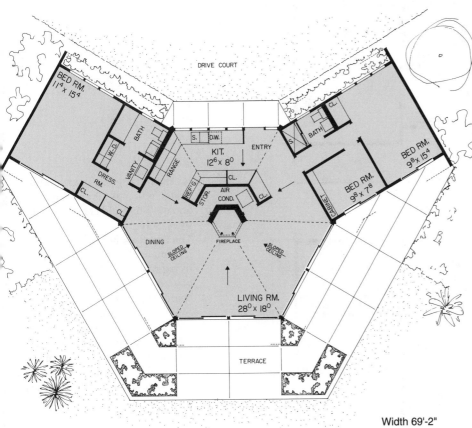

DRIVE COURT

BED RM.
11⁴ x 15⁴

BATH

W.D.

VANITY

DRESS. RM.

RANGE

CL.

CL.

CL.

S.

D.W.

KIT.
12⁶ x 8⁰

ENTRY

S.

BATH

CL.

REF'G

STOR.

CL.

AIR COND.

CABINET

BED RM.
9⁸ x 7⁸

BED RM.
9⁸ x 15⁴

DINING

SLOPED CEILING

FIREPLACE

SLOPED CEILING

LIVING RM.
28⁰ x 18⁰

TERRACE

Width 69'-2"
Depth 39'-11"

Design BB1404
Square Footage: 1,336

● Here is an exciting design, unusual in character, yet fun to live in. This design, with its frame exterior and large glass areas, has as its dramatic focal point a hexagonal living area which gives way to interesting angles. The spacious living area features sliding glass doors through which traffic may pass to the terrace stretching across the entire length of the house. The wide overhanging roofs project over the terraces, thus providing partial protection from the weather. The sloping ceilings converge above the unique, open fireplace. The sleeping areas are located in each wing from the hexagonal center.

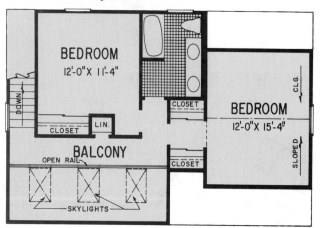

BEDROOM
12'-0" X 11'-4"

DOWN

CLOSET

CLOSET

LIN.

BALCONY
OPEN RAIL

CLOSET

BEDROOM
12'-0" X 15'-4"

CLG.

SLOPED

SKYLIGHTS

Design BB4153

First Floor: 893 square feet
Second Floor: 549 square feet
Total: 1,442 square feet

L **D**

● The rectangular shape of this
design will make it an economical
and easy-to-build choice for those
wary of high construction costs.
The first floor benefits from the
informality of open planning; the
living room and dining room com-
bine to make one large living
space. The partitioned kitchen is
conveniently adjacent yet keeps the
cooking process out of the living
area. Also downstairs is the master
bedroom and bath. The second
floor houses two large bedrooms, a
full bath and a balcony over the living room. Notice the skylights.

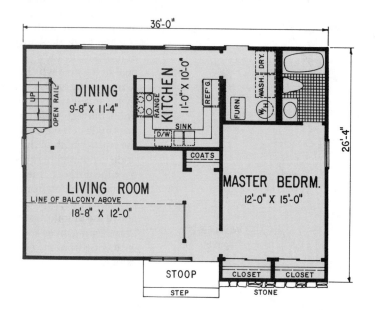

36'-0"

UP

OPEN RAIL

DINING
9'-8" X 11'-4"

KITCHEN
11'-0" X 10'-0"

RANGE

REF'G

SINK

D/W

FURN.

WASH. DRY.

W H

COATS

26'-4"

LIVING ROOM
LINE OF BALCONY ABOVE
18'-8" X 12'-0"

MASTER BEDRM.
12'-0" X 15'-0"

STOOP

STEP

CLOSET

CLOSET

STONE

Design BB2464

First Floor: 960 square feet
Second Floor: 448 square feet
Total: 1,408 square feet

● This economical-to-build leisure home boasts a wealth of features to satisfy the most discerning tastes. The list begins with a wood deck just outside the sliding glass doors of the 31' living area. The list continues with the U-shaped kitchen, the snack bar, the pantry and closet storage wall, the two full baths (one with stall shower), three bedrooms and the raised-hearth fireplace. Perhaps the favorite highlight will be the manner in which the second floor overlooks the first floor. The second-floor balcony adds an even greater dimension of spaciousness and interior appeal.

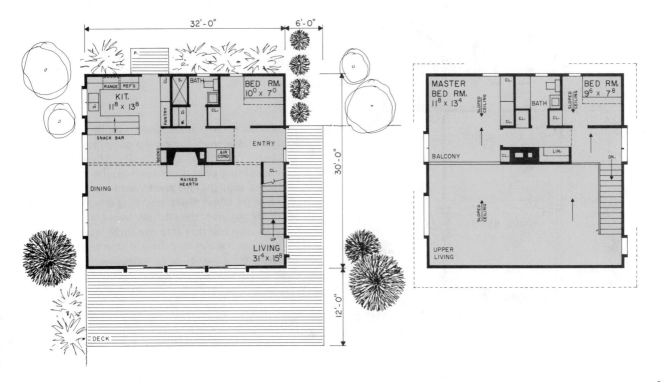

Design BB4114

Main Level: 852 square feet
Upper Level: 146 square feet
Total: 998 square feet

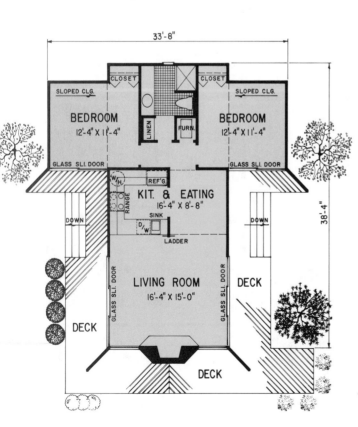

● This home was designed with the outdoors in mind. A large, wraparound deck provides ample space for sunning and relaxing. Huge windows and sliding glass doors open up the interior with lots of sunlight and great views — a must in a vacation home. Open planning makes for relaxed living patterns; the kitchen, living, and eating area flow together into one large working and living space. An upstairs loft provides added space for a lounge or an extra sleeping area.

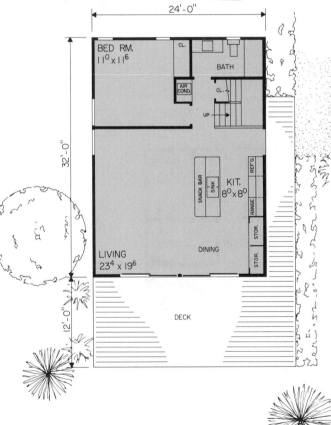

24'-0"

BED RM.
11⁰ x 11⁶

CL.

BATH

AIR COND.

CL.

UP

32'-0"

SNACK BAR

SINK

KIT.
8⁰ x 8⁰

REF'G.

RANGE

STOR.

STOR.

LIVING
23⁴ x 19⁶

DINING

12'-0"

DECK

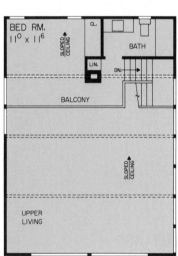

BED RM.
11⁰ x 11⁶

CL.

SLOPED CEILING

BATH

LIN.

DN.

BALCONY

SLOPED CEILING

UPPER LIVING

Design BB1496

First Floor: 768 square feet
Second Floor: 288 square feet
Total: 1,056 square feet

● Make your mountain getaway—or any getaway at all—a reality with this delightfully planned vacation home. A wooden walkway opens to a deck just outside the living and dining areas of this home—entry is also gained via a side door to the kitchen area. Dual storage closets off the kitchen will hold all of your necessities as well as your recreational items. The kitchen utilizes an island work space that doubles as a snack bar. Two bedrooms and full bathrooms grace this fine home. One of the bedrooms, on the second floor, enjoys a balcony overlook to the living room below.

Design BB1486
Square Footage: 480

● For that prime piece of property, this little house will delight all vacationers. Two sets of sliding glass doors open to the living and dining area. A kitchen with a double sink, closet and porch door is just a step away. Two bedrooms share the same dimensions while utilizing a full hall bath. Whether you decide to build this house on your own or with the aid of professional help, you will not have long to wait for its completion.

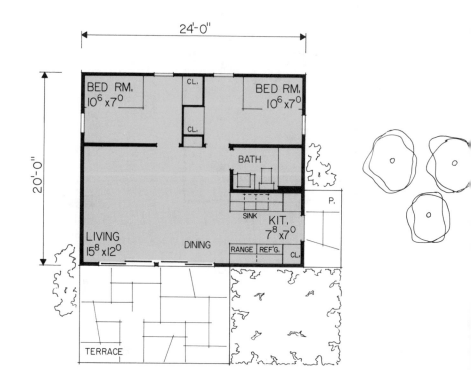

Width 34'-8"
Depth 48'

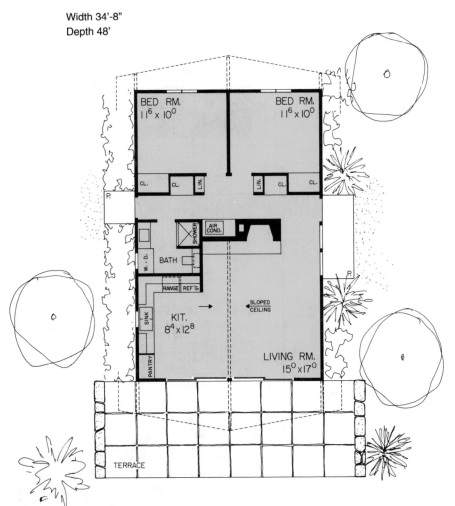

Design BB2423
Square Footage: 864

● A true vacationer's delight, this two-bedroom home extends the finest modern livability. Two sets of sliding glass doors open off the kitchen and living room where a sloped ceiling lends added dimension. In the kitchen, full counter space and cabinetry assure ease in meal preparation. A pantry stores all of your canned and boxed goods. In the living room, a fireplace serves as a nice design as well as a practical feature. The rear of the plan is comprised of two bedrooms of identical size. A nearby full bath holds a washer/dryer unit. Two additional closets, as well as two linen closets, add to storage capabilities.

When You're Ready To Order . . .

Let Us Show You Our Home Blueprint Package.

Building a home? Planning a home? Our Blueprint Package has nearly everything you need to get the job done right, whether you're working on your own or with help from an architect, designer, builder or subcontractors. Each Blueprint Package is the result of many hours of work by licensed architects or professional designers.

QUALITY

Hundreds of hours of painstaking effort have gone into the development of your blueprint set. Each home has been quality-checked by professionals to insure accuracy and buildability.

VALUE

Because we sell in volume, you can buy professional-quality blueprints at a fraction of their development cost. With our plans, your dream home design costs only a few hundred dollars, not the thousands of dollars that custom architects charge.

SERVICE

Once you've chosen your favorite home plan, you'll receive fast, efficient service whether you choose to mail or fax your order to us or call us toll free at 1-800-521-6797.

SATISFACTION

Our years of service to satisfied home plan buyers provide us the experience and knowledge that guarantee your satisfaction with our product and performance.

ORDER TOLL FREE 1-800-521-6797

After you've looked over our Blueprint Package and Important Extras on the following pages, simply mail the order form on page 221 or call toll free on our Blueprint Hotline: 1-800-521-6797. We're ready and eager to serve you.

Each set of blueprints is an interrelated collection of detail sheets which includes components such as floor plans, interior and exterior elevations, dimensions, cross-sections, diagrams and notations. These sheets show exactly how your house is to be built.

Among the sheets included may be:

Frontal Sheet
This artist's sketch of the exterior of the house gives you an idea of how the house will look when built and landscaped. Large ink-line floor plans show all levels of the house and provide an overview of your new home's livability, as well as a handy reference for deciding on furniture placement.

Foundation Plan
This sheet shows the foundation layout includ-

Sample Package

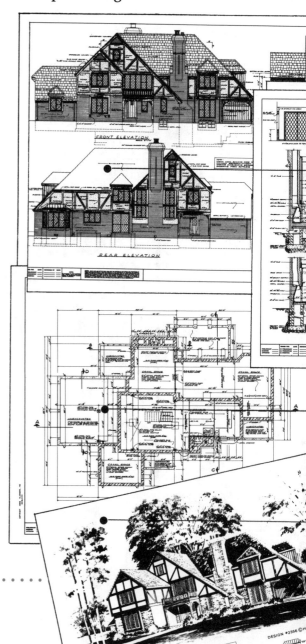

ing support walls, excavated and unexcavated areas, if any, and foundation notes. If slab construction rather the basement, the plan shows footings and details for a monolithic slab. This page, or another in the set, may include a sample plot plan for locating your house on a building site.

Detailed Floor Plans

These plans show the layout of each floor of the house. Rooms and interior spaces are carefully dimensioned and keys are given for cross-section details provided later in the plans. The positions of electrical outlets and switches are shown.

House Cross-Sections

Large-scale views show sections or cut-aways of the foundation, interior walls, exterior walls, floors, stairways and roof details. Additional cross-sections may show important changes in floor, ceiling or roof heights or the relationship of one level to another. Extremely valuable for construction, these sections show exactly how the various parts of the house fit together.

Interior Elevations

These large-scale drawings show the design and placement of kitchen and bathroom cabinets, laundry areas, fireplaces, bookcases and other built-ins. Little "extras," such as mantelpiece and wainscoting drawings, plus moulding sections, provide details that give your home that custom touch.

Exterior Elevations

These drawings show the front, rear and sides of your house and give necessary notes on exterior materials and finishes. Particular attention is given to cornice detail, brick and stone accents or other finish items that make your home unique.

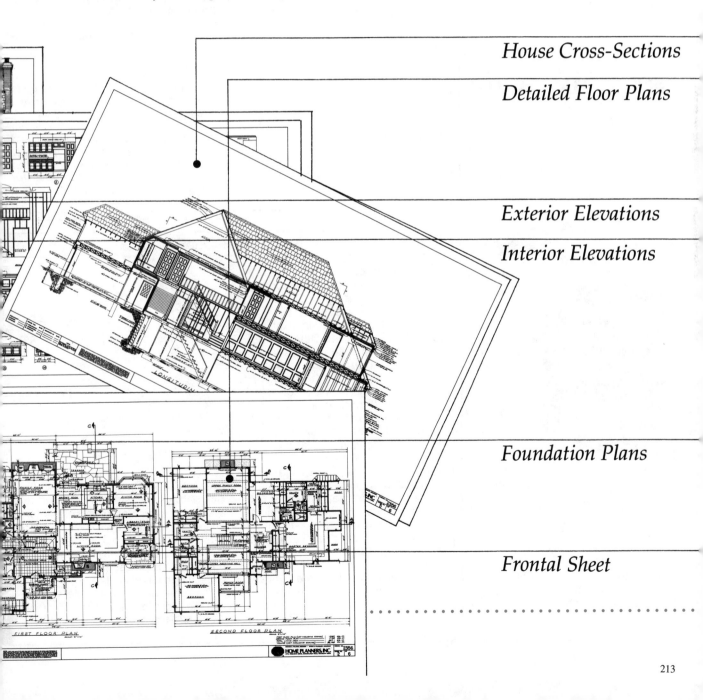

House Cross-Sections

Detailed Floor Plans

Exterior Elevations

Interior Elevations

Foundation Plans

Frontal Sheet

Important Extras To Do The Job Right!

Introducing eight important planning and construction aids developed by our professionals to help you succeed in your home-building project.

MATERIALS LIST & DETAILED COST ESTIMATE

The **Materials List** outlines the quantity, type and size of materials needed to build your house. Included are framing lumber, windows and doors, kitchen and bath cabinetry, rough and finish hardware, and much more. This handy list helps you or your builder cost out materials and serves as a reference sheet when you're compiling bids.

The **Quote One™ Detailed Cost Estimate** matches line for line over 1,000 items in the Materials List (which is included when you purchase this estimating tool). It allows you to determine building costs for your specific area and for your specific home design. Space is allowed for additional estimates from contractors and subcontractors. (See **Quote One™** below for further information.)

The Materials List/Detailed Cost Estimate package can be ordered up to 6 months after a blueprint order. Because of the diversity of local building codes, the Materials List does not include mechanical materials. Detailed Cost Estimates are available for select Home Planners plans only. Consult a customer service representative for currently available designs.

Make informed decisions about your home-building project with a customized materials take-off and a Quote One™ Detailed Cost Estimate. These tools are invaluable in planning and estimating the cost of your new home.

SPECIFICATION OUTLINE

This valuable 16-page document is critical to building your house correctly. Designed to be filled in by you or your builder, this book lists 166 stages or items crucial to the building process. It provides a comprehensive review of the construction process and helps in making choices of materials. When combined with the blueprints, a signed contract, and a schedule, it becomes a legal document and record for the building of your home.

QUOTE ONE™

This new service helps you estimate the cost of building select Home Planners designs. Quote One™ system is available in two separate stages: The Summary Cost Report and the Detailed Cost Estimate. The Summary Cost Report shows the total cost per square foot for your chosen home in your zip-code area and then breaks that cost down into ten categories showing the costs for building materials, labor and installation. The total cost for the report (including three grades: Budget, Standard and Custom) is just $25 for one home and additionals are only $15. These reports allow you to evaluate your building budget and compare the costs of building a variety of homes in your area.

The Detailed Cost Estimate furnishes an even more detailed report. The material and installation (labor + equipment) cost is shown for each of

over 1,000 line items provided in the Standard grade. Space is allowed for additional estimates from contractors and subcontractors. This invaluable tool is available for a price of $110 ($120 for a Schedule E plan) which includes the price of a materials list. Must be purchased with a Blueprints set.

To order these invaluable reports, use the order form on page 221 or call **1-800-521-6797**.

CONSTRUCTION INFORMATION

If you want to know more about techniques—and deal more confidently with subcontractors—we offer these useful sheets. Each set is an excellent tool that will add to your understanding of these technical subjects.

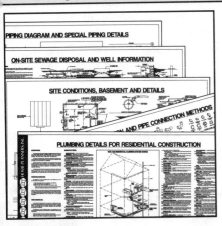

PLUMBING

The Blueprint Package includes locations for all the plumbing fixtures in your new house, including sinks, lavatories, tubs, showers, toilets, laundry trays and water heaters. However, if you want to know more about the complete plumbing system, these 24x36-inch detail sheets will prove very useful. Prepared to meet requirements of the National Plumbing Code, these six fact-filled sheets give general information on pipe schedules, fittings, sump-pump details, water-softener hookups, septic system details and much more. Color-coded sheets include a glossary of terms.

ELECTRICAL

The locations for every electrical switch, plug and outlet are shown in your Blueprint Package. However, these Electrical Details go further to take the mystery out of household electrical systems. Prepared to meet requirements of the National Electrical Code, these comprehensive 24x36-inch drawings come packed with helpful information, including wire sizing, switch-installation schematics, cable-routing details, appliance wattage, door-bell hookups, typical service panel circuitry and much more. Six sheets are bound together and color-coded for easy reference. A glossary of terms is also included.

CONSTRUCTION

The Blueprint Package contains everything an experienced builder needs to construct a particular house. However, it doesn't show all the ways that houses can be built, nor does it explain alternate construction methods. To help you understand how your house will be built—and offer additional techniques—this set of drawings depicts the materials and methods used to build foundations, fireplaces, walls, floors and roofs. Where appropriate, the drawings show acceptable alternatives. These six sheets will answer questions for the advanced do-it-yourselfer or home planner.

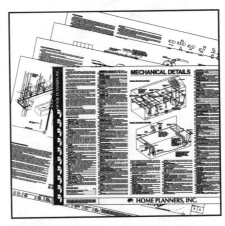

MECHANICAL

This package contains fundamental principles and useful data that will help you make informed decisions and communicate with subcontractors about heating and cooling systems. The 24x36-inch drawings contain instructions and samples that allow you to make simple load calculations and preliminary sizing and costing analysis. Covered are today's most commonly used systems from heat pumps to solar fuel systems. The package is packed full of illustrations and diagrams to help you visualize components and how they relate to one another.

Plan-A-Home®

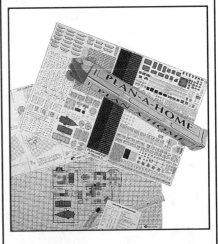

Plan-A-Home® is an easy-to-use tool that helps you design a new home, arrange furniture in a new or existing home, or plan a remodeling project. Each package contains:

- **More than *700 reusable peel-off planning symbols*** on a self-stick vinyl sheet, including walls, windows, doors, all types of furniture, kitchen components, bath fixtures and many more.

- **A reusable, transparent, *1/4-inch scale planning grid*** that matches the scale of actual working drawings (1/4-inch equals 1 foot). This grid provides the basis for house layouts of up to 140x92 feet.

- ***Tracing paper*** and a protective sheet for copying or transferring your completed plan.

- A ***felt-tip pen***, with water-soluble ink that wipes away quickly.

Plan-A-Home® lets you lay out areas as large as a 7,500 square foot, six-bedroom, seven-bath house.

To Order, Call Toll Free 1-800-521-6797

To add these important extras to your Blueprint Package, simply indicate your choices on the order form on page 221 or call us Toll Free 1-800-521-6797 and we'll tell you more about these exciting products.

The Deck Blueprint Package

Many of the homes in this book can be enhanced with a professionally designed Home Planners' Deck Plan. Those home plans highlighted with a **D** have a matching or corresponding deck plan available which includes a Deck Plan Frontal Sheet, Deck Framing and Floor Plans, Deck Elevations and a Deck Materials List. A Standard Deck Details Package, also available, provides all the how-to information necessary for building *any* deck. Our Complete Deck Building Package contains 1 set of Custom Deck Plans of your choice, plus 1 set of Standard Deck Building Details all for one low price. Our plans and details are carefully prepared in an easy-to-understand format that will guide you through every stage of your deck-building project. This page contains a sampling of 12 of the 25 different Deck layouts to match your favorite house. See page 218 for prices and ordering information.

SPLIT–LEVEL SUN DECK
Deck Plan D100

BI-LEVEL DECK WITH COVERED DINING
Deck Plan D101

WRAP–AROUND FAMILY DECK
Deck Plan D104

DECK FOR DINING AND VIEWS
Deck Plan D107

TREND–SETTER DECK
Deck Plan D110

TURN–OF–THE–CENTURY DECK
Deck Plan D111

WEEKEND ENTERTAINER DECK
Deck Plan D112

CENTER–VIEW DECK
Deck Plan D114

KITCHEN–EXTENDER DECK
Deck Plan D115

SPLIT–LEVEL ACTIVITY DECK
Deck Plan D117

TRI–LEVEL DECK WITH GRILL
Deck Plan D119

CONTEMPORARY LEISURE DECK
Deck Plan D120

L The Landscape Blueprint Package

For the homes marked with an L in this book, Home Planners has created a front-yard landscape plan that matches or is complementary in design to the house plan. These comprehensive blueprint packages include a Frontal Sheet, Plan View, Regionalized Plant & Materials List, a sheet on Planting and Maintaining Your Landscape, Zone Maps and Plant Size and Description Guide. These plans will help you achieve professional results, adding value and enjoyment to your property for years to come. Each set of blueprints is a full 18" x 24" in size with clear, complete instructions and easy-to-read type. Six of the forty front-yard Landscape Plans to match your favorite house are shown below.

Regional Order Map

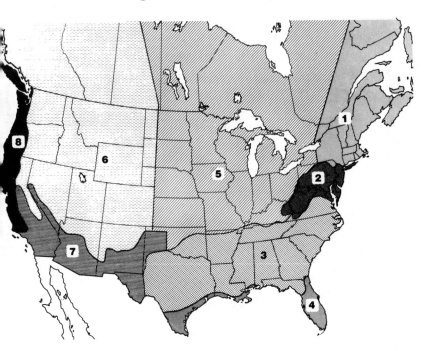

Most of the Landscape Plans shown on these pages are available with a Plant & Materials List adapted by horticultural experts to 8 different regions of the country. Please specify Geographic Region when ordering your plan. See page 218 for prices, ordering information and regional availability.

Region	1	Northeast
Region	2	Mid-Atlantic
Region	3	Deep South
Region	4	Florida & Gulf Coast
Region	5	Midwest
Region	6	Rocky Mountains
Region	7	Southern California & Desert Southwest
Region	8	Northern California & Pacific Northwest

CAPE COD COTTAGE
Landscape Plan L202

GAMBREL–ROOF COLONIAL
Landscape Plan L203

CENTER–HALL COLONIAL
Landscape Plan L204

CLASSIC NEW ENGLAND COLONIAL
Landscape Plan L205

COUNTRY–STYLE FARMHOUSE
Landscape Plan L207

TRADITIONAL SPLIT–LEVEL
Landscape Plan L228

Price Schedule & Plans Index

These pages contain all the information you need to price your blueprints. In general, the larger and more complicated the house, the more it costs to design and thus the higher the price we must charge for the blueprints. Remember, however, that these prices are far less than you would normally pay for the services of a licensed architect or professional designer.

Custom home designs and related architectural services often cost thousands of dollars, ranging from 5% to 15% of the cost of construction. By ordering our blueprints you are potentially saving enough money to afford a larger house, or to add those "extra" amenities such as a patio, deck, swimming pool or even an upgraded kitchen or luxurious master suite.

House Blueprint Price Schedule
(Prices guaranteed through December 31, 1996)

	1-set Study Package	4-set Building Package	8-set Building Package	1-set Reproducible Sepias
Schedule A	$280	$325	$385	$485
Schedule B	$320	$365	$425	$545
Schedule C	$360	$405	$465	$605
Schedule D	$400	$445	$505	$665
Schedule E	$520	$565	$625	$725

Additional Identical Blueprints in same order................$50 per set
Reverse Blueprints (mirror image)...................................$50 per set
Specification Outlines ....$10 each
Materials Lists:
     Schedule A-D $50
     Schedule E $60
Materials Lists are not available for California Engineering Service.

Deck Plans Price Schedule

CUSTOM DECK PLANS
Price Group	Q	R	S
1 Set Custom Plans	$25	$30	$35

Additional identical sets ....$10 each
Reverse sets (mirror image)...$10 each

STANDARD DECK DETAILS
1 Set Generic Construction Details............................$14.95 each

COMPLETE DECK BUILDING PACKAGE
Price Group	Q	R	S
1 Set Custom Plans, plus 1 Set Standard Deck Details	$35	$40	$45

Landscape Plans Price Schedule

Price Group	X	Y	Z
1 set	$35	$45	$55
3 sets	$50	$60	$70
6 sets	$65	$75	$85

Additional Identical Sets ....$10 each
Reverse Sets (mirror image)...$10 each

Index

To use the Index below, refer to the design number listed in numerical order (a helpful page reference is also given). Note the price index letter and refer to the House Blueprint Price Schedule above for the cost of one, four or eight sets of blueprints or the cost of a reproducible sepia. Additional prices are shown for identical and reverse blueprint sets, as well as a very useful Materials List for some of the plans. Also note in the Index below those plans that have matching or complementary Deck Plans or Landscape Plans. Refer to the schedules above for prices of these plans. Some of our plans can be customized through Home Planners' Home Customizer ® Service. These plans are indicated below with this symbol: 🏠. See page 221 for information. Some plans are also part of our Quote One™ estimating service and are indicated by this symbol: 🏠. See page 214 for more information.

To Order: Fill in and send the order form on page 221—or call toll free 1-800-521-6797 or 520-297-8200.

DESIGN	PRICE	PAGE	CALIFORNIA PLANS	CUSTOMIZABLE	QUOTE ONE™	DECK	DECK PRICE	LANDSCAPE	LANDSCAPE PRICE	REGIONS
BB1404	A	205								
BB1424	A	197								
BB1438	A	201								
BB1440	A	204								
BB1472	A	200								
BB1475	B	196								
BB1482	A	202								
BB1486	A	210								
BB1496	A	209								
BB1499	B	198								
BB1754	B	105								
BB2170	B	61						L221	X	1-3,5,6,8
BB2212	D	153						L217	Y	1-8
BB2423	A	211								
BB2427	A	203								
BB2431	A	199								
BB2439	A	194								
BB2464	A	207								
BB2485	B	193								
BB2488	A	191	✔	🏠	🏠	D102	Q			
BB2490	A	35		🏠	🏠					
BB2493	C	131								
BB2500	B	20				D100	Q	L204	Y	1-3,5,6,8
BB2505	A	70		🏠	🏠	D113	R	L226	X	1-8
BB2510	A	10				D105	R	L200	X	1-3,5,6,8
BB2528	B	83				D100	Q			
BB2563	B	11		🏠	🏠	D114	R	L201	Y	1-3,5,6,8
BB2565	B	56			🏠	D101	R	L225	X	1-3,5,6,8
BB2573	C	116	✔			D114	R	L220	Y	1-3,5,6,8
BB2581	C	32								
BB2594	C	109				D120	R			
BB2597	B	51			🏠	D114	R	L226	X	1-8
BB2606	A	65		🏠	🏠			L221	X	1-3,5,6,8
BB2607	A	64						L220	Y	1-3,5,6,8
BB2615	D	160			🏠	D106	S	L211	Y	1-8
BB2671	B	85			🏠	D114	R	L234	Y	1-8
BB2672	B	44			🏠	D112	R	L226	X	1-8
BB2699	C	156						L211	Y	1-8
BB2707	A	74		🏠	🏠	D117	S	L226	X	1-8
BB2708	C	29				D112	R			
BB2721	C	110								
BB2729	B	30						L234	Y	1-8
BB2753	B	82				D112	R			
BB2771	C	33								
BB2778	C	107				D120	R			
BB2781	C	144				D121	S	L230	Z	1-8

DESIGN	PRICE	PAGE	CALIFORNIA PLANS	CUSTOMIZABLE	QUOTE ONE™	DECK	DECK PRICE	LANDSCAPE	LANDSCAPE PRICE	REGIONS
BB2782	C	142				D101	R			
BB2784	C	108								
BB2789	C	106				D117	S	L228	Y	1-8
BB2791	D	141								
BB2795	B	81								
BB2802	B	60		✔	✔	D118	R	L220	Y	1-3,5,6,8
BB2805	B	75				D113	R	L220	Y	1-3,5,6,8
BB2806	B	76				D113	R	L220	Y	1-3,5,6,8
BB2807	B	77				D113	R	L220	Y	1-3,5,6,8
BB2809	B	89								
BB2818	B	84		✔	✔	D101	R	L234	Y	1-8
BB2822	A	126	✔					L229	Y	1-8
BB2827	C	125						L229	Y	1-8
BB2828	B	124								
BB2857	D	143						L239	Z	1-8
BB2858	C	101								
BB2864	A	88	✔	✔	✔	D100	Q	L225	X	1-3,5,6,8
BB2869	B	53								
BB2871	B	80				D117	S			
BB2873	C	100								
BB2877	C	117				D114	R	L220	Y	1-3,5,6,8
BB2878	B	50	✔	✔	✔	D112	R	L200	X	1-3,5,6,8
BB2880	C	120		✔	✔	D114	R	L212	Z	1-8
BB2884	B	27						L228	Y	1-8
BB2887	A	127								
BB2888	D	157						L211	Y	1-8
BB2892	B	26								
BB2902	B	86			✔			L234	Y	1-8
BB2905	B	28				D121	S	L229	Y	1-8
BB2913	B	87				D124	S			
BB2915	C	103	✔		✔	D114	R	L212	Z	1-8
BB2920	D	139	✔	✔	✔	D104	S	L212	Z	1-8
BB2921	D	159	✔	✔	✔	D104	S	L212	Z	1-8
BB2922	D	136	✔		✔					
BB2930	B	98		✔						
BB2931	B	54		✔						
BB2947	B	52	✔		✔	D112	R	L200	X	1-3,5,6,8
BB2948	B	177	✔	✔	✔					
BB2949	C	173	✔	✔	✔					
BB2950	C	176	✔	✔	✔					
BB2962	B	114		✔	✔					
BB2964	B	17								
BB2967	B	16						L217	Y	1-8
BB2995	D	158	✔		✔	D106	S	L217	Y	1-8
BB3302	A	14		✔	✔			L205	Y	1-3,5,6,8
BB3310	C	40			✔	D111	S	L227	Z	1-8
BB3311	D	138			✔	D109	S	L220	Y	1-3,5,6,8
BB3314	B	46	✔		✔			L200	X	1-3,5,6,8
BB3315	D	22			✔			L200	X	1-3,5,6,8
BB3319	C	96		✔	✔	D112	R	L217	Y	1-8
BB3321	C	23		✔	✔	D116	R	L209	Y	1-6,8
BB3323	C	129			✔			L223	Z	1-3,5,6,8
BB3330	A	24			✔					
BB3331	A	15	✔		✔			L203	Y	1-3,5,6,8
BB3332	B	119	✔		✔			L200	X	1-3,5,6,8
BB3334	C	155			✔			L207	Z	1-6,8
BB3340	B	113			✔			L200	X	1-3,5,6,8
BB3343	C	12			✔			L202	X	1-3,5,6,8
BB3344	D	178			✔			L211	Y	1-8
BB3345	B	68		✔	✔			L220	Y	1-3,5,6,8
BB3346	B	112		✔				L204	Y	1-3,5,6,8
BB3347	D	34			✔			L230	Z	1-8
BB3348	C	118	✔		✔			L200	X	1-3,5,6,8
BB3351	C	21			✔	D115	Q	L209	Y	1-6,8
BB3353	C	154			✔	D113	R	L206	Z	1-6,8
BB3355	A	66		✔	✔	D117	S	L220	Y	1-3,5,6,8
BB3357	D	111			✔	D115	Q	L211	Y	1-8
BB3360	D	149			✔			L207	Z	1-6,8
BB3366	D	151			✔			L220	Y	1-3,5,6,8
BB3368	C	102			✔	D104	S	L220	Y	1-3,5,6,8
BB3373	A	62	✔		✔	D110	R	L202	X	1-3,5,6,8
BB3374	A	62			✔	D110	R	L202	X	1-3,5,6,8
BB3375	A	63			✔	D110	R	L202	X	1-3,5,6,8
BB3376	B	73			✔	D114	R	L205	Y	1-3,5,6,8
BB3377	C	115			✔	D110	R	L203	Y	1-3,5,6,8
BB3378	E	152			✔	D115	Q	L211	Y	1-8
BB3396	C	134				D111	S	L207	Z	1-6,8
BB3397	D	147	✔			D110	R	L209	Y	1-6,8
BB3400	C	175		✔	✔			L236	Z	3,4,7
BB3401	C	174		✔	✔			L233	Y	3,4,7
BB3402	D	172		✔	✔			L236	Z	3,4,7
BB3403	C	42	✔		✔			L237	Y	7
BB3404	C	145			✔			L230	Z	1-8
BB3405	D	169	✔	✔	✔			L236	Z	3,4,7
BB3408	C	95			✔			L230	Z	1-8
BB3411	C	184		✔	✔			L233	Y	3,4,7
BB3413	C	180		✔	✔			L238	Y	3,4,7,8
BB3414	C	166		✔	✔			L233	Y	3,4,7
BB3415	C	183		✔	✔			L233	Y	3,4,7
BB3416	A	188		✔	✔			L239	Z	1-8
BB3418	A	165		✔	✔			L239	Z	1-8
BB3419	B	187		✔	✔			L239	Z	1-8
BB3420	B	164	✔	✔	✔			L233	Y	3,4,7
BB3421	B	182		✔	✔			L238	Y	3,4,7,8
BB3422	B	186		✔	✔			L239	Z	1-8
BB3423	C	181		✔	✔					
BB3426	C	163		✔	✔			L233	Y	3,4,7
BB3428	C	162		✔	✔			L238	Y	3,4,7,8,
BB3430	C	179		✔	✔			L233	Y	3,4,7
BB3431	B	170	✔	✔	✔					
BB3433	C	171		✔	✔			L213	Z	1-8
BB3435	D	167		✔	✔			L227	Z	1-8
BB3436	C	168		✔	✔			L227	Z	1-8
BB3438	C	5			✔			L209	Y	1-6,8
BB3440	C	94		✔	✔	D120	R	L233	Y	3,4,7
BB3441	C	41	✔	✔	✔			L239	Z	1-8
BB3442	A	67		✔	✔	D115	Q	L200	X	1-3,5,6,8
BB3450	C	128		✔	✔	D106	S	L229	Y	1-8
BB3453	A	90			✔			L238	Y	3,4,7,8
BB3454	B	91			✔	D110	R	L220	Y	1-3,5,6,8
BB3455	B	36			✔	D105	R	L238	Y	3,4,7,8,
BB3458	C	39			✔	D105	R	L222	Y	1-3,5,6,8
BB3460	A	48	✔	✔	✔			L200	X	1-3,5,6,8
BB3461	B	8			✔			L204	Y	1-3,5,6,8
BB3462	B	6			✔			L207	Z	1-6,8
BB3465	A	47			✔			L205	Y	1-3,5,6,8
BB3466	B	45		✔	✔	D110	R	L207	Z	1-6,8
BB3467	B	19		✔	✔			L203	Y	1-3,5,6,8
BB3468	B	4			✔			L209	Y	1-6,8
BB3475	D	137		✔	✔			L236	Z	3,4,7
BB3481	B	69		✔	✔			L200	X	1-3,5,6,8
BB3505	E	146			✔			L204	Y	1-3,5,6,8
BB3550	D	148			✔	D112	R	L220	Y	1-3,5,6,8
BB3557	D	140			✔	D105	R	L228	Y	1-8
BB3558	C	38			✔	D105	R	L203	Y	1-3,5,6,8
BB3559	C	97	✔	✔	✔	D111	S	L217	Y	1-8
BB3560	B	99	✔		✔			L234	Y	1-8
BB3566	C	9			✔	D111	S	L207	Z	1-6,8
BB3569	B	92			✔	D105	R	L238	Y	3,4,7,8
BB3573	D	130			✔	D111	S	L233	Y	3,4,7
BB3575	D	150			✔			L205	Y	1-3,5,6,8
BB3600	C	104		✔	✔			L200	X	1-3,5,6,8
BB3602	C	185		✔	✔			L220	Y	1-3,5,6,8
BB4027	A	192								
BB4061	A	190	✔			D115	Q			
BB4114	A	208								
BB4115	B	122								
BB4153	A	206				D115	Q	L202	X	1-3,5,6,8
BB4293	B	195				D120	R			
BB4308	C	123						L231	Z	1-8
BB4334	B	31						L231	Z	1-8
BB8888	C	79								
BB8889	A	58								
BB8890	B	59								
BB8891	C	13								
BB8892	B	7								
BB8893	B	78								
BB8894	A	25								
BB8895	A	72								
BB8896	B	37								
BB8897	B	18								
BB8898	C	132								
BB8899	C	133								

Before You Order . . .

Before filling out the coupon at right or calling us on our Toll-Free Blueprint Hotline, you may want to learn more about our services and products. Here's some information you will find helpful.

Quick Turnaround
We process and ship every blueprint order from our office within 48 hours. Because of this quick turnaround, we won't send a formal notice acknowledging receipt of your order.

Our Exchange Policy
Since blueprints are printed in response to your order, we cannot honor requests for refunds. However, we will exchange your entire first order for an equal number of blueprints at a price of $50 for the first set and $10 for each additional set; $70 total exchange fee for 4 sets: $100 total exchange fee for 8 sets. . . *plus* the difference in cost if exchanging for a design in a higher price bracket or *less* the difference in cost if exchanging for a design in a lower price bracket. One exchange is allowed within a year of purchase date. **(Sepias are not exchangeable. No exchanges can be made for the California Engineered Plans since they are tailored to your specific building site.)** All sets from the first order must be returned before the exchange can take place. Please add $10 for postage and handling via ground service; $20 via 2nd Day Air; $30 via Next Day Air.

About Reverse Blueprints
If you want to build in reverse of the plan as shown, we will include an extra set of reverse blueprints (mirror image) for an additional fee of $50. Lettering and dimensions will appear backward. Right-reading reverses of Home Customizer® plans are available. Call 1-800-521-6797, ext. 800 for more details.

Modifying or Customizing Our Plans
With such a great selection of homes, you are bound to find the one that suits you. However, if you need to make alterations to a design that is customizable, you need only order our Customizer® kit or call our Customization representative at 1-800-521-6797, ext. 800 to get you started. We strongly suggest you order sepias if you decide to revise non-Customizable plans significantly.

Architectural and Engineering Seals
Some cities and states are now requiring that a licensed architect or engineer review and "seal" your blueprints prior to building due to local or regional concerns over energy consumption, safety codes, seismic ratings or other factors. For this reason, it may be necessary to talk to a local professional to have your plans reviewed. In some cases, Home Planners can seal your plans through our Customization Service. Call 1-800-521-6797, ext. 800 for more details.

Compliance with Local Codes and Regulations
At the time of creation, our plans are drawn to specifications published by the Building Officials and Code Administrators (BOCA) International, Inc.; the Southern Building Code Congress (SBCCI) International, Inc.; the International Conference of Building Officials; or the Council of American Building Officials (CABO). Our plans are designed to meet or exceed national building standards. Some states, counties and municipalities have their own codes, zoning requirements and building regulations. Before building, contact your local building authorities to make sure you comply with local ordinances and codes, including obtaining any necessary permits or inspections as building progresses. In some cases, minor modifications to your plans by your builder, architect or designer may be required to meet local conditions and requirements. Home Planners may be able to make these changes to Home Customizer® plans providing you supply all pertinent information from your local building authorities.

Foundation and Exterior Wall Changes
Most of our plans are drawn with either a full or partial basement foundation. Depending on your specific climate or regional building practices, you may wish to change this basement to a slab or crawlspace. Most professional contractors and builders can easily adapt your plans to alternate foundation types. Likewise, most can easily change 2x4 wall construction to 2x6, or vice versa. For Home Customizer® plans, Home Planners can easily make the changes for you.

How Many Blueprints Do You Need?
A single set of blueprints is sufficient to study a home in greater detail. However, if you are planning to obtain cost estimates from a contractor or subcontractors—or if you are planning to build immediately—you will need more sets. Because additional sets are cheaper when ordered in quantity with the original order, make sure you order enough blueprints to satisfy all requirements. The following checklist will help you determine how many you need:

_____Owner

_____Builder (generally requires at least three sets; one as a legal document, one to use during inspections, and at least one to give to subcontractors)

_____Local Building Department (often requires two sets)

_____Mortgage Lender (usually one set for a conventional loan; three sets for FHA or VA loans)

_____TOTAL NUMBER OF SETS

Have You Seen Our Newest Designs?

Home Planners is one of the country's most active home design firms, creating nearly 100 new plans each year. At least 50 of our latest creations are featured in each edition of our New Design Portfolio. You may have received a copy with your latest purchase by mail. If not, or if you purchased this book from a local retailer, just return the coupon below for your FREE copy. Make sure you consider the very latest of what Home Planners has to offer.

Yes! Please send my FREE copy of your latest New Design Portfolio.

Name _____

Address _____

City_____State_____Zip _____

HOME PLANNERS, INC.
3275 WEST INA ROAD, SUITE 110
TUCSON, ARIZONA 85741

Order Form Key

TB33NDP

he Home Customizer®

ny of the plans in this book are customizable
ough our Home Customizer® service. Look for
s symbol ⌂ on the pages of home designs. It
licates that the plan on that page is part of
e Home Customizer® service.

ome changes to customizable plans that can be
de include:

- exterior elevation changes
- kitchen and bath modifications
- roof, wall and foundation changes
- room additions
- and much more!

f the plan you have chosen to build is one of our
stomizable homes, you can easily order the Home
istomizer® kit to start on the path to making your
erations. The kit, priced at only $29.95, may be
dered at the same time you order your blueprint
ckage by calling our toll-free number or using
e order blank at right. Or you can wait until you
ceive your blueprints, spend some time studying
em and then order the kit by phone, FAX or mail.
you then decide to proceed with the customizing
rvice, the $29.95 price of the kit will be refunded
you after your customization order is received.
e Home Customizer® kit includes:

- instruction book with examples
- architectural scale
- clear acetate work film
- erasable red marker
- removable correction tape
- ¼" scale furniture cutouts
- 1 set of Customizable Drawings with floor
  plans and elevations

he service is easy, fast and *affordable*. Because
e know and work with our plans and have them
ailable on state-of-the-art computer systems, we
n make the changes efficiently at prices much lower
an those charged by other architectural or drafting
rvices. In addition, you'll be getting custom changes
rectly from Home Planners—the company whose
dication to excellence and long-standing profes-
nal experience are well recognized in the industry.
Call now to learn more about how simple it can be
have the *custom home* you've always wanted.

 Toll Free
1-800-521-6797, Ext. 800

alifornia Customers!!

r our customers in California, we now offer
alifornia Engineered Plans (CEP) and California
ock Plans (CSP) to help in meeting the strict
alifornia building codes. Check Plan Index for
mes that are available through this new service or
ll 1-800-521-6797 for more information about the
ailability of the service and prices.

LUEPRINTS ARE NOT RETURNABLE

 HOME PLANNERS, INC., 3275 WEST INA ROAD
SUITE 110, TUCSON, ARIZONA 85741

THE BASIC BLUEPRINT PACKAGE
Rush me the following (please refer to the Plans Index and Price Schedule in this section):
_____ Set(s) of blueprints for plan number(s) _____. $_____
_____ Set(s) of sepias for plan number(s) _____. $_____
_____ Additional identical blueprints in same order @ $50 per set. $_____
_____ Reverse blueprints @ $50 per set. $_____
_____ Home Customizer® Kit(s) for Plan(s) _____ @ $29.95 per kit. $_____

IMPORTANT EXTRAS: Rush me the following:
_____ Materials List: $50 Schedule A-D; $60 Schedule E (not available
for CEP service) $_____
_____ **Quote One**™ Summary Cost Report @ $25 for 1,
$15 for each additional, for plans _____. $_____
Building location: City _____ Zip Code _____
_____ **Quote One**™ Detailed Cost Estimate @ $110 Schedule A-D;
$120 Schedule E for plan _____. $_____
(Must be purchased with Blueprints set; Materials List included)
Building location: City _____ Zip Code _____
_____ Specification Outlines @ $10 each. $_____
_____ Detail Sets @ $14.95 each; any two for $22.95; any three
for $29.95; all four for $39.95 (save $19.85). $_____
(These helpful details provide general construction
advice and are not specific to any single plan.)
❏ Plumbing ❏ Electrical ❏ Construction ❏ Mechanical
_____ Plan-A-Home® @ $29.95 each. $_____

DECK BLUEPRINTS
_____ Set(s) of Deck Plan _____. $_____
_____ Additional identical blueprints in same order @ $10 per set. $_____
_____ Reverse blueprints @ $10 per set. $_____
_____ Set of Standard Deck Details @ $14.95 per set. $_____
_____ Set of Complete Building Package (Best Buy!) Includes
Custom Deck Plan _____ plus Standard Deck Details.
(See Index and Price Schedule) $_____

LANDSCAPE BLUEPRINTS
_____ Set(s) of Landscape Plan _____. $_____
_____ Additional identical blueprints in same order @ $10 per set. $_____
_____ Reverse blueprints @ $10 per set. $_____
Please indicate the appropriate region of the country for
Plant & Material List. (See Map on page 185): Region _____

POSTAGE AND HANDLING		1-3 sets	4+ sets
DELIVERY (Requires street address - No P.O. Boxes)			
•Regular Service (Allow 4-6 days delivery)		❏ $8.00	❏ $10.00
•2nd Day Air (Allow 2-3 days delivery)		❏ $12.00	❏ $20.00
•Next Day Air (Allow 1 day delivery)		❏ $22.00	❏ $30.00
CERTIFIED MAIL (Requires signature)			
If no street address available. (Allow 4-6 days delivery)		❏ $10.00	❏ $14.00
OVERSEAS DELIVERY		fax, phone or mail for quote	

NOTE: ALL DELIVERY TIMES ARE FROM DATE BLUEPRINT PACKAGE IS SHIPPED.

POSTAGE (From box above) $_____
SUBTOTAL $_____
SALES TAX (Arizona residents add 5% sales tax;
Michigan residents add 6% sales tax.) $_____
TOTAL (Sub-total and tax) $_____

YOUR ADDRESS (please print)
Name _____
Street _____
City _____ State _____ Zip _____
Daytime telephone number (_____) _____

FOR CREDIT CARD ORDERS ONLY: Please fill in the information below:
Credit card number _____
Exp. Date: Month/Year _____ Check one: ❏ Visa ❏ MasterCard ❏ Discover Card
Signature _____
Please check appropriate box: ❏ Licensed Builder-Contractor ❏ Homeowner

 ORDER TOLL FREE!
1-800-521-6797 or 520-297-8200

Order Form Key
TB33BP

Helpful Books & Software

Home Planners wants your building experience to be as pleasant and trouble-free as possible. That's why we've expanded our library of Do-It-Yourself titles to help you along. In addition to our beautiful plans books, we've added books to guide you through specific projects as well as the construction process. In fact, these are titles that will be as useful after your dream home is built as they are right now.

COUNTRY

1 200 country designs from classic to contemporary by 7 winning designers. 224 pages $8.95

BUDGET-SMART

2 200 efficient plans from 7 top designers, that you can really afford to build! 224 pages $8.95

FAMILY HOMES

3 200 stylish designs for today's growing families from 7 hot designers. 224 pages $8.95

NARROW-LOT

4 200 unique homes less than 60' wide from 7 designers. Up to 3,000 square feet. 224 pages $8.95

REGIONAL BEST

5 200 beautiful homes from across America by 7 regional designers. 224 pages $8.95 NEW!

EXPANDABLES

6 200 flexible plans that expand with your needs from 7 top designers. 224 pages $8.95 NEW!

BEST SELLERS
7 NEW! Our 50th Anniversary book with 200 of our very best designs in full color! 224 page $12.95

NEW ENGLAND
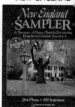
8 260 of the best in Colonial home design. Special interior design sections, too. 384 pages $14.95

AFFORDABLE

9 430 cost-saving plans specially selected for modest to medium building budgets. 320 pages $9.95

LUXURY

10 154 fine luxury plans-loaded with luscious amenities! 192 pages $14.95

ONE-STORY

11 470 designs for all lifestyles. 860 to 5,400 square feet. 384 pages $9.95

TWO-STORY

12 478 designs for one-and-a-half and two stories. 1,200 to 7,200 square feet. 416 pages $9.95

VACATION

13 345 designs for recreation, retirement and leisure. 312 pages $7.95 NEW!

MULTI-LEVEL

14 312 designs for split-levels, bi-levels, multi-levels and walkouts. 320 pages $6.95

OUTDOOR

15 42 unique outdoor projects. Gazebos, strombellas, bridges, sheds, playsets and more! 96 pages $7.95 NEW!

DECKS
16 25 outstanding sing double- and multi-level decks you can build. 112 pages $7.95

ENCYCLOPEDIA

17 500 exceptional plans for all styles and budgets—the best book of its kind! 352 pages $9.95

MODERN & CLASSIC

18 341 impressive homes featuring the latest in contemporary design. 304 pages $9.95

TRADITIONAL

19 403 designs of classic beauty and elegance. 304 pages $9.95

VICTORIAN

20 160 striking Victorian and Farmhouse designs from three leading designers. 192 pages $12.95

SOUTHERN

21 207 homes rich in Southern styling and comfort. 240 pages $8.95 NEW!

WESTERN

22 215 designs that capture the spirit and diversity of the Western lifestyle. 208 pages $8.95

EMPTY-NESTER
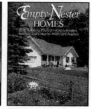
23 200 exciting plans for empty-nesters, retirees and childless couples. 224 pages $8.95

STARTER

24 200 easy-to-build plans for starter and low-budget houses. 224 pages $8.95

Landscape Designs

FRONT & BACK

25 The first book of do-it-yourself landscapes. 40 front, 15 backyards. 208 pages $12.95

BACKYARDS

26 40 designs focused solely on creating your own specially themed backyard oasis. 160 pages $12.95

EASY CARE

27 NEW! 41 special landscapes designed for beauty and low maintenance. 160 pages $12.95

Design Software

BOOK & CD ROM

28 NEW! Both the Home Planners Gold book and matching Windows™ CD ROM with 3D floor-plans. $24.95

HOME ARCHITECT

29 The only complete home design kit for Windows™. Draw floor plans and landscape designs easily. Includes CD of 500 floor plans. $59.95

Interior Design

HOME DECORATING

30 Special effects and creative ideas for all surfaces. Includes simple step-by-step diagrams. 96 pages $8.95

BATHROOMS

31 An innovative guide to organizing, remodeling and decorating your bathroom. 96 pages $8.95

KITCHENS

32 An imaginative guide to designing the perfect kitchen. Chock full of bright ideas to make your job easier. 176 pages $12.95

Planning Books & Quick Guides

| TRIM & MOLDING | PAINTING | ROOFING | WALLS & MORE | FLOORS | PATIOS & WALKS | WINDOWS & DOORS | PLUMBING |

33 Step-by-step instructions for installing baseboards, window and door casings and more. 80 pages $6.95

34 Tips from the pros on everything from preparation to clean-up. 80 pages $6.95

35 Information on the latest tools, materials and techniques for roof installation or repair. 80 pages $6.95

36 A clear and concise guide to repairing or remodeling walls and ceilings. 80 pages $6.95

37 All the information you need for repairing, replacing or installing floors in any home. 80 pages $6.95

38 Clear step-by-step instructions take you from the basic design stages to the finished project. 80 pages $6.95

39 Installation techniques and tips that make your project easier and more professional looking. 80 pages $6.95

40 Tackle any plumbing installation or repair as quickly and efficiently as a professional. 160 pages $9.95

| ADDING SPACE | HOME REPAIR | TILE | WALLPAPERING | BASIC WIRING | HOUSE CONTRACTING | VISUAL HANDBOOK | CONTRACTING GUIDE |

      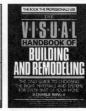 

41 Convert attics, basements and bonus rooms to useful living space. 130 pages $9.95

42 An owner's manual for your home. Sound advice on home maintenance and improvements. 256 pages $9.95

43 Every kind of tile for every kind of application. Includes tips on use installation and repair. 176 pages $12.95

44 Use the book the pros use. Covers tools and techniques for every type of wallcovering. 136 pages $12.95

45 A straight forward guide to one of the most misunderstood systems in the home. 160 pages $12.95

46 Everything you need to know to act as your own general contractor...and save up to 25% off building costs. 134 pages $12.95

47 A plain-talk guide to the construction process; financing to final walk-through, this book covers it all. 498 pages $19.95

48 Loaded with information to make you more confident in dealing with contractors and subcontractors. 287 pages $18.95

FRAMING

49 For those who want to take a more-hands on approach to their dream. 429 pages $19.95

Additional Books Order Form

To order your books, just check the box of the book numbered below and complete the coupon. We will process your order and ship it from our office within 48 hours. Send coupon and check (in U.S. funds).

YES! Please send me the books I've indicated:

☐ 1:FH $8.95	☐ 26:BYL $12.95
☐ 2:BS $8.95	☐ 27:ECL $12.95
☐ 3:FF $8.95	☐ 28:HPGC $24.95
☐ 4:NL $8.95	☐ 29:ARCH $59.95
☐ 5:AA $8.95	☐ 30:CDP $8.95
☐ 6:EX $8.95	☐ 31:CDB $8.95
☐ 7:HPG $12.95	☐ 32:CKI $12.95
☐ 8:NES $14.95	☐ 33:CGT $6.95
☐ 9:AH $9.95	☐ 34:CGP $6.95
☐ 10:LD2 . . . . $14.95	☐ 35:CGR $6.95
☐ 11:V1 . . . . $9.95	☐ 36:CGC $6.95
☐ 12:V2 . . . . $9.95	☐ 37:CGF $6.95
☐ 13:VH $7.95	☐ 38:CGW $6.95
☐ 14:V3 . . . . $6.95	☐ 39:CGD $6.95
☐ 15:YG $7.95	☐ 40:CMP $9.95
☐ 16:DP $7.95	☐ 41:CAS $9.95
☐ 17:EN $9.95	☐ 42:CHR $9.95
☐ 18:EC $9.95	☐ 43:CWT $12.95
☐ 19:ET $9.95	☐ 44:CW $12.95
☐ 20:VDH $12.95	☐ 45:CBW $12.95
☐ 21:SH $8.95	☐ 46:SBC $12.95
☐ 22:WH $8.95	☐ 47:RVH $19.95
☐ 23:EP $8.95	☐ 48:BCC $18.95
☐ 24:ST $8.95	☐ 49:SRF $19.95
☐ 25:HL $12.95	

Additional Books Sub-Total . . . . $_____
ADD Postage and Handling . . . . $ 3.00
Ariz. residents add 5% Sales Tax; Mich. residents add 6% Sales Tax . . . . $_____
YOUR TOTAL (Sub-Total, Postage/Handling, Tax) $_____

YOUR ADDRESS (Please print)

Name _____

Street _____

City _____ State _____ Zip _____

Phone (_____) _____ — _____

YOUR PAYMENT
Check one: ☐ Check ☐ Visa ☐ MasterCard ☐ Discover Card
Required credit card information:

Credit Card Number_____

Expiration Date (Month/Year)_____ / _____

Signature Required _____

Home Planners, Inc.
3275 W Ina Road, Suite 110, Dept. BK, Tucson, AZ 85741

TB33BK

Design BB3332

OVER 3 MILLION BLUEPRINTS SOLD

"We instructed our builder to follow the plans including all of the many details which make this house so elegant... Our home is a fine example of the results one can achieve by purchasing and following the plans which you offer... Everyone who has seen it has assured us that it belongs in 'a picture book.' I truly mean it when I say that my home 'is a DREAM HOUSE.'"

> S.P.
> Anderson, SC

"We have had a steady stream of visitors, many of whom tell us this is the most beautiful home they've seen. Everyone is amazed at the layout and remarks on how unique it is. Our real estate attorney, who is a Chicago dweller and who deals with highly valued properties, told me this is the only suburban home he has seen that he would want to live in."

> W. & P.S.
> Flossmoor, IL

"Your blueprints saved us a great deal of money. I acted as the general contractor and we did a lot of the work ourselves. We probably built it for half the cost! We are thinking about more plans for another home. I purchased a competitor's book but my husband wants only your plans!"

> K.M.
> Grovetown, GA

"We are very happy with the product of our efforts. The neighbors and passersby appreciate what we have created. We have had many people stop by to discuss our house and kindly praise it as being the nicest house in our area of new construction. We have even had one person stop and make us an unsolicited offer to buy the house for much more than we have invested in it."

> K. & L.S.
> Bolingbrook, IL

"The traffic going past our house is unbelievable. On several occasions, we have heard that it is the 'prettiest house in Batvia.' Also, when meeting someone new and mentioning what street we live on, quite often we're told, 'Oh, you're the one in the yellow house with the wrap-around porch! I love it!'"

> A.W.
> Batvia, NY

"I have been involved in the building trades my entire life... Since building our home we have built two other homes for other families. Their plans from local professional architects were not nearly as good as yours. For that reason we are ordering additional plan books from you."

> T.F.
> Kingston, WA

"The blueprints we received from you were of excellent quality and provided us with exactly what we needed to get our successful home-building project underway. We appreciate your invaluable role in our home-building effort."

> T.A.
> Concord, TN

77 530IDA 0949
FS 0147
11/95 30910-44